Charles

Selected Letters Volume 2
1965–1970

Other books by Charles Bukowski available from Virgin Books:

Post Office
Factotum
Women
Pulp
New Poems Book 1
New Poems Book 2
New Poems Book 3
Selected Letters Volume 1

Charles Bukowski

Selected Letters Volume 2
1965–1970

First published in 2004 by
Virgin Books Ltd
Thames Wharf Studios
Rainville Road
London
W6 9HA

Previously published in the USA by Black Sparrow Press in *Screams from the Balcony* and *Living on Luck*

A catalogue record for this book is available from the British Library.

ISBN 0 7535 0936 9

Typeset by Phoenix Photosetting, Chatham, Kent
Printed and bound in Great Britain by Clays Ltd, St Ives PLC

Editor's Note

This second volume of Bukowski's letters begins in the 1960s. As that decade ends, Bukowski is liberated from the drudgery of his post office job and embarks with some trepidation on his career as a professional writer, encouraged by a small regular stipend from his publisher John Martin, who undertook to pay him $100 a month to enable him to write full-time.

As in volume 1, the letters have been selected and transcribed from photocopies furnished by libraries and individuals. Bukowski's correspondence was astonishingly voluminous, and only selections are given from most letters. Editorial omissions are indicated by asterisks in square brackets, thus: [* * *]. Ellipses in the original letters are indicated by three dots. Bukowski often typed in CAPITALS for emphasis or for titles. Here, book titles are printed in *italics*, poem titles in quotes, and emphatic capitals in SMALL CAPS.

Dates are regularized and sometimes supplied from postmarks or guessed at from other evidence. A few spelling errors have been silently corrected. Salutations and signatures are for the most part omitted, except for a few examples that give the characteristic flavor. Some attempt is made to preserve Bukowski's layout, which at times includes multiple margins, but a printed book cannot reproduce such effects unaltered. As in the previous volume, a few letters have been printed verbatim to give the flavor of a completely unedited letter.

References to *Hank* in the editorial matter are to Neeli Cherkovsky's biography of Bukowski, published by Random House in 1991.

Acknowledgments

The editor and publisher thank the following institutions for supplying copies of some of the letters in this volume:

University of Arizona, Special Collections

Brown University, Providence, John Hay Library
The University of California, Los Angeles, Special Collections
The University of California. Santa Barbara, Special Collections
Centenary College, Samuel Peters Research Library, Shreveport, Louisiana
The State University of New York at Buffalo, Poetry/Rare Books Collection
The University of Southern California, Rare Books Collection
Temple University Library, Special Collections

• 1965 •

At Bukowski's instigation, Purdy had sent poems to Douglas Blazek for Ole.

[To Al Purdy]

July 5, 1965

yes, I wouldn't have wanted your poems for *Ole* if I didn't think the mag was a kind of powerhouse, and that's why I like to stick my stuff in there when I can . . . I guess you read the essay I wrote about a part of my youth for *Ole* #2; it was kind of a loose thing, but have gotten more comment on that than on anything I have written, and I doubt that any other mag slick slim or snobbish would have run it. They are also going to bring out a booklet thing, prose I wrote. *Confessions of a Man Insane Enough to Live with Beasts*, which I also don't think anyone else would publish, and christ, if you don't have outlet, you choke. I believe that rejection is good for the soul if you are not a quitter, but my soul has had plenty of that. [⋆ ⋆ ⋆]

[To Douglas Blazek]

July 8, 1965

[⋆ ⋆ ⋆] a small sparrow in the bush outside the window, reambeaking his feathers in the 4 p.m. sun, and I've got to take a shit. just got a tune-up on my '57 plymouth and the thing runs worse than ever. what the fuck? well it's good to have a car like that. once in a while somebody'll say, 'why don't you come over for dinner?' and I can just say, 'Car won't make it.' I don't have to tell them that time is scarcer than young pussy around here. and I don't mean time to write POETRY. I mean time to lay in bed, alone, and stare up at the ceiling and not think at all, not at all, not at all. . . . [⋆ ⋆ ⋆]

William Wantling contributed to many of the same magazines as Bukowski and had a book published by Douglas Blazek. An ex-convict who had spent five years in San Quentin, he took an interest in matters such as capital punishment and penal reform (see Hank, *p. 164).*

[To William Wantling]

July 9, 1965

no, haven't made a dime on poetry but am supposed to get 10 cents a copy on all *Crucifix*'s sold and there were over 3,000 of them printed but I don't know if I can trust Park ave. I never saw the contract. Also supposed to get 10 percent from *Poems Written Before Jumping from an 8 Story Window* and am supposed to get 50 percent from a BORDER PRESS book of drawings, both of these supposedly to be issued this Fall. but, after all, I've only been writing poetry since I was 35 – about ten years ago, and I figure about ten cents a year would be very good pay. hell, that reminds me, I did get $2 for a poem once, a horrible thing in *Flame*. and Garner of the extinct *Targets* sent me checks of $10 or more 3 times for large groups of poems – so shit, I did make my dime on poetry. and when I was young and used to go the short story – $25 for one from *Story* and ten bucks for one from *Portfolio*. so I've made around $80 writing and no end in sight except the a-bomb.

I don't know about this anarchist handbook, I really wouldn't know who to burn or who to put in if I tore down the works. the way I see it you ream out one piece of shit and substitute another for it. in the human mechanism – soul, balls, brain – there simply isn't enough there; it's a bad party, good guys in or not. . . . [★ ★ ★] everything here sags. now toothache. out of beer. car stalls in streets and they honk honk honk and I push it to the curb and think it's time they dropped the god damned hydrogen bomb and got everything over with. there's your anarchy – it'll come from the top and they won't know it. except the few big fat fuckers who get away on that space ship to another planet. I hate teeth. shit's all right if it's yours, but teeth, no, soulless shirks of things, fangs into brain center pulling . . . puking. [★ ★ ★]

[To Tom McNamara]

July 14, 1965

yours was a good letter in courage but no more than I would expect from a guy like you living on the edge of hell, you've got it, and I could no more give a damn whether you were a latent or an unlatent homo or a desk drawer – although one always gets a little touchy about this subject and feels as if he were saluting the flag, and if you talk enough about it somebody points a finger at you and says, 'you are a homo yourself!' same with Shannon – what he is as a sexual weapon or tool or plant doesn't matter to me – he writes a good letter and had a beer with me, and to hell with it.

bad day at track today, hot sweaty hot crotches of whores and maidens and men and jocks and newsboys stank and I made some bad plays against my reason, feeling my 45 years jumbling in my balls and getting a little down with EFFORT, the old death-wish assuming its effrontery, and I drank too much out there and sun came down and the whole world stank.

I guess it works like this in Spain too, or The United Arab Republic, and I have some sketches to make for a book of sketches drawings due in Nov. and I can't get rolling, I think of ants and garters and wire of cheese, and madmen dicing up committees of kangaroo, wawa, didn't d. h. lawrence write a bad one about a kangaroo? a novel? well, who cares? he hadda eat, I hadda eat, I do things I do not like to do either but not yet on a typing machine although I guess there's not much difference if you hold it under strong glass . . . christ, I'm tired. think of all the piss pissed away today; not the shit, just the piss. momentous. think of all the poems written today, then if you want to, think of all the shit. I donate. when the cat comes home in the morning I'll have 3 pears on my head.

I am pretty well on the way and listening to some Beethoven; (on radio) – with music I like what I care for, and sometimes it's jazz or whatever or sentimental or sound that strikes against my arms under electric light just right, awwha, you ever get that guy fucking with your mailbox?

Find a way to survive that does not cut too much of a hole in you or anybody else, said the holy man, and then he lifted out his palm and I dropped in the pecan shell and the lighted cigarette butt, and victory is not what you capture but rather what you don't want to capture, and I've wanted to be a monk but the robes are hot and they itch and I'm afraid I'd meet the same men there too – dressed differently. conch auszieh tusche schwarz! this is a dull one! like I told you, I am on the way. and the woman's in the bathroom and the baby fell, YAAAH!!! more death on a fork.

by midnight I will know no more; I will be sitting naked on the edge of the bed spitting invective out of my broken teeth out of the m.g.'d psyche, slabs of fat rolling like bread dough white and gummy over my gut, my face hacked with the bad years, my eyes sucked out by the snakes, I will be sitting on the edge of the bed . . . mumbling, twitching, shading myself against the walls, shading myself against my self, the elves, the whores, taxes, love and demolition, it will be a more drab-plink night than the one before and finally it will be a little while safe in the barbwire of sleep. sweet picture of groveling snail can't breathe.

I used to lean slightly toward the liberal left but the crew that's involved, in spite of the ideas, are a thin & grafted-like type of human, blank-eyed and throwing words like vomit. essentially they are *very* lonely. the secret is really that they have not put society down but that society has put them down and so now they gather and hand-hold through 1/4 souls and play at tinkertoy games with 1/8 minds. there's nothing left to do except admit that they are slugs, worms, and they are not going to do that. I do not say that these people do not sometimes do things for the betterment of mankind; I only say that they give me a pain in the ass when I have to sit in the same room with them. I am essentially a loner and now that I've got hung with child and woman a lot of people are coming through my door (her friends) that I would never have to look upon. christ, this is a bitter letter. maybe it was the phone call. she's still talking, 'yes, the writer needs to make such a thing *vivid*, give it *vividness*. . . .' it's the same old swill I heard on campus so long ago. god damn, Tom, am I insane? it seems to me as if everything is the same mouth saying the same thing over and over again from all these bodies and faces that also look the same. sometimes I feel sick, sick, disgusted. you get your faith up again and again; then it's like trying to climb a mountain for a good hot piece of ass or a fifth of good scotch at the peak, and what do you find? a basketful of worms.

I'm going to get something to drink. you slam through that novel.

> the realest part of the leg is
> where is ends, like the mind
> becoming soul or an apple thrown into
> the sea

p.s. – christ, don't get me wrong. I'm no John Bircher or am I for the power boys at all. nine, nine, I only like time to lay around and stare at the ceiling for a while without voices around or bodies with voices. like that.

The following letter is printed entire and verbatim.

[To Douglas Blazek]

[July 14, 1965]

July 14 in 1965 in Los Angeles in America in a kitchen drinking beer and smoking a Dutch Master panatella, and lost $8 at the races today, and listening to Schumann I think . . .
aye, Blazer:

you're right, I have been feeling down DOWN and almost did the Big Thing last Sunday, but that's talk, Krist, I'm still here with 14 half-quarts of beer, stocking feet, red-eyed, misty of brain, gaga fk goofy, and the man on the radio asks me:

'Have you made your will yet?'

I don't answer him.

MORE THAN THE BLUES, MORE THAN A SPIDER
CRAWLING NEAR THE CORNER OF THE WALL:

quite quite quite
quit quit quit
I want to quit
I am not brave
I do not want to fight
I want to stay under the covers and
  cry cry cry
I don't want to see a
  human
I want to sleep

I will stay here until they come and
get me
or the meat disappears from the
bones and I am
beautiful
again

this is a free poem to hang in your bathroom in case you run out of paper.

I will send the letters I will send the letters I will send the letters, it is only that I have been a little goofy and some things going wrong – no need a list – I am being chewed to pieces by everything, and if I were a smooth gentleman I would not admit this – but I eat hash, hate policemen, baseball, squaredances, nuns, factories, goatees, barbers and old women who want respect only because they are old women. I will send the letters, only like I said most of them are not so good, god damn it. yours, Purdy's, and then that's it. I will send yours in seperate envelope so as not to defile their good guts. it's a matter of getting to a postoffice and I will be very haappy when i get up the verve to seeit done. I am half-assed weak or something lately. how about death by cannon, Blaz? shit. great, eh man? completely blown apart in the public square, in the park on a Wednesday afternoon under a statue of Grant or Lincoln or Beethoven or Lee! in the sunshine! poems blown to pigeons. I've never seen a statue of Christ in the park, any park, I guess they don't want the birdshit on his brain, I saw one once in a glass case and I was drunk and felt like getting up in there with him, it was night and he was undera small blue light but I didn't get in there with him (Him, I mean). I was too much in a hurry to get to my place and knock off a piece of ass from this longlegged wino whore I was living with at the time, she's dead now, poor slit. which reminds me – once I was drunk in Inglewood and I was walking down the street and I saw this mortuary, it was 2 a.m. in the morning and you know how mortuaries are out here, the big ones, those long flat steps leading up to a kind of white colonial granduer and they keep the bright big lights on all night, and I climbed up on the top step and stretched out and passed out on those mortuary steps until thepolice came and got me. and when the judge sentenced me he not only sentenced me for drunkenness but also for BLOCKING TRAFFIC! – ain't that the shits? you know there aren't many cars at that time of the morning but so many of them stopped to look at the body on the top step that it caused a jam. I guess they thought I was dead and that's what I wanted them to think, chop up the smooth jugular vien of their sleep-within-Life, the fuckers. I don't do this so much anymore because there is this ten-month old kid as an excuse, and I shouldn't use it; but you know I used to conk out everywhere. there was one of my favorite hills, I believe it was Westview street just above 21st. and the hill was very steep a dark steep street going straight down without lights, and I'd get drunk and just lay myself down in the center of the street right near the top and pass out. a car never got me. although once a woman came by and screamed when she saw me out there and it brought me to and I lifted my head and looked at her and said, 'Don't worry, baby, I don't want to FUCK you, you are too ugly, you are a shitty ugly looking human being because you live like a roach!' she disgusted me so much that I got up and staggered after her until she ran into a house. then there was an alley behind a bar in Philly, I think the bar was at 16th. and Fairmount, a real piss hole and I ran errands for sandwiches and begged for drinks and shook the pinball machine for drinks and talked for drinks (I *used* to be a good talker) and about noon I'd go into my first phase of drunkeness and walk out into the alley and lay down, and I knew these trucks used the alley to deliver and pickup stuff from the warehouses but since it was noon or one p.m. they had some chance to see me, and they had little houses in there that the blacks lived in and the kids would come out and throw rocks at me or poke me in the back with sticks, and I'd hear the mammy's voice finally, 'Now you childrens leave dat man alone!!' and the truck didn't come by. I am writing you now and I have 12 beers left. I been thinking about Wantling. got a rather (what?) knifey postcard from him today because I had told him in a letter that I was rather disappointed with anarchy and revolution because the way I saw it shit was only replaced with more shit. he inferred that I was getting old and – 'that terd yr carrying in your pocket, throw it out. somebody might throw you back a diamond.' I don't intend to argue with him; yet it's true that I don't have much hope. I don't disrespect either his hope or his energy, or his work. I give money to people on the streets. a woman stopped me the other night. I know I shouldn't. it doesn't help. maybe I should have fucked her. I am tired of pain. mass anarchy is more pain, more error. I don't know what to do. shit, I know about the corruption, the lie of office and govt., but these are only men and if we put them in different jars with different labels they will remain only men, and the process is slow, most surely almost 2,000 years wasted, but I don't know if i could kill a man or even say that I thought I was right about anything.

and even tho W. infers that I am old, I infer that he is YOUNG in spite of the 5 and one half years he did, and there goes *that* argument. I suppose now that I will be referred to as an extreme rightist and that I voted for Barry while I was disguised in a stocking mask. – yet, W. is right: our anarchy is best served in the poetry we write. do you think we'll all end up writing stuff for *The New Yorker* and *Esquire*? how much ya wanna bet some of us do? and *Evergreen Review* is halfway there.

Got your flyer on *Ole* and the chapbooks, and well done, baby, well done. although reading about myself this CHARLES BUKOWSKI, seems very strange. I seem to see some pisser done up in white robes and tilting a winebottle. where is he? sitting in the ants? tickling his belly with red turpentine?

look here, Bensenville, from *Mo tzu*:

5. Seven causes of anxiety: bad city walls, no allies, careless expenditure, incompetent officials, overconfidence of sovereign, failure to recognize loyal officials, crop failures. Reduce expenditures and be prepared.

14. 16. Love everybody uniformaly.

17. 19. Against offensive war.

26. 28. Will of Sky.

(oh shit, I just spilled beer over my cigars! will of Sky? lucky they in cellophane. me drunk again? Blaz, you're only person I know who is worse speller than I. you must be good person, yes. you are not interested in hopscotch while the walls are on fire.)

31. Ghosts.

35–37. Against belief in Fate.

39. Against Confucianists who love narrowly, like music, and believe in Fate.

(if I were Wantling I would say that Fate is an excuse for lack of courage and disorder. I'll say it anyhow, although it's too simple – and not always so.)

(Stevenson died. I saw the headlines. when E. E. Cummings died somebody told me – 5 days later.)

(ho, I am growing old old, silver threads amongst the gold, the kid keeps crawling in and I sit her up here and she bangs against the keys. and I am the man who once sneered at babies in carriages and dull-faced men walking along with their dull-faced wives.)

oh hell, I have been reading some shit about summoning a gamekeeper with a hat of feathers. it should not be done. you use a hat of fur. good gamekeeper will not come (I mean appear) if you summon them with a hat of feathers, even if it means they will be shot. they just didn't go for that hat of feathers jazz.

of course I am almost drunk now, and fine, and I think reverence and adoration is horseshit, there is no man that I adore, or a chance that I will; there are men that I would want to drink beer with, there are women I would want to fuck. that is as far as my love goes. we are contaminated by nearness. I say I love this child that has been on my lap but if I say this it also means that I do not love some child that I cannot see because if I can't see her she surely does not exist, and although only what exists is that which is near us or what we can see – it traps us into error – like murder, war. the 8 or 12 hour job, the house, the flag, the love of the greasy tablecloth that we puked upon just last night. it is certainly logical to seek for the things which make us happy and safe and drunk and immortal and christlike and comecrazy but we are all banging heads to satisfy the teeth of our own souls – anarchists, rightists, leftists, religionists, judo practicers, horseplayers, drunks, chess players, all, all, . . . lost in the tilting glob of self. what the hell can we do? I have often thought that much more than suicide that MADNESS was the answer! think the sweetness! battering against rubber walls, screaming great poems and Nobody hearing! cold showers when you don't want them. WATER? WATER, WATER!! wires jammed into the-back of your neck jammed with electric shock. the TRUTH AT LAST: YOU DID NOT *FIT*. you are therefore crazy because we as members of society have practiced various standard devices that make us safe and you unsafe. nobody takes his pecker out in a stadium of 90,000 people and shouts SHIT ON AMERICA! that man must be crazy. he's been treated so good. what the hell does he want? *we* can live without protest, what's all this *protest* SHIT? so he lost his job? so he's worried about the bomb? so he writes madrigals on the sleeves of his dirty shirts? some PANSY who wants GOOD? real men don't fuck with good; real men are tough; real men can take it. the stockpiles of bombs don't bother us. shit, we got more an' they got. and we'll figure a way to handle those chinks. Remember Teddy R.? a big stick and a soft woice. I mean, Blaz, I am ready to go crazy not because I think the good guys are not winning but because the good boys are almost the same as the bad boys, I mean it's jazz and waste and holler, and all this expenditure and not even a young Portoguese girl say 19 licking my cock with her sandpaper tongue while whilst I lay back upon a mass of blue pillows while the VULTURE winks.

your stuff about letters, your u putting out these letters I don't quite know about because men seem to lie in their letters as while well as in their poems, theonly thing bing being that maybe the lies in the letters are the more relaxed lies. this helps. and of course, the letters the pomes are maybe the best of the sorid worst of us, but I keep thinking of everybody shitting and then getting up to wipe their asses, dabbing in the paper, holding it in the hand, looking tat the smear smears of brown and then the terds and the n flushing it away, looking at the swirl of guggling white anhi hi hoping tit high that it does not stuff up that the mackeral holy get it so we can eat it again and jam it down and out, hurrah. I give top shit advice so listen, I am one eight eighth of your heart, and I say, you';l get some good ones, the very worst and best of men come clean sometimes, but really, mostly, I guess as your finding out – you'll get flashes and flares, but mostly sandin the motor, crap, hackneyed, and it being loose will often be worse, and so that's more hell, yet we are used to that, so I'd say (the voice from above) that you should try to pick the meat, the avocado, I mean EXCERPTS, baby, you read? sure you do. of course, like thaat ass C.C. would say, all my letters are good, but if you printed *all* my letters y'd probably make a fortune and I'm not quite ready to spill I mean spoil you yet.

the rats are drunk and the bluebells dance upon the top of WITHERED TITS.

not being shit, but I wish you could get hold of the 50 or 60 letters I wrote CORRINGTON, but doubt that he'll let you peek. do I guess right here? Willie all right, mostly more so once, but gone off on tangent of success and power, and maybe he's right, shit, I don't know, I don't know, we did not get on wll in new Orleansin that room full of prefessers and laymen hymen lawyers and bigwigs, and I didn't say anthihing which was cowardly, but on the other hand, they didn't give me much a chance too. all that exposition of brilliance and nobody really wanting to get drunnk. I just get the toothache of everywhere, these people sitting around matching wits and in the pocket brilliances . . . I sometimesdo think that I am XRA CRAZY because I am tired and do not seem to care, although actually I do care, andI remember Williams, Miller Williams was hard but kind and gave me a book of his poems, but even Jon gave me a tough time – holding things against me that I said anddid while drunk, and I think this is amatuer, and I keep thinking of the boys who did a lot of TIME up there and I keep thinking they haven't learned basics – the 8 or 9 whores I shacked with knew more about me drunk than Jon could understand. what good's the lockup if you come out like a little boy with a blackboard? you and Jon Webb and Louise Webb are the only living editors that I know in this world – yet if if it comes to a break I will go elsewhere – and not be published. God, I guess I give a lot of shit and ask forgiveness, but I've

what? whet where am I?

the woman just camein and asked me to fk readone
of her pomes. o.k. pome but title way off, I had to tell her so. all right?
man, I can barely findthe keys where was I?
woman came in and said we she was almost outa cigarettes
I said go get some I'll watch t h e kid
and I pray that this is what keeps us from conquering room
Rpm Rome I mean or not being a tetrander

I guess by now that you gather by now that I my my am a nut case instead of the true inspirational ½ poet, but I do not think that this bothers you, so far you are the only man I can trust, and I do not mean some kind of fictional handholding duressof gag ignomy, when you rot or I ror rot roar, it will be time enough to let go, where was I???

o, yes –

a native American citizen must submit with his application for transport: a birth certificate, or, if such a certificate is is not obtainable, a bapistmal certicite or a certified cop y of the record of

bastardism.

god, thanks for your invite to sleep u ½ on your rug when the human beasts close in, but I cannot accept mostly because I love yor wife and your children and your walls, and also my love for you goes too deep to allow myself to die prick thing or wounded dove within your gentle hands, and now christ I've said p5ickthing andnow you think it's my prick between your hands and that I am jiving you, god god I mustn't drink so much exce t I want to, what I mean to say, my sorrow nose a way to end get off the head when it hurts enough, I got the secret, you know what I mean.

look, don' ever send me money: I will take it
it's not lack of money keeps me from sending letters
shit written to me it's only that after reading the
letters I am scard scared thatnobody has written to
me. it came as a kind of shcok I keep dying up and
down, dull-eyed sacroscant mar macarroni of self

I don't think anybody knows
and it is really very much like
being lockedin a closetful of
socks and wrinkled shirst
and hearing the breadman's whistel
at noon and no way to get out
to buy a taffy-roll or a green smock
full of warm woman bending over a cupcake
whileher husband dies in a Kansas City
electrodude of shock
and victory.

another free pome for your shithouse . . .
your furnish the paper and I'll furnish the
HA HA HA hahaha

rest,

baby.

what seems the cunt mock intonation of the gravity of my sadness is not a play game   it is eyow HEAVY

and I do not promise you suicide or anything that *must*
be cone snapped intto turtle's mouth

done

only what I've got to do want feel now here hear you cotton-stainer
long-haird squash bug ally in
pn pendulous necktie drifting

HOSUMMA!

I've run out o   of my children
(they keep playing Gustave Hotlz 'The Planets'
becauw of these space cocksuckers and I grow very
tired of bad music and plentifuf timing)

I lost it.

look, don't worry about paper for *Asshole Insane Enough to Live Between Breasts*, I am most happy that you understood the manuscript but I can't write any novel I think, unless I feel like it and I just don't feel like it and maybe never will, andso here we go on being poor, novels means dollars, and I still envision the smashed face not giving in, stoking in the cigar, lighting it, saying fuck you, and all escxuxses of later times if I even am around will call me a homo a coward a fink a seller of cowardice, and who knows? maybe I am all or any of hell these, yet I sometimes think of those who makethe decisions, I sometimes think of what they are and where they are and I do not

feel so good

now Richard Wagner.

they stoked off Wagner and tossed him in the corner, these laterists, an expelled jackoff kid, and even an anti-Wagner school, and he had certain ways, of grandeur of malicious exploitation of sound but shit, don't they all? every man who arrives upon the scene thinks he knows it and most of them do, like Corrington, but they know too god damned much, and what they missed was the fact that Wagner had

MUSCLE
ENERGY
HEART
and the guts to fill 40,000 pigs,
or 80,000
human?
beings.

see Hon Jonathan Swift
see Schopenhauer
see Orpahn Anney.

I am going to close this letter while I am drunk and this is the onl y way to do it otherwise we choose sides of ourselves to see

I HOPE THAT YOUR PORCH STEPS HAVE SPLINTERS

I HOPE THAT YOUR BALLS ACHE WHEN THE MOON IS HIGH HIGH HIGH

I HOPE THAT THEY KILL THE FACTORIES
AND THE ALREADY DEAD
I HOPE THAT THEY KILL THEM SOMEMORE SO
THAT MY $$$# EYES MAY SEE
MERCY

within them
within
me.

bathroom poem.

something about Jean's Journal. you were good man not too attack too hard, cd. have told the bitch she shd have named dog after her pussy.

I guess Stravinsky Pound
John Fante to be the best men
of our age
with the early Saroyan
even then lying to himself
but wide and lovely style of flaoting

yet to go down in the muck when the war began

WORLD WAR 2

he did not follow his dream and
he therefore died

and I am trying to pick up some of the strings from the best of M9lton dante inferno big nose wax mustache death of them all

somebody once took me into seeing this old and almost famous poet andI did not want to go u know fuck u but I got drunk enough and we went, the id kid with the scarf around and and around his neck and me I went with some whore some woman and the great poet finally leaned forward and he said to me:

I THOUGH YOU WERE YOUNGER THAN YOU ARE.

and we watched his young boy who looked like a woman
pa. play
the piano and he p.a played it good good
I got icehole asshole chills on t into the dark of me,
he was good
yet he was pitiful –
like a srouge a stranger trained to die a certain way,
and his mother knew
as , I said goodbye
she said
he's so strange, he's so little man, I don't think
he's ever kissed a
girl.

don't worry, mama, I told her, your little boy is
beautiful, and goodnight, and I stole
one of there gentle little statutes of
pewter
and then gabe it very much back and
smiled

and they, Mr.Bukowski, I'm very sorry we do not
drin herem , but good to meet you we've
read your work
somewhere.

. . . look blaz not much good
list ning to Srav Strav
and trhing to fond i find
k e y s

I better leave
now.

if I could piss only be
the shadow of this
man's
giant.

I've got to wake up to that yellow ;pro mise of action and I w n't certainly bd be ready.

think of the
breadmaan,
Buk

[To Steven Richmond]

July 23, 1965

[★ ★ ★] I am reading Celine, who is somebody else who writes better than I do, and I find this *comforting*, I like to be led along, I like somebody else to do THE DIRTY WORK. there are so few people that I *can* read – Camus' *The Stranger*, the early Sartre, the few poems of that homo Genet; Jeffers; Auden before he got comfortable; the early Shapiro (and then with a sense of distrust); Cummings when he didn't get too *too* fucking cute; the early Spender –

'the living or the dying,
this man's dead life or
that man's life
dying.'

Patchen's got a little too much sugar for me, too much melodramatic bravado which makes me feel as if I had been crying in a movie house, but

I find his drawings innocent and lovely and they continue to appear that way to my eye at this stage.

Of course, the Dickey boys, Allen Tate, the whole South Kenyon Sewanee snob cocksuckers of the blood of Life, they write so very well, and they are real bastards, they know the game, it's a power game, and they know the language and the history, but they are truly a bad people, the worst people of all in the worst game of all: conning men out of their souls. Last March in New Orleans I met a couple of Southern profs who had once been men and I could see that they were gone, and didn't speak, or that is, they spoke. one had acquired a whole new line of degrees, had gone to England and written a batch of research on James Joyce (but history will find, I say, that he wrote only one decent book: *Finnegans Wake*), and this boy had even been given a grant to do this, and the other one had been given a grant too and he went somewhere and translated somebody in South America (hell! vallejo again? or the other one? can't think, can't think), and one had a fine red beard and the other a beret and they shouted across the room arguing various things of university power – degrees, control of magazines, publication credits, all that shit, my god, jesus, all that shit, and there was some lawyer who had come over to the Quarter and this lawyer collected John Crowe Ransom, Allen Tate, Y. Winters, the mess, and I thought sure they would all leap together in the center of the room and kiss and ream and kiss and feel each other's balls if they had any. yet, in a sense, I was hurt, let's admit it: they did not admit the reality of my existence and soon forgot me. I should have known because I have been cooled all my life – beginning with my 2 bugged-up parents and down through the schoolyards and into the alleys with the winos and down through the women and the years and the living I was either always something to laugh at or forget, which was all right with me, I almost liked it, and still almost do, being alone, being alone here now with the girlchild screaming and the woman flushing the toilet . . . [★ ★ ★]

Blaz fucked-up again – this time not strike but something worse, I can't tell you; maybe he will, and it's really none of my horse, but I keep thinking that he is the Great Romantic Caught in the Spider Dream, and worse yet the kid has got to begun believing that I am some source of wisdom or Life-long Kool, you know, and I think he expected me to o.k. his latest, but Christ, I can't walk a straight line most of the time myself, and if I had to straight-talk him I'd say 2 things at the same time:

a) take what you want, take what's good for you, take what keeps you alive

b) but don't kill anybody ever in the process in this process who has ever loved you depended on you or saved *your* life.

if you take a without b you don't make it and whatever you take will kill you because you are as phoney as that which you wish to overthrow. the weakest men take that which seems immediately better; the strongest men hurt themselves (if hurt has to be), and wait. I'd never say this if I were sober, of course, but I'm seldom sober, of course. [⋆ ⋆ ⋆]

[To Jim Roman]

July 23, 1965

I really believe that *Cold Dogs* will be issued [⋆ ⋆ ⋆]

No, I didn't see Jonathan Williams when he hit town. I have a reputation as a vicious and nasty drunk (not entirely unfounded) and somebody gave him the word prob. when he asked. That's all right. [⋆ ⋆ ⋆]

oh yes, Stuart hung with 3100 copies of *Crucifix* but he'll unload and at $7.50 too. now I am fairly high on beer, typing this in the kitchen while the woman and the ten month old girl sit in the front room listening to Russian poetry on the FM radio. I can't listen because almost all poetry is bad for me; it irritates; me makes me twitch and have spasms. I don't understand it, I feel as if I were being reamed in a pig pen. [⋆ ⋆ ⋆]

p.s. Finally reading Celine and it's about time. A master, no doubt of it.

[To Jon and Louise Webb]

July 26, 1965

[⋆ ⋆ ⋆] Did Corrington show before you left town? if so, I think we gotta give him points. I think I have g.d. been too hard on too many people. to hell with KNOCK CORRINGTON. to hell with KNOCK SHERMAN. this is small and I am sick of myself. I can disagree with some of their principles and ways and manueverings, but, hell, no man knows when he is right and when he starts thinking he is always right and that the universe is his apple, then he might as well either start a whorehouse or become a preacher. he's got rocks. [⋆ ⋆ ⋆] I am still growing up and I'm very much afraid that when I reach full size that I will be dead.

Marina keeps yanking at me and I lift her up and she sits here in her yellow pajamas

> banging at the typewriter
> grabbing for my cigar and beer
> tiny hand sea-blue eyes
> she thinks me a monster of heroic proportions,
> my god such a sweet DOLL!!!
> she breaks me and breaks me up again and again
> as I peer at her out of my
> evil face.

the faucet drips. and on and on I write, it's so easy when drunk. the poems are flowing again, poems, poems, and good or bad they may be, I am now easier to live with, I'd suppose. those 2 books, they almost froze me. It's like somebody wrote me, 'Well, you might as well kill yourself now and go out clean.' I know what he means. but what about Marina? I think she likes me very much, she does seem to, so suppose I left now? a dirty trick I'd think. you should see her eyes. what eyes what eyes what eyes!!! [★ ★ ★]

look here, if Henry Miller liked *Crucifix* that's good enough for me, that's the best critic there is – a man who has lived that hard that long just can't learn to lie and also has no need to. Christ, Jon and Lou, isn't life *really* strange??? that a man like Henry Miller would be speaking about all of us? we are truly lucky, we are in touch with the gods, and I am happy for us all. god damn, that was a *good* phone call, you LIFTED ME RIGHT UP WITH YOUR HAPPINESS and that is why I keep drinking and write on and on. Frances has fixed me something to eat but I keep saying no no, I am busy, to hell with food! oh shit, everything is so strange; it's so good to know the good people, but do you know what else??? we must be wary, we must be careful, we must follow our own guts . . . or else the poems will quit, we will quit and we will forget where we are. look, the world is still, I think (so far), a very horrible place filled with horrible people (am I snitching?) (I keep opening beers and drinking them and lighting cigars like a madman), look, look, it's only next poem or the way we walk or the way we act or respond to the next situation. all we've done beforehand DOESN'T COUNT IF WE WASTE IT! and this is what gets me: so many writers, artists, people, begun well who turn to shit when in the beginning they knew what SHIT was. but all it takes is a letter from the editor of *The New Yorker*.

and they sell. thank god I still had the nerve to tell an editor of some big publishing house, last year or so, that I simply did not feel like writing a novel upon his request. I keep thinking of Corrington (I'm snitching again), and thinking of death. look, I am crazy with everything, I am confused but it seems to be quite simple to me – the line is drawn, either you're on this side of the line or that. they say any man can be bought. I deny this. they say that any man, any man has his price. I don't have a price. it may be the biggest laugh of the century. they may buy me with a lollipop. poverty is bad enough but poverty that you drag others into beside yourself is what makes them win, what makes you sell out. yet I believe that this beautiful little girl with the beautiful eyes would become less instead of more beautiful if I sold out. that's the way it works. backwards. it really takes more than 2,000 years of Christianity or anti-Christianity for a man even to get a half decent bearing. and 65 or 75 years of life are not enough. hardly a beginning. I began at 35 which leaves me nothing, and the way I drink and have lived, certainly less than half, perhaps. not even another lousy Summer or 2. well, I have talked long enough. [★ ★ ★]

[To Ruth Wantling]

August 10, 1965

[★ ★ ★] the heat has me goofy too. and I get these pains in my neck and back and chest, I feel like screaming, 'oh Christ, let's start the bloody Crucifixion!' I don't know what I've got. but last night I sat there working with a black foreman glaring at a spot at the back of my neck and the human race went down like lumps of gravy mixed with dung and spittle. I played a little game last night – each person I saw I asked myself, IF YOU HAD THE POWER TO ORDER THE DEATH OF THIS PERSON, WOULD YOU DO SO?

and as they walked by, man and woman, I'd say to myself:

that one, sure!

and that one, MOST SURELY!

and look at that pig, that gross manure, runs through with conceit! death to that!

and look, that one thinks it's pretty! ugg.

and that one must go and that one, and that, and look at THAT ONE – a sore in the eye of the sun, kill him!

anyhow, nobody got by. it was very sad. no nobility. no grace of walk. not a flower. not a leaf. not even a water spaniel. just bugs, pigs, worms, ant-eaters, gorillas, monkeys, pageboys, so on so. on.

I hope it's a better night tonight, I hope that I see somebody whether the pains stop or not.

you go easy now. not much sense to anything, of course. your husband writing better as the years prop him up, but hope he does not get too well-known. this usually flips them over the side and does them in. [* * *]

The books by Ginsberg, Kerouac, Corso, and Burroughs that Bukowski lists below were in fact in print in 1965. Carl Larsen's Plot to Assassinate *. . . was published by Seven Poets Press in 1962.*

[To Jim Roman]

August 14, 1965

[* * *] my god, I know, I know little about Patchen, I know the *name*, and that's all. this is the hell of it with people who come out in small chapbooks, small books of poetry, editions of 200–500. they are soon swept up and the years go by, and then there's just the sort of a ring of a name somewhere. I'd like to see some publisher reissue some of these – *Howl, On the Road, Gasoline, the Naked Lunch, The Plot to Assassinate the Chase Manhattan Bank, It Catches My Heart in Its Hands* . . . I don't have any of these myself except the last one. and then there's Patchen. and what he has written, drawn. Maybe *Outsider* #4 will throw some light where it's needed. [* * *]

it's been searing hot here for a week running, between 95 and 100. race riots in the streets. stores burning and looted, automobiles burning; whites and police beaten. whole blocks on fire. fireman shot at. all hell. I guess they'll clean their area out and then come up here looking for me. I've got my black face ready, ready. '*Mammy! Mammy!*' 'motha-fucka!' of course, I've got nothing for them to steal except a couple of books of poetry but I'm surrounded by a lot of white meat they'd just love to beat on. hell, I know they've had it rough; I have too. the only difference being that they want a lot of things that I don't want. anyhow, it's hot and there's FUN in town. they caught a white guy the other night and beat him, beat him until one of his eyes was hanging from a thread out of the socket. I keep thinking it's a good thing the whites didn't do this to a BLACK or there'd be a national uproar. the whole thing, I think, is just the human monster showing teeth, shitting upon itself every chance it gets. the social workers and professors can talk about conditions and background and all the big glib vacant words, but it's just the humanthing with hands and feet and bloody flat brain and soul letting go in another direction. shit will always find a direction out, and if it doesn't, they'll operate or blast it out. I mean black shit, white shit, brown shit, yellow shit. I need me a wall, oh, I need me a 12 foot wall. with beer inside, with me inside. oh, I need me a 12 foot wall.

well, like I said, it's hot and we're all a little off in the noodle today. [* * *]

[To Douglas Blazek]

[August 15?, 1965]

[* * *] this is Sunday. I've drunk about 2 six packs tall and still feel quite sober although I am gradually growing deaf. will be 45 years old on the 16th., my god my god my god. don't think I don't remember being young – the bars, the fights, the alleys, everything – refusing marriage, work, country, culture, literature, the sum total. now I sit trapped in a little by everything; the heart got soft, I slipped here and there, finally. and that's how they trap the fox and the madman.

I wonder about you out there and I know that you have been going through your own particular type of HELL, the Blatt thing, the factory, everything, and that I have been very little use to you. I am sorry; mostly I only write poems, and many of these – as you know – not so good. Wantling tells me this and you tell me this about *Crucifix*, and I know that it is true. I knew that when I was down there in New Orleans, I knew I sensed that old man Webb wanted more and better poems but I couldn't do it. I just kept wandering the streets a drunken jackal of self, wandering drunk, and I could not come up with it. and then they charge $7.50 a copy; well, they had their makeup and format and their artist – only the poet dipped between the slabs. so fuck it. I've died before. why lift me upside-down? why strain at me? I think that what might have held the pages down was a more clever poet, practiced. I only mourn and dip within my own ink tears. I don't know the rules. and I get the side whispers around here from the woman's poetry-group finks who slip in through the doors while I am asleep? 'he's slipped.' 'um, this is really not as good as *It Catches.*' so, what the hell do they want? we all slip. we slip all the way into the grave and then we stretch out straight and no more vomit no more bluebirds no more busrides to East Kansas City and a blow job by a maid with a lisp and a big ass for 3 dollars. the woman now in here sliding a big knife into a mayonnaise jar, clank clank clank, smiling a sunlight smile and not realizing that I am writting to the great Blazek. hello to Alta, by the way, and that I'd suggest that she hang close, you'll make it, hell, you've got to, jolly old chopper, I'd like *you* at my funeral, don't you see? a few sharp mad words. are you still there? all right, I'll no longer ask you to 'hold' but you must have known what I meant when I said it. the other night, coming out of the slave pit, here was this long freighter load behind an electric motor dragging this body, one ball here one ball there, cock sliding into the moon, asshole like a gnome, fingers and arms spitting at the sky, a letter to mother in the back pocket like a dirty sex picture, some bum had gotten caught and dragged beneath the wheels . . . blood of course, the human body is mostly blood and mystery and sadness . . . a dirty game . . . and a voice shouted out: STOP THE TRAIN!

later, after they examined the shreds, they found it was o.k. 'Just a transient,' they said.

just think if it had been a United States congressman. or president Johnson. but to my mind this man could have easily been a better man than any of them. and probably was. and this is the insaneness of our times: that only what you KNOW or are TOLD ABOUT can be hurt. all else is either shit or the enemy or useless. says who? what the fuck is this? I am getting tired of it. [★ ★ ★]

I almost never think of suicide anymore. what would be the sense in killing this cuckold, this fat demented flabby body, this distilled eye, this color of YELLOW. I've got a yellow streak running up and down my back that would make the Sahara Desert look like a children's sand pile. else I would have killed myself long ago.

so here I sit like a shit
writing a 23 year old kid I never met
and I get drunkeran drunker
and jam the beer down down
the sunlight is all gone
and the cigars too
I go to the woman's cigarettes
and light one after the other

like a jackal imbecile
and I don't know where I am
and a small light burns over my head
a touch of endurance up there
and it makes me almost smile
but the world's out there humming
and the world's not right for me
which makes me a de-balled oxen in the
poverty of myself
and that's sweet enough for me
and I lift the beercan and
drink.

what I mean is, kid, where do we from here? relief rolls? the bloody razor blade? Eartha Kitt, that voice, through a foggy radio? that foreman's face like God, cut from wood, from glass, seeming to know but knowing nothing nothing . . . and so, such poor fuckers as you and i? you and I? we turn to the immortals and the immortals hand us a hot turd, the smell of shit. what a sweet mad game! tricked all the way. – and the most famous poets of our Age, they appear in the pages of the New Yorker, silk white, and you read the poems again and again; and the poems say

NOTHING.

except they are kinda nice. eyow eee yes. how they work the word. this takes training and culture. not everybody can do this. the slip of the word like the knife into Caesar.

let me make up a New Yorker poem as drunk as I am I asshole may not get it, anyhow –

mass effusion darkens my brain –
Clymentia, where are you –
with the silver goatherd
or emptying the glass of
me?
swish, swish the coattails of the
Ark, never by god gone never gone
by god, sweet please, Clymentia,
the dark boys coming over the hill
into a machinegun fire
that would moon-strike gorgeous

teacups from
Georgia to Abeline.

and so on. this they consider poetry because it's pretty and it's a con game and they think that we CAN'T write it, but we can, we simply refuse to, we simply refuse to give more to an Age that already stinks like an old garbage can, and that after Pound there has to be somebody and after Eliot there has to be somebody, and it's a shame but – Ginsberg, Corso, the rest have been sucked in playing their entrails across the applause of the crowd, and they are dead and they know that they are dead, it's useless, they've skipped across listened to the applause of half-drunk freaks too long too long, too long have they taken the bait, and I think of one of Corso's poems: 'I Hate Old Postmen!' this sounds nice, but I predict that when Corso reaches the age of 45 he won't be writing at all. of course, I will be dead so it won't matter. but the Ginsberg, Corso crew (and they write well) will die because they can't resist the delicacy of being forever known forever touched forever heard NOW before 20, 18, 45 people applauding their stuff. they are weak and lack STEEL GUT. I learned in barrooms of the world who the men were. those who spouted the worst were the lousiest fighters. the quiet man was always another kind of job. I don't want to talk like Hemingway, but my face is not only scarred because of disease. I've caught some good ones.

I am an ugly man, surely, but I've also learned that there other kinds of ugliness; and that some beatings that I have taken in alleys, or from a friend across the room, these do not diminish me.

Blaze god damn it, I am SORRY SORRY I could not help you in the Blatt thing. fuck poetry. poetry makes me vomit. and I am tired of fights on the front lawn. I've had enough of that Hemingway stuff to last me 300 years, 2 men on the front lawn punching the living shit out of each other, blood going, we should be punching Johnson right into his fat Texas map for killing us *all*, for trying to be a shadow of Frankie D. what a tent show we put on, eh?

and then we open the *New Yorker* and here's one of the Dickey boys – who knows the difference. –

of course, I keep getting drunker and drunker and this makes less and less sense.

I think I'll chop it off and just fall forward over the keys. BROOKS TOO BROAD FOR LEAPING. good night, babe.

[To Douglas Blazek]

August 24, 1965

the shits around here all discussing the race riots but they are all in the limbo theory, hacking around and vomiting all over their minds and enjoying it listening to the sounds of their own voices, but they are all cotton, cotton-shit with paper faces worse than any halloween masks, and it all ends up like a skeleton trying to fuck a 500 pound ape-gorilla . . . they just don't just can't make it. I speak of certain friends of the woman's who come around. my friends are different, hahah ha! the few of them. at least they don't get out beyond the depth of a dripping cunt until they've thought awhile. I can't think of thinking as an *activate* sort of thing like throwing a ball, even if you've studied the target a long time. thinking is very strange; mostly *it* thinks you and it takes its time. that's why these people who warble their ideas for hours make me want to walk away from them – they are all unpacked loose. besides one of them ate my steak. I left the other night for work and here was this Stanley from her Writer's Group warbling on the couch. he's the one who claims that his writer's group writes better poetry, better stuff than any of the stuff printed in the littles. and they claim they don't send their stuff out, any of them, and that's why you don't see it in print. the magazines are not good enough, real enough, to recognize them. sweetheart, I have not only seen and listened to some of these but have also read some of their stuff. it is weak, weaker than weak; trivial, flat, washed-out. their egos can't face rejection so they gather together each week, chatter and praise each other, scream at each other, haggle, and make up the dreamthing that their stuff is good. better than. anyway, I came home from work, balls-tired and looked in the refrig. 'hey, where's my steak? where'd ya put my steak?' 2 hours overtime and I was thinking of that steak sandwich and a beer and the yellow light over my head as I read the race results. 'oh, Stanley ate your steak,' she said. 'he can't cook at his place and I don't think he's working a full-time job.' I didn't say anything, but when that monkey starts getting into my beer and whiskey, somebody's gona get hurt.

I wrote Henry Miller the other day to twist 15 bucks from a patron of his who promised same if I mailed Henry 3 more *Crux*. I undersell Stuart and it buys whiskey and some horsebets. like I've got a $70 brake repair bill. the *car* isn't worth that. anyhow, I was drunk and inferred that Henry shake his patron out of his money tree. the 15 arrived from one source today and the Miller letter from another: partial quote: 'I hope you're not drinking yourself to death! and, especially not when you're writing. It's a sure way to kill the source of inspiration. drink only when you're happy *if you can*. Never to drown your sorrows. and never drink alone!' of course I don't buy any of this. I don't worry about inspiration. when the writing dies, it dies; fuck it. *I drink to keep going another day*. and I've found that the best way to drink is to drink ALONE. even with a woman and a kid around, I'm drinking alone. can after can laced with a half pint or pint. and I stretch wall to wall in the light, I feel as if I were filled with meat and oranges and burning suns, and the radio plays and I hit the typer maybe and look down at the torn and ink-stained oilcloth on the kitchen table, a kitchen table in hell; a life, not a season in hell; the stink of everything, myself aging; people turning to warts; everything going, sinking, 2 buttons on shirt missing, belly working out; days of dull clubbing work ahead – hours running around with their heads chopped-off, and I lift the drink I pour in the drink, the only thing to do, and Miller asks me to worry about the source of INSPIRATION? I can't look at anything, really look at anything without wanting to tear myself apart. drinking is a temporary form of suicide wherein I am allowed to kill myself and then return to life again. drinking is just a little paste to hold on my arms and my legs and my pecker and my head and the rest. writing is only a sheet of paper; I am something that walks around and looks out of a window. amen. [★ ★ ★]

my god, did I cry that you didn't like my poems?? I musta been drunk. this is really amateur, old ladies' sewing, circle tears. it's as silly as walking in dogshit. forgive me. we all stumble, even old iron-head here. [★ ★ ★]

[To Jim Roman]

August 28, 1965

[★ ★ ★] it seems like everybody and his grandma's dog now own a mimeo machine and is putting out a magazine, and most of them are bad, but a few are good. I yearn for the old days when everything came out in clean print and we knew where everything was. some of the mimeo boys put out faded half-hearted almost unreadable pages, and some of the big boys drop off their crap in here – stuff they can't get to go elsewhere. and the little boys too. I tend to do it. yet there are a few good mimeos and there are some many bad print jobs, and the essence, the secret, is content. [★ ★ ★]

[To Jon and Louise Webb]

September 7, 1965

I had 5 days off (Labor Day + 4) and a hell of a five, and I'm glad I wasn't with you because my mind drew a blank and I fell all over myself, drunk in the streets, I am now lousy bloody bruised – each knee and elbow a blash and scab of blood where I landed each time, drunk, dumping myself like damn keen garbage – what a mess, and no sense to it, I know. my new system seems to work but no good because as soon as I make it I blow it, give it away on the streets, burn it burn it, my god sometimes I think I am truly crazy, but hell, here I sit, trying to shape up for tomorrow to go back in if the job is still there, and I never know – I have a habit of showing in places like that and raising a lot of shit. lost my job at the Biltmore hotel that way. no matter. and it's my teeth too, I've got a half dozen them aching and I can't sleep – but why all these complaints? I bring on my own woe. I keep thinking of Crane jumping off the back of that ship. of course, Crane was a homo, but he was also human. I don't think anybody but a drunk can understand the terrible the horrible horrible BLUES!!! a hangover can bring! of course, I am no longer hung now, am fairly high, and even enclose a half-dozen poems I batted off tonight. not that it matters that they are good or not; what matters is a little juice is flowing, good or bad, there's a little flowing again. I had a hell of a period, it was like steel walls built all around me. but now a little song and dance. it's not excellence we want, it's a kind of going-on, a clown's gesture. it took some deciding to come to this. I think we are all too careful. fuck reputation. if I have a reputation it's only the dirty work of others. I have a right to go on. nobody has the rights to rope and bind me. fuck 'em.

so the eagle came over the San Marcos mountain like a horse and I sat under a busy and rolled a cigarette just like in the old days with Minnie and Mary and Jane in the cheap rooming houses, and it's cigarettes like this and comic strips and radios that work badly and a clean pair of stockings and something to laugh at that keep a man going – even something like Joe Conrad or Tolstoy and they are pretty bad; even something like Faulkner and he's horrible. an eagle over the San Marcos. a cup Hem drank coffee out of. a photograph of your father shooting golf in knickers. Herbert Hoover, alive, without wrinkles. victrolas you had to pump. Icemen with leather shoulders. God on the dole. Mickey Rooney in a tent getting whipped by Wallace Beery. so the eagle came over the San Marcos.

the san marcos. and I read where India and Pakistan are fighting, something about a border. but it's not something about a border. it's something about us. we don't make it. I don't make it. I stink. I am ashamed of myself. I am not ashamed of you, I can never be ashamed of you. a cigarette. bad writing. more bad writing. Jane told me that I couldn't write. when Burnett wrote back – 'all your people seem to die in their own excrement,' dear Jane thought this was wonderful criticism. 'That RIGHT, that's RIGHT!' she screamed, 'ALL YOUR PEOPLE DIE IN THEIR OWN SHIT!' I only told her, 'For Christ's sake, drink your wine and shut up!' I had always thought that all people died in their own shit; it wasn't until Jane and Burnett told me that I thought there would be an alternative?? and the eagle came over the San Marcos and stopped to shit and was killed by a most agile wildcat, looked something like me.

as bad as I feel sometimes it comes pretty close to the end but I remember reading a Norwegian somewhere??? I was much younger. something called the suicide. *The Suicide*. This Icelander could write much better than I; married 3 or 4 times, born children, plowed the land, gone crazy, sucked up years of the sun, I think he finally died an old age, maybe in prison or embarrassment for being a political dupe – became so because he went to the underdog, what was his name? his name? no matter. the SUICIDE wanted to live so badly that given the final great and stereotyped chance, he wouldn't buy it. but this isn't any secret. many men who want to kill themselves only wish to do it because they are tired of being born in an age that will not let them live. I fall in love with my own limbs, my head ugly as it may be, my cock, my balls, my writes by merely being around them, by being with them, awake and asleep, my head, my breathing, my sense of the sun and walls; but when these things become too greatly violated by outside forces I will make the choice, and then finally the choice will not be now when but how?

I have met garbage men with more soul than President Johnson; and this is not sad, this is the way it should be. Johnson is trying to stir alive the soul of Franky D. – which was War and Economic Justice. well, that's the same chapter. I am not much on these history-makers, these killers; but I'd like to see just one pop up: non-war and economic justice. but this is the hell of too much thought. I sit here writing you tonight with 6 teeth aching the living christ outa me and only 2 beers left and the landlord will want his $85, even tho once a week she or he will come down and get me and ask me to get drunk with them and so I'll get drunk with them, we'll talk, and then we'll sing corny songs, songs of their choice, and I'm glad to see them happy but they don't help my happiness much except that they drink and I drink and we sit there in their breakfast nook until Frances brings the kid and the kid cries and Frances says, 'come home, come home!' so I come home, fuck it, and it's a beautiful little girl, tho, and I think she loves me. that's hell. [* * *]

[To Ruth Wantling]

September 11, 1965

in response to your last letter, which I realize was a lot in jest but not entirely – yes, I prob. do carry around my little wooden cross of pain and wave it a bit too much, and even feel foolish defending it . . . for it's up to a man to create art if he's able, and not to talk about it, which, it seems, he's always more than able. I'm nuts, yes, reamed-out and sick; a lot of it shows in the poems. I am an anti-man, pretty sick of the show, yet I have not killed myself, so you have me there; but if you think my way is bad, you ought to try the other – I mean the life-is-good, God-is-good, life-is-beautiful crew. Mostly midwest with names like Irma Tremble Stockholder or Bobby Poots West. they vomit continual Affirmation at a sickening rate, and just because you don't see the magazines around (I doubt Bill reads them) doesn't mean that they don't exist. don't get the idea that everybody writes like Wantling (they can't) or Bukowski. they don't. just for a laugh to jack-off the fleas I once sent a couple of poems into one of those golden hymn singing outfits. they took them. but I had to pay the price. a long letter came along: 'I know your type, brilliant but a drunkard, a gambler, unhappy, disbelieving in God . . .' (so on, so on). 'I awaken every morning to the sound of birds outside my window and I have birds inside too, my canaries, and I have joy and peace, and my magazine pays for itself.' the letter was 4 or 5 pages long in the handwriting of an old woman. I took all her guff until she mentioned that was her policy to make contributors pay for their issue. I wrote back an ass-scorcher and got my issue free. full of hundreds of 3 or 4 lines poems. a photo of a man (poet?) in airforce uniform on cover. so this is the way it works: she thinks I'm sick and I think she's dull. how do we know who's right as I sit here listening to E. Power Biggs pound out Handel?

then, too, there's something else. In America, everybody's supposed to be making it. if you don't make it, that's all right too – only *play* like you're making it. riots are accidents. refuse to think. you know how it works. somebody will pass you on the sidewalk, say a neighbor, and he'll say (sure, he will), 'Good morning, nice day, isn't it?' and you're supposed to say, 'yes, it is a nice day,' and that ends it. but if you say, 'no, it isn't a nice day,' or the answer to the other question (how are you today?) with 'I don't feel so good,' he will act as if struck across the face. you aren't playing the game, and this is *not* just a little voice game, it extends all up and down and across through life. phonies, galore, phonies walking around under the same sun that makes roses, that makes wheat. now, I am not a mad seeker after TRUTH, god damn all that; but I can and do get a bellyful of phonies, and although I don't care to machine gun them down I'd like to get away from them but I can't because I must live with them, work in their factories, fuck their women and drink their booze and kick their dogs and eat their beans. about the only chance a punk like me has to say anything is on a piece of paper called a poem, someplace in between sleeping, eating, batting a woman off what's left of your soul and turning a screw in a factory. so if it comes out as a scream sometimes it really is because the pinch is too tight, the Bastard keeps tightening the vise and smiling and you're supposed to sing The Jelly Roll Blues or say a couple of Hail Marys, but it doesn't work. we are dying inch by inch, being chopped-up and killed by the minute by the hour. I keep looking at that clock, doing the same dull things over and over and over again with my hands, looking at the clock, and doing the dull thing over and over much faster than I want to in order to keep up with production so I can keep my job and die some more, and I keep looking up at the clock, and I die a minute at a time . . . ALL THOSE MINUTES THAT I COULD BE SHIT SHIT USING FOR MYSELF!!! . . . never to be gotten back again, and all around me my fellow-workers laugh a continual hysterical almost female laughter while bragging on their virility as MEN!!!, or there's the tough type full of hatred, nothing but hatred hatred and not even knowing why, swaggering to the latrine thinking he's cool, cool, but what a face on this type of job – a kind of flat shiny deadness with 2 little piglet eyes peering out. and everybody TALKING TALKING about . . . nothing. sports lifts them. they can talk baseball all night, getting fighting mad, or insane, and still not knowing anything about the game. jabber, jabber; my hands moving, moving, the clock hands stuck like arrows in the wall. self-pity? why not? but if we could only do the job quietly without the neurotic jabbering, the fear, the lies, the back-stabbers, the swine, the slickers . . . and I watch the clock and it finally gets there, and if I am lucky they do not call one or 2 or 3 or 4 hours overtime. the only time I am free is driving from the job to where I live in the early a.m. all other times somebody is getting at me. so I get home (home? 2 rooms? a woman, man and child in the same bed?) (I want riches! I want to fuck Elizabeth Taylor's maid!) so I get home and I can't sleep, I can never sleep. I just lay there and listen to the woman and the kid snore. it's beautiful. and I watch the light change from black to gray to red to orange to yellow and finally it's morning and I still stay in bed like an invalid and about noon I go to sleep and about 4:30 p.m. I have to get up again and go to work. nuts? sure, I'm nuts. what do I care about sending kids off to school if the world does not fit around them? President Johnson looks like all the idiot and unfeeling men I've worked for and quit from and been fired from. bombs like walnuts on a row of trees. the clock, the clock, death riding me home in the car repeating the little dirty jokes of my fellow working man. and some x-whore operating a poetry magazine in the Midwest and giving me a lot of jazz about sparrows singing, the angels of God awakening her. if I don't crash through with a poem now and then, I am finished. drink alone is not enough. staring at the ceiling is not enough. my little wooden cross. sure. and yours,

[P.S.] my god, it's all so terrible: all our self-importance; we'll all soon be dust, and that's not news, not news. less even than the smell of shit.

[To William Wantling]

September 11, 1965

as ya can see, I've burned myself out writing a letter to your wife (enclosed) when I should be out building little bird-houses for the approaching winter and those little bastards too lazy to leave this Goldwater territory.

where the riots have just about said quits and the committees are in dividing govt. poverty program funds among contractors, engineers, bullshitters and companies to train janitors – or as they now are called Floor Engineers. I was a janitor for a while but I can never imagine a man calling himself a Floor Engineer when he has to walk into the woman's crapper and clean up what they leave behind. I couldn't get a hard-on for a year after working in that place. what they leave behind. and on the floor. and in that little compartment behind the seat. or alongside of it. or wherever it was.

knives, guns? you're one deep beyond me. I can understand drilling wood with a bit, tho. that's fetching. your problem, of course, is not that you're insane but that you are entirely too sane. through war, jail, dope, woman you're still twitching to find something to hang your hat onto and you probably don't wear one until it snows. I guess, if I can guess, that what hurts is that no matter what men go through, little changes them. they may change an inch for a moment, then snap back, then snap to. the centuries and the training are too jesus much for them. you want victory now, not in your grave where it doesn't count. I'm too tired for victory. I fight a slow withdrawal. I can't make it. if your wife only realized that while you are drilling into that ladder that what is left of your soul is falling back into place. I can see you out there now in the middle of the night, a small light bulb like a crazy sun hanging near your ear and you are smelling the wood and the burning oil from the bit, jesus, what sweetness, nobody around, not even people you love, and if the people you loved would leave you alone you'd come to them with eyes shining in your head so beautiful they'd cry cry cry, but the average woman and no matter how good she is, is only more or less average and the Art they help create is the child and that is enough and too much for me; the average woman wants a constant reminder of love and fuck, and from their angle, I can't blame them – they figure we've been off to a big ball game in hell, tough, yeah, but how about that long cock now, daddy? you haven't told me you loved me since I burned my hand making strawberry jam in 1961. yet, love is confining if you hold it too close to your own belly. I read somewhere a week or so ago that the food America throws into its garbage cans could feed two-thirds of a world and that two-thirds of the world is starving. think how many lovers have thrown their garbage to the pits. love is, in a sense, only a form of selfishness, a form of recognition, usually between 2 people. I do suppose when you are drilling that wood in the middle of the night that all this has occurred to you, but just to let you know that I have thought of it too, and that you are not insane, and that the faces you'd think of machine-gunning on the boulevards are only dead and you only want to bury them bury them, not kill them, for it can't be done, even tho y'd be charged with murder. Your problem, our problem, of course, has been faced before most strongly in the 3 novels (I hesitate to use the world great, they are more than that, for they are beyond the Bible, man's saving little stamping ground) *Crime and Punishment* via Dos, and Camus' *The Stranger*, and, I think, the strongest of them all: Celine's – *Journey to the End of the Night*. where the hell was I? [★ ★ ★]

all right, I'm not much of a man. you've busted them out of their high caves with grenades, with air power, and they've come out ready to meet their slant-eyed God while screaming a banal language and you got to them, aimed, took them out, got some taken out. people like Mailer and Hem made money (and Hem *some* Art, earlier) writing about it, but where does it leave us and what??? [★ ★ ★]

listen, Bill, listen to me, stay off the stuff. [★ ★ ★] only Ginsberg can smoke pot and advertise it and get away with it because his name has become BIG enough so that he'd love to get busted just to help push the circulation of his fading poetry, and also he'd be able to blow the screws after lights out. a man who WANTS to get busted can't get busted because the orders are in. it's like sometimes I've wanted to get fired but I couldn't get fired yet some guy with 6 kids busting his ass and sweating his balls would get layed off. that's the way it works. [★ ★ ★]

[To Jim Roman]

September 26, 1965

[★ ★ ★] A Charles Bukowski checklist/bibliography? why not? for all I've written I seem to remain like a monk fornicating a goose in a coal mine. of course, this is to my advantage too. it allows me to go on working, chipping at the block without interruption. of course, I die in my own vomit, but quietly, and that counts. the gods have been good to me, very very good. if you want to know anything, ask me – I have kept every mag that has published me except one – *Portfolio* II, which went for $10, a Caresse Crosby Black Sun Press thing, very akin to Webbwork, lavish with love and color, I had 2 copies, a short story of mine in there, around 1944, 45? – I remember Caresse writing me – 'Who are you to write this story? I have never heard of you.' even a ten buck check, and there I was in with all the famous fucks – Sartre, Lorca, Miller and on and on . . . I was on the bum and needed the ten. I got drunk. came to the door of my parents weighing 135 pounds. my usual weight around 200. they hated my guts. charged me room and board, atrocious prices, while I got a job and paid it back in. or looked for a job. anyhow the old man stole *Portfolio* II, both copies, and got himself a better job at the L.A. County Museum by claiming that he was Charles Bukowski, and I often wonder, as the years went on [★ ★ ★] what the people thought of him. he was such a beastly stupid prick. 'there goes Charles Bukowski,' I can hear them saying. well, that's all over and he's dead dead dead, thank god.

the date of issues of *Story* that published my short story was March-April 1944, vol. XXIV, no. 106. I remember I was in New York at the time and walking down the street broke and I looked up and there was the god damned magazine in a rack at a corner drugstore. a hell of a feeling, believe me, when you're 24 and half mad. a hell of a feeling anytime, I'd imagine. [★ ★ ★]

Blazek planned a book of Bukowski letters but the project never reached completion. Some letters, however, were included in the Bukowski Sampler *that he published in 1969.*

[To Douglas Blazek]

September 30, 1965

[★ ★ ★] I thought you were thinking of a general book of letters but if you want to do an all-bukowski thing, shit, I'd like to see what I have written too. honor, honor, like a crippled cat fighting off a bulldog or police dog while backed to the fence. (this is good scotch). if we should somehow get some fancy publisher and there's any $$$, I'd suggest we split the god damned loot 3 ways: Blazek, Blatt, Buk. the mighty bees. I don't look for such luck, however. [★ ★ ★]

given a choice, 9 times out of ten a woman would rather sleep with money than talent. given a choice, 7 times out of ten a woman would rather sleep with money than genius. given a choice, ten times out of ten a woman would rather sleep with more money than less money. [★ ★ ★]

Younger readers may need reminding that this letter was written before the widespread availability of the xerographic copying machine.

[SENT TO DOUGLAS BLAZEK]

[ca. September, 1965]

an open letter to those who hold my letters to their bellies in the dark closets their lives . . .

Dear mr. miss, mrs. queer, lesbian and so forth,

what the hell, they are stacking the stuff up to smear us like fly smear and you hold onto a couple of ten cent baubles. these editors are attempting to *collect a collection*, that's profound enough, and a dog with 3 legs staggers. dogs, flies, ach! what I mean is, don't be that way – when I wrote you to begin with, I wrote you because I thought you were a real person not a real estate salesman of sorts, and look look, I am drinking here now and I think the sky will fall down, I look around in panic, 45 years dripping from my belly and you hold onto a couple of letters. it's this, it is a collection, and, shit, it *may* be YOUR LAST CHANCE AT IMMORTALITY, ah haha ha!

when I wrote these letters I wrote them to you and I wasn't thinking about a collection because as you must know I was mostly very poor and very unknown and still am. yet, some find interest in these drunken wailings. are you going to kill me like being a screw in a jail? are you going to half-kill me like a whore taking my wallet while I sleep? are you going to fire me like the factory foreman because orders have fallen off? are you going to kick me out like the landlord because I can't pay the rent. WHAT I AM TRYING TO SAY IS THIS: ARE YOU GOING TO BE LIKE THE REST OF THE WORLD OR ARE YOU GOING TO BE LIKE THE PERSON I THOUGHT I WAS WRITING TO? if this sounds like I am begging, then I am: I am begging for faith and a little bit to go on with.

I don't know the actualities. maybe a big name publisher, maybe just shit smeared onto toilet paper with fingernails. but when I wrote you I felt you, the sound and realness of you, the you you you, myself directing the arrow the heart the crooked music of what was left after the factory the racetrack whatever whatever. I can't feel you'll let me down; I can't feel you've grown that dead. if it's only money money, my god, I'll try to send you a little each day each week each month; whatever I have.

I ask you out of whatever is left of my soul, out of what tiny bit of gentility and mirror of a sweat shot of sun I have left, please send in your letters and you'll be received where you should be received: where I met you, say, peeling an orange and talking about Picasso, anything, guts, spirals, pawnshop brokers, rain, *almost* love, broken doors, donkeys without names. I guess I must sound like a cocksucking preacher. I am tired. I only want all the parts to be all the parts like the river running after the 6 horse. I can't say anymore. your move and the night grows dank with the sweat of violets pimping.

love, ya ya ya.

[To William Wantling]

[Early October 1965]

thanks for the Dos thing, I will comb it like I did the same central caves of the novel, only what bothered me about *Brothers* [*Karamazov*] was this unreal division of the brothers into those cast types like chessmen, each with his own move. a wonderful diveboard for stunting but I wonder about the critics who rate the *Brothers* Dos's #1 work. *Crime* seemed the more evil and normal and natural work. I think that Dos wanted to say a lot more than he did in *Crime &* but lost his guts, his nerve and his senses. a great novel, still. and since I haven't written a nearby companion piece I had better shut up. [* * *]

it is 5 a.m. as I write this yet the woman snores over and through Mozart. I cannot help thinking that snoring is an infirmity of the soul, a true voice speaking through sleep. my father was the most vile beast I ever met and he snored louder and with more ugliness than anybody I have ever heard. [* * *]

I was never good with the women, never really tried to be, couldn't get my back up to go through the prelims, the fake talk. it cost me too much. then, too, a kind of withered pride. they all looked kind of pukey to me, even those the boys called 'fine.' too much battle. I settled for the old ones. those nobody wanted. a fifth on the dresser, a little talk, a kind of dead fuck (tho, not always), then more drink, more easy talk and then another fuck. but not much strain or pretense. kind of a wearisomeness. I just just can't pay the price of tight new pussy, and won't, it's too high. always was. for me. [* * *] but it's all shit in pink drawers and squatting to piss, finally. [* * *]

[To Douglas Blazek]

October 10, 1965

been playing with the little girl for an hour and a half on the rug after work and now I am like a burned city, but, shit, so? & Thursday at 12:30 p.m. I swing onto the CHIEF #20 for Lamay, New Mexico with 2 pints of scotch and then a bus on into Santa Fe, 7 a.m. Friday morning if I do not die or fall off the cliff of myself before then, and I have bummed for years until this crotch of a life grabbed me on this job for 8 years, my god, but a little space again, a shot of light, and then back, or a shot of agony – I do not make it with people, I can't help it. and I can't sleep on trains, I can't even sleep on a bed, the only way to sleep is to drink yourself senseless.

you get people together and they sit around in a room and look at each other and try to think of things to say; it's ugly and senseless. or somebody gets on the make. or somebody vomits in the back porch. or somebody screws the dog. I am not all there in conversation; sometimes I think I am made of some kind of hard and unfriendly stone. most things disgust me; I don't know what I want. then I begin thinking that I am insane, that I can't see what they see, that I can't understand what they understand; that they are naturally warm and that I am a dribbling fake. and then, in the next flash, I suddenly think that they are damned fools and I don't give a damn what they think. all my strings fight in discord; my cock is trying to screw my brain, or the other way. then I look down and my belly is flopping out, my sides are flopping out; my zipper is coming undone, China crawls in a teacup like a worm; everybody looks handsome and clean and there is dirt under my fingernails and a stink rises from my soul. a bad fix all the time – perhaps a little exaggerated but not too much.

now the kid is crawling under my feet and the woman says PEEK A BOO! I SEE YOU!!!

no, I don't want a steady stay in N.M. those things don't work. the battle I have here now is killing me but that one would kill me faster. I have to go by instinct. actually I am not trying to write mainly poems or a novel. actually poems are only toothpicks that hold me up a little. [★ ★ ★]

you might have guessed by now that the literary gang is an unclean mob – dollar crazy as any manufacturer, as any pimp, as any anything. and cold, and cold. they pretend to have intelligence, and they write so seemingly of justice and life, almost as if they knew something. but the dirty cocksuckers would sell you off in a minute; a pawnbroker has more conscience and more heart. the Arts, generally, are the hiding place of the weak and the imbecilic. I know I know I know. I am not knocking Art as a contrivance, as a good bell ringing inside my hollow head; I am knocking the polluted stream, the turds. you know.

yet maybe I am just talking talking talking. the longer I live the less I know. maybe death is just eliminating everything – life is a turd – you pop it out and you are ready. I mean, each day I get a little simpler: I believe less, I feel less, I realize less. I like to watch flies now or look at coffeepots or listen to refrigerator sounds, sounds like god-voices. I hear. isn't this what a child does? I want it easy; I don't even want to win. of course, there has been a lot of this. even when I am fighting a man and he is intent upon killing me, I cannot believe him, I cannot believe what is happening and I cannot become truly angry. there are 2 things that bother me, that make me weak in the world:

1: I have never been lonely.

2: I have never been angry.

and the third thing:

I fuck with the Arts.

drinking is only to jell the parts that have been taken apart by factories or whores or a faceful of busses. I mean, that it brings me back to the basics of myself, whatever those basics may be. if drinking destroys the brain, fine. for what my brain has seen it yearns destruction.

god, I wish I had the guts and style and cement and vastness of a Jeffers – clean through rock into an eagle's eye, and then behind stone, hacking, sounding. I have some of this but not enough, and meanwhile I jump through all sorts of weird hoops at others' behest, and I get rapped and trapped bit my god by bit until I am hanging by a finger, by a thin gut-string in the middle of an empty sky. get me? melodramatic? o, hell yes – 96,000 SEASONS IN HELL ON OVERTIME. [* * *]

and here I go down to poke my smashed head into a doorway. I really don't want to go. I don't want to do anything. I lose 3 days at the track, harness races, sunshine, the quiet drink from my flask on the grandstand steps, the looking at the legs of women I don't know the name of. I could weep for my quiet freedom, yet somebody sends me a railroad ticket and I play it through. maybe it is that I have seen enough hell; maybe it is that I don't want to see anymore. yet, I guess, there I will be getting on that train 12:30 p.m. thursday, my face twisted into nothing, sitting down, waiting for the thing to roll, wondering what ass I will draw for a seat partner and very glad the 2 pints are in the cloth bag over my head.

wish me luck, baby, wish me everything; I am sad, I got the blues the blues the green blue purple blues. my my my.

[To Al Purdy]

October 11, 1965

[* * *] people keep sending me poems and novels to read and collections of poesy – I mean people I have never written to or heard of – and all the stuff is bad, bad, bad. I wonder if you realize how much bad stuff is written in all earnestness? and they'll keep right on with it. thinking that

they are undiscovered genius. I rec. a beautifully printed book of poems, fine paper, hardcover, and inscribed 'to Buk . . .' and etc. an honor, sure, but I can't even write this person and thank him because the poems are so flat and drivelling that they are not even bad – they don't even exist. if you know the type I mean. yet I don't throw a book away when it is sent to me in this way and I don't know what to do with them. I guess there'll be another one in the mail tomorrow. there are a lot of dead men sitting at typewriters. I would have quit long ago but when I saw the truly bad stuff that was being done, I couldn't let go. [* * *]

[To Douglas Blazek]

October 23, 1965

[* * *] it has been 100 degrees for 3 or 4 days and everybody smells like shit and everybody is, of course. in from track, medium day, plus $32. the human race is an empty egg out there. the crowd is a dog made of sausage. I could not think of fucking or singing out there, or dreaming; only murder. – now back in the trough: cigar, beer, old hat bit. my guts are dropping out and I sit here pecking at the keys like a propped-up Hemingway with matchstick soul. and the typer seems shot. hope you can read.

back from Santa Fe, ya. [* * *] I was sick most of the time I was there but did hunk down quite a bit of beer and scotch and got into a little trouble. Webb always flips a bit when the image does not fit the peg but I can't be bothered. one night I was quite drunk and locked out in the icy rain and knocking on doors but nobody wanted to let me in. somebody finally relented and gave me a long angry speech. shit on that. my father is dead. I am dead. [* * *] I got on the train and my foot began to swell. I walk around barefoot when drunk and all the glass and steel I had picked up decided to play death. I found a sadist doctor when I got into town and he sliced my heel open and dug and probed and dug. no shot, of course. German accent: 'Vell, vell, you took it like a man!' 'You enjoyed it more than I did,' I told him. 'Nine, nine! you see I vuz only interested in seeing vat was in dere, I did not enjoy . . .' 'make out the bill.' and that, was Santa Fe. [* * *]

the average person has largely and finally already left the earth, my friend. they generally leave about the age of 5, although some stay a bit longer. tough for you, mother, but you are still here. your letters and poems get better, better, as I shrivel up into bologna-string walking. have you ever seen a bologna-string walking? Death is 2 balls without a head. Death is not being able to possess a good woman because I am dirty from factories and alleys and sluggings and hospitals and marriages and shack-jobs, and poor, poor, poor, poor crippled dirt. wine bottles, nights of a steaming light bulb, scribbling on little slips of paper and unable to read them in the morning or at noon or ever.

> death is all this waiting without screaming
> death is bread rotting in the heat
> and 90 million rats and roaches
> death is a sea of piss
> death is a sophisticated afternoon in Santa Fe
> with nobody saying what they are thinking

maybe it's the heat, kid, I am really snarling through these thin rented cardboard walls. how much separates me from the loony bin? sometimes down at work I feel like slugging somebody. no hatred, only the zero complex. I want to bust something. sometimes it happens by itself. same thing happened to somebody that happened to me in 53 or 54 or whenever it was. the belly broke open and the blood came out, out, out. he was dead by the time he reached the hospital. the bad life. I whine before I turn out the lights; I pray for spastics and dwarfs, Pal, I pray for scrub women, Pal, I pray for frightened women of some seeming beauty who play their hand and exchange one rich man for a richer man. I pray for the nail that enters the hand that enters the wood, I pray that that nail may not be rusty. Pal.

a couple of old wrinkled-up women down at work are trying to fuck me. they know that I am whipped. one of them has a young girl's ass and legs but she must be a thousand years old. 'I am getting a new Mustang. will you teach me how to drive?' 'I'll drive you, baby, I'll drive you!!' 'he, hehe, hehehe, that's what I thought! an' I want ya ta meet my sister too!' looks like I gotta fuck the whole family. I'll probably pass. it's a hairy drippy drizzling game. it's only when I get drunk that I imagine that I am the lover. what nonsense. and Rupert Brooke wrote better too. but he didn't have any sense and decided to go to war. and try to be lucky. bullets are built for poets. I knew this one guy, not a bad writer or human being either (sometimes there's a difference) who said, 'But suppose some stupid cocksucker points a machinegun at me and squeezes the trigger?' 'if you go, he will.' he went – it happened. m.g. slugs. but they'll always find an excuse for another war, that's all right. but they'll bust you for a little game of pot. or jail a whore for selling her pussy. or blame a homo for being a homo. or fire a man for being 10 minutes late to work. or jail you for being drunk on the streets. or run a woman out of the country for not believing in God (Mad Murray) and saying so and getting them to ban prayer in schools because she figured the kids should have a choice. but War? stockpiles? shit??? why not? listen, I don't mean to preach here but a little drunk a little tired – up all night at work and then the racetrack today and now almost midnight, no sleep, so the seams ripping a bit.

something on from the Three Penny Opera. Brecht does not help me too much. I do not trust his melodrama; a god damned horse thief. the social structure bit. I mean, he holds a good hand . . .

the little girl runs up and pokes me with her finger. I sit in my shorts. 'uts DAT?'

'dat's fat.'

'uts DAT?'

'dat's my bellybutton.'

. . . because he speaks plainly, that's a good thing, but he turns it on too much. there are other basics besides a Jewish nose. clarity of delivery can trap you as much as obtuseness because you can kid yourself that you always *seem* to know what you are saying. (See Hemingway, Dos Passos, Sherwood Anderson, E. E. Cummings.) but I know a lot of guys down at work who have a plain clarity of delivery and they never say anything.

tell me, Blaz, do you think the dead get hard-ons?

do you think the worms and maggots will ever crawl the body of your Love in that closet down there in the dark? what did that fly mean? why did it affect me? why all the sunlight? and the horse standing under the tree? will I live another ten years? [* * *] a siren goes now, ambulance, then fire trucks earlier, the town is on fire, and earlier today coming in from the track I drove thru the Negro section of the x-riots and they were shining their cars and sitting on their steps, they'd had their drunk, and now it was back to it. my god, not a chance for any of us. white or black, living or dying, we are snot, driven helpless snot before a brainless moon of God. seesee, see the Martini Life! the homes in the hills! 14 bathrooms, 17 fireplaces, & 7 great muddy garages while buying 2 more homes over the telephone, one with a winding staircase marvelous like a lighthouse thing for your guests to fall down drunk upon after drinking their *own* liquor.

well, 6 more bottles of beer and then to sleep, maybe. [★ ★ ★]

now they play the Blue Danube and I snap the radio off.

now everybody is here in the kitchen and the whole kitchen is hollering. they talk about making OATMEAL! don't say that I don't properly feed these broads.

so we go on. no death in the road. no Nobel. 5 bottles of beer. a typer that wobbles on 3 legs and wants to kick off. my my. there goes a fly. [★ ★ ★]

I am spreading wall to wall, fat and stupid, hardly feel the pain – translate it mostly, I do, into shots of blue and green light. a formula. I didn't mean to lay it on you, baby. I remember the bit about (who was it?) Flaubert telling DeMass to keep on clerking, practice on his writing and not to become a journalist. so de Mop clerked and Flub wrung his hands in the light of his (Flaubert's) fame. sometimes I think it might have been to remove competition? anyhow, DeMop took it out on his rowboat and mad he went because of the siff and mostly because of clerking, although they won't admit that. [★ ★ ★]

there is a poet-novelist who said, 'Bukowski worries about his soul.' this is too pat of course and puts em in a neat box. but I have packed the meat on my shoulder and have seen the threads come out of statues. I don't need a soul; all I need is a light bulb, some beer and a chair to sit in. but some want to take that from me. now I have been shipped the poet-novelist's latest book of poems and I am supposed to review the bit for a mag. I don't know what to do. it looks very much as if my friend has not worried about *his* soul. christ, how we snipe! should I shoot him down? we are all a bunch of bitches. dying is often a slow process. why rack a man because his poems have started to fail anymore than rack a man because his eyesight is failing or his teeth falling out or his pecker failing to get hard? we gotta have a winner, what? yet, in another sense, there are some men who sell too easy; one second a man is his brother's keeper and the next second he is Brutus. [★ ★ ★] then too, you might figure it this way: a real man is gonna lose his teeth his hair and his balls long before the soul??? it is confusing. yet I keep looking at faces, I keep watching ways things are done. I'm no Virgin. I've rolled and been rolled and yet, in a certain sense, there is just so far that you ought to go, just so much that you should do. I don't speak of morality and code – that jazz has held the world back too long. I speak of simple things, although I can't say just what they are but you know them when they come upon you. Genet's seeming immorality and depravity are nothing of the sort. because he is neither depraved nor immoral toward himself. he does what is proper toward himself. the greatest immorality is going for gold against the grain of yourself when you don't need the gold, the possession – like taping dead oranges on an orange tree. of course, most of us figure we need some of the gold. there's always an excuse to die: the wife, the baby, the girlfriends; there is always an excuse to go to the cowardice that most men are naturally inherent to because his father was inherent to it and his father's father etc. there's always an excuse to be a prick. it even seems clever. graft. babes with long legs and tights pussies. new cars. then often immorality and immortality lock legs and you've got jism all over the bed. Oxford. grants. lectures. poetry readings. mouth, mouth, mouth. we are sucked forever into the traps. I've always found the face and the ways and the honesty of a ditch digger more alive than any English prof. of course, nowadays even the ditch diggers are getting sophisticated. trouble everywhere. what am I saying? I've lost the string. good. good, then. [⋆ ⋆ ⋆]

catch? fine. the critics say that I am non-cerebral. I think the same thing of them. I think that they are patsies to the dupe, playing some kind of con-game, not because I *don't* understand their words but because I do. they and Grandma may call it carnal but I call it wet pussy and prostitution. I am as cerebral as any of them (at least so) and if they want to talk about Government or God or Plato or the Meaning of Man, or any of those useless things, have them pour me a couple of glasses of bourbon and I'll take them up alleys they've never seen and roll them out of their minds. Everything is basically simple – especially the critics, especially my critics. and, thus, having unloaded this load of come I move on to other things.

do you think, my son, that I will ever get a job teaching Creative Writing at the University of Columbia? I would very much like to fuck some young coeds or have *them* fuck me. [⋆ ⋆ ⋆]

I guess that so many problems come in upon a man that he finally dismisses them all and becomes a rock. the world is full of rocks. but the beer goes down down down. Wagner's *The Ring* on now. Wagner goes good with me. Shostakovich. the Russians, the German in the Arts. The French, the English, the Spaniards do me little good. the Italians, halfway. why is it? of course, there's Knut Hamsun. Norway? wherever the hell. [⋆ ⋆ ⋆]

Kirby Congdon was editor of Magazine *(New York). A letter from Bukowski appeared in no. 3 (see below).*

[To Tom McNamara]

October 25, 1965

[★ ★ ★] have you ever met Kirby Congdon? he seems bright enough to set torches to the world. almost seemingly classical, yet lived, and learned, and not to be bullshitted. I understand he is going to Key West or somewhere. there are so many good people I'd like to get drunk with, not so much as to talk myself, but to see them sitting in chairs and talking. Each man seems to come up with something good, something to make me laugh, and they do it so easily and with grace and honesty. Christ I am a pig, Mac, so often so tight, so often so untrusting.

if I could only realize that right now there are at least 1,000 people on earth better than Christ was; I mean, if Christ was not a fable; I mean, people who don't do tricks like raising the dead and being glorious and so forth. these people stay hidden. they know that contact means the plague. this is what disgusts me with the Ginsberg/Corso mob. they suck to the human adulation bit and are soon swallowed. Corso died rather quickly because his only mainstay was a simplicity of purpose and some type of message that he thot important. It has taken Ginsberg a little longer, but he is swallowing the same bloody bait – via Behan, via D. Thomas. The woman here is full of words and the child runs around. but I am still insane. She says Thomas drank himself to death because he felt his talent was waning. Bullshit. Thomas drank himself to death for the same reason that I do: he loved his drink, it lifted him where he belonged, where we all belong, where we all should be if the stream of people weren't such asses and didn't believe in homes and new cars and all that junk. I have almost died of drink several times, once very close, it was sweet and didn't matter, and they finally stood me up and walked me out of a door to do it again. fuck em. I am ready to die. I am ready to wilt. [★ ★ ★]

[To Ann Menebroker]

[Late October 1965]

umm, yes, I am a dog, of course & therefore and forevermore and I have not written but you wouldn't want me to send you a letter that didn't walk around on the paper . . . wouldn't a halfass babbling be an insult? we all die and are stuffed with standard formality, and, of course, now that I've said this, you have a fine springboard to leap upon me with. Christ, that almost sounds sexy! we have to be careful. at least, you have to. anyhow I just got in from Santa Fe, sick, of course, silly and boozed and nowhere further along anywhere. sure, I remember the good old days when you used to ship me a half dozen 50 cent pieces for one of my books, and enclose a trinket or a rose with eyes, sure sure, and I am the same ass. nothing has altered me. I crash through a headful of shoulders and find myself in a marble bathtub with dirt rings, bell rings, blue rings, red rings, the saliva of myself dribbling into lukey water without goldfish, and the world is shot, and I breathe and wait to die, I breathe and wait for November or Rapid Transit or a young girl sitting on bus stop bench with a lot of leg showing. I drink continually and it keeps me going or it kills me and it doesn't matter, it is all the same. [* * *]

the old life was very satisfying, of course. Please do not become too relaxed watering plants, baking cookies, putting out the diaper pail to remember the rest. I don't know exactly what price you are paying for your safety. me, I'm paying a pretty high price for mine and the mirrors turn their backs from me now. I prefer to cover them with towels to spare them the sight of my death. I have joined the walking living dead upon the avenues, in the saloons and everywhere else. but it's 4 a.m. and the police are driving by and I hear voices outside and we all live very close together here and I am a coward, I am afraid of jails, I hate jails, and so I turn Wagner down a little on the radio, sip my next to last beer and wish you the love of memory and the love of love or whatever there is, dear one.

Neeli Cherkovski, then known as Neeli Cherry, was a poet and editor of Black Cat Review. *He later was to write Bukowski's biography,* Hank.

[To Neeli Cherry]

[?1965]

[★ ★ ★] I was in a mellow mood (rare for me) when I wrote the intro to Sherman's stuff, and I felt a little kind and comradely. It is easier to feel that way when Sherman is at a distance. Outside of the poem form I do not much buy his antics. I believe I made this clear in my poem 'Letter from the North.' Yet everything I said in the intro to his poems I said out of the truth of myself, whatever truth I could find. It's a scurvy word anyhow. Actually I do not think J. writes as well as he used to . . . never fulfilled the early promise and all that hogwash, except maybe with the poem 'Montgomery Street' which I think is a great poem, and if a guy can write a poem like this, I will forgive a lot of his nonsense in actual life.

[To Neeli Cherry]

October 28, 1965

[★ ★ ★] my thanks for the emotive 'An Invitation,' good flow here. although the truth factor in some lines disturbs me: 'to combat all the yellow-bellies who are sucking us dry. and they are, they are.' 'but the only alternative is not to fight, and my god! we couldn't do that.' sounds like you've been hornswoggled. if you really think about it, it is the white-bellies who are sucking you dry. but, then, to have a war it is always best to believe you are the Good guy and the other is the Bad guy. it runs more smoothly. death needs help sometimes.

then, too, I think you might have written your lines in jest, in satire, and that I missed the point. [★ ★ ★]

[To William Wantling]

[?1965]

[★ ★ ★] I keep drinking beer and scotch, pouring it down, like into a great emptiness . . . I admit that there is some rock stupidity in me that cannot be reached. I keep drinking, drinking, am as sullen as an old bulldog. always this way: – people falling down, off their stools, testing me, and I drink them down, down, down, but really no voice, nothing, I sit I sit like some stupid elf in a pine tree waiting for lightning. when I was 18 I used to win $15 or 20 a week at drinking contests and this kept me alive. until they got wise to me. there was one shit, though, called Stinky who always gave me a hard go. I'd outpsyche him sometimes by drinking an extra in between. I used to run with these thieves and we were always drinking in a vacant room, a room for rent, with a low light . . . we never had a place to stay, but most of these boys were tough, carried guns, but I didn't, still was square, still am. I thought Stinky had me one night and I looked up and he wasn't there and I went in to heave and I didn't even heave, there he was in the bathtub, out out, and I walked out and picked up the money. [★ ★ ★]

[To William Wantling]

October 30, 1965

[★ ★ ★] It isn't any secret to myself that I am a rather backward man, lived, baby, but still culling and never sure, always goofed, no answer, and I learn this more and more down at the pits where I work. trying to be one of the boys I will crack wise but it seems to me that I am always topped. christ, the clock is long enough without being topped mentally and spiritually by your fellow-workers. but they always seem to edge me; I get this look of eye and I drop back into silence, once more the defeated asshole, my god. I am always under somebody's whip. a father. a highschool principal. a fine-looking and lying whore. a bottle. a cigar. a flat tire. rent. a child. rain. constipation. insomnia. a screw at Moyamensing, a trusty in the drunk tank. [★ ★ ★]

and yet we learn. there is a whiner down at work. he cries cries but his crying is like some suckerfish, it is not a clean cry and I have listened to all his strickenness, I have listened to hours to years of his mewking and it has taught me – a good man can learn from a good fool. even a not so good man can learn. what I mean is that we all have extremities of unfulfilled wanting. we are toys to whatever has created us. we will never get there, and even if we get halfway, the ending will be the same: smashed cat's guts on the boulevard or the last drip of sour blood into the bedpan, hurrah!! I mean

> we've got to live with loss like we used to
> maybe still do
> live with a bad
> whore

but
we know all along what it is
we take is standing like Hemingway
or we dismiss it like
Camus
but we know
about it

this is the way it works and
we wind our clocks and we
wait on
midnight or the carnival
a hamburger sandwich or the
garbage man.

we live with it we live until we
die.

how's that for hot shit? I throw in free poems that will never be used. I am a truly tough spit baby crying outa a blinkin' blinking eye thing. [★ ★ ★]

Veryl Blatt, together with her husband Jean Rosenbaum, was planning to gather and edit a collection of Bukowski's letters.

[To Veryl Blatt]

November 9, 1965

[★ ★ ★] It's too bad Corrington and Webb won't let go of their letters – the bulk of everything is here – but I felt from the beginning that Corrington would hold out. he has changed very much in the last 2 years – ever since getting his doctorate and writing his first novel. He has stepped up out and away from me. I got worried about him near the end when he said, 'I am going to use your letters to help send my son through college.' Through college for what? *we* are trying to live now. It's strange how cold things can become and how, basically, so many poets are like real-estators, holders of stock, investors . . . C. has plenty of money; he ought to loosen his grip; he won't. the fact is, that I was writing to the wrong man. [★ ★ ★]

Wantling must have requested some quotable aphorisms.

[To William Wantling]

November 11, 1965

They beat you down with their factories, their booze, their women until you are no longer of any use to them or yourself.

– Bukowski

The trouble with women is that in creating new men they tend to destroy old ones, and you and I know that women are not very good artists.

– Bukowski, again.

[* * *]

I have never met a man that I have truly liked. I have met men that I would drink with, laugh with, fight for – but only in a manner of hope instead of reality.

– B.

I only loved one woman and, unlike all the others, she was the only one who never demanded or asked for the spoken word of it. and even over her grave I said nothing, not even in my head, but the sunlight knew and my shoelaces and [*illegible*].

– B.

[* * *]

I don't want to play the image of the drunk; it is only that I get so sick of what I remember.

b.

Social consciousness is what keeps me from raping little girls of eleven – that, and the chance of getting caught. Yet I cannot conceive of anybody raping my own little daughter – her eyes are so blue and holy that God himself might awaken to destroy the offender. Yet what keeps us going while we are racking up our own cruelties is the almost certain knowledge (instinct) that God is asleep during our acts. I am as guilty as any, for the desire to act and then not-to-act is the same as acting; the only factor lacking between them being courage, and yet I must beg off at times through a seeming sympathy for an intended victim, which might only be an inbred Christianity or cowardice. The greatest problem is, however, that no intended victim of rape, robbery, murder, the worst of acts, is *innocent* at all – they have all died or slipped or slurred or murdered something themselves along the way – even eleven year old girls. I think that the best principle for a strong man (if

I may invent a term?) is not to get involved with the creatures because the creatures are a swamp. There will be certainly enough involvement, without voluntary explorative involvement, to last you a lifetime and to wear you down and kill you before you are 37 years old.

– buk

happy birthday you 32 year old dog [⋆ ⋆ ⋆]

[⋆ ⋆ ⋆] and we all know about our Great President Honorable Rancho Hot shit Johnson, he talks outa one side of his mouth and shoots a loaded 45 into the back of an innocent man with the other. I go on record that he is a Liar. I've met and worked for his types in all the slave mills from Atlanta, Dallas, New York, any city you can name. I hate his face. he is the final great o o o intruder elected to mutilate society at society's behest. what a hell kind of a democracy is this, that gives you one face, and then gives you the knife?

the United States Government keeps increasing its hardness by the surety of its strength, and it keeps getting harder and harder and tougher and tougher until it is almost like some crazy kind of wart or cancer gone mad. I keep getting the thought that this is happening everywhere in all governments all countries . . . christ, we are all so ugly. Is this the meaning of Govts? to get uglier? so, we have the French Rev. which slowly faded back into its cage. and now we have found that even the American Civil War was meaningless . . . an exchange of ariel courtesies . . . while the poor black remained the poor free?? black, and even more hollow doughnuts, this Watts strike which I witnessed and work with most of the blacks, even the blacks have conspired into silence, for Christ's sake, tell them about a few committees, a poverty program wherein not one wino gets 10 cents for a drink of wine, just salaries for officials who have already beat the game by getting into the machine of the game fuck it fuck it. I am lost. and I knew all during the riots that it would be lost . . . that even the words of the rioters would fall back. . . . no new world, never. Just the guy on top looking and talking like the guy on the bottom and thinking the same things and the same way. all lost, forever. my hands on a small torn white tablecloth, my white hands, my drink, my cigarette, hoping verily for a wake up of Big Prick God but knowing all along it would not be so. Keep your grenades, 32 year old tough guy, I have done time too, but I guess all our dreams are going to leak out of a salty piss pillow, and I never had no hope and if you think it hard to be 32, you are correct. it is hard to be anything.[⋆ ⋆ ⋆]

[To Douglas Blazek]

[?November, 1965]

[* * *] I've got to say one thing for ALL THE WOMEN I've lived with, they couldn't care less. it's only when the blade falls and we are sitting out on the street on a piece of cardboard that they seem to question. I remember one of them saying, 'But I thought you knew what you were doing!' 'Baby, baby,' I told her, 'what ever gave you such an idea?' this one I walked South into the city with, she knew somebody – 'he'll let me stay. I only hope he makes his balls quick. I can't stand the son of a bitch.' I walked her to the door, watched her make up her face, she gave me the sad death kiss and then knocked, 'It's me, Kelly, honey.' and some big fat swine of a businessman, 285 pounds of gold wrapped his arms around her and I walked off. to the streets. I didn't have a pussy.

the woman is off to her little poetry reading group at his church or other. Neeli Cherry is down there too. he likes to mouth his stuff but they won't let him read right off. he's got to suck in. he'll shoot some mouth tho. I can see Frances now, 'And now, I want to introduce Neeli Cherry, editor of the *Black Cat Review*.' and the little butterball, 20 years of him, will try to get up and say something clever. I'll have them all on my back next Sunday – Neeli, Frances, the kid; I'm going to drive them down to see the Richmond madhouse EARTH, if the old car makes it, and I take F. to drive me back. the judge told me last time, 'one more drunk driving rap and you might as well measure up for a loose-fitting pinstripe.' only not in that terminology. but I read him, the monster. Neeli keeps telling me, 'I don't care for Richmond's stuff,' and not being an arguer or a man for detail in vocal transmission, I always give him the same, 'Richmond writes some good stuff.' which, of course, is so. Richmond writes a clean and easy and a clear line. all those fuckers write well: Richmond, Cherry, Wantling, the whole screwy suffering houseful. I just hate to see them scratch each other. well, god damn them anyhow, I travel alone.

scratch, scratch.

very strange happening today, was sitting going over my horses today before going to track, red-eyed, sucking on a beer, shivering, sick with 2 hours overtime and no sleep, sitting in the torn chair by the door and the doorbell rings and here is the mailman with a registered letter from one Heinrich Fett, 547 Andernach a/Rhein, Privoit Strs. 1, Germany. that's where I was born, sweetheart. what an odd feeling. and here in broken English was a letter from my Uncle (my dead mother's brother) who said,

'By chance I got your address on October 22, 65.' only it was my old address at 1623 N. Mariposa Ave. where I did some good whoring and maybe some good writing too. anyhow, the letter, short and simple, damn near knocked the beer outa my hand, tho not quite. I'll write him tomorrow and tell him that I am very old and very tired. [★ ★ ★]

[To Ann Menebroker]

November 17, 1965

[★ ★ ★] It seems like I've written a hell of a lot of drunken letters, maybe more letters than poems, and somebody got the idea it might make a book. Feelers in from some publishers already even tho book is still gathering. I would like your letters – mine to you – included, the best ones, unless you feel that in some of them there was something extra personal. But I have nothing to hide. the letters are yours tho, please do as you wish. I am hoping that you will let them look at most of them, maybe all of them. All letters are returned, of course. Please understand that. and my letters to you are, of course, more personal than to many but I am hoping that anything I said was universal as well as personal. I do hope that you will let them look at most of them? if you do, my more than thanks, of course. for since we have gotten into this thing I would like it to be as complete a selection as possible. [★ ★ ★]

[To Douglas Blazek]

November 24, 1965

[★ ★ ★] I haven't heard from you on the 2 long poems I sent. Please return if they don't fit you. I have been rejected before. besides, one poem must have a portion *eliminated* anyhow. I remember slamming Eisenhower but since his recent heart attack & obvious decline, I have decided to lay off. no need to attack the sick and the aged – there's bigger game in the brush.

now must try to get some rest. please forgive tired letter. and again, much thanks, your master job on *Confessions*.

[To Ruth Wantling]

[November 25, 1965]

[* * *] no no no, I don't like snowstorms, I almost died in one, and I am now too old to die. death is only for the young. o christ, forgive me. I keep opening my mouth. you know, I am always in a jam. anyhow, since you know I am an ass, I'll go on. there was one winter, I think it was in Philly. I am sitting in this very tiny bar and the bartender starts spouting Shakespeare and I am making it with a couple of women in there but this makes me angry, this Shakespeare, so being a blackheart by nature I started bragging on Hitler, Mussolini, so forth, and the next thing I knew I was evicted and instead of being guided to one of the warm pads of one of the whores to be fucked and rolled or maybe just rolled I was walking along in the snow, then stopped and decided to piss against the side of a church. this worked nicely. finished. put it away. then decided on a shortcut across the churchyard. all fine. big moon. ice cold. I have a room somewhere anyhow. I am walking along plenty drunk and then I trip over this wire they have strung across the yard about ankle high. down I go. too drunk to raise up. I lay there knowing I will freeze. I laid there a long time. but it must have been the coldness of the snow on my face that revived me. I got up and made it on in. but, remembering this the next morning, I decided to get out of the snow country and stay out. suicides are desperately vain: they like to choose the time and place. there's a great difference between dying when you want to and dying when you don't want to. I know that it amounts to the same thing yet there remains a kind of difference in how the soul or what's left of the soul enters the earth of the sky or whatever it enters.

listen!!! will you stop this god damned lovely dental technician shit and what great gobs of nicety these dentists . . . these paid torturers of the haunted human race . . . are. all other areas of science have moved forward and these fuckers are still working with a pair of pliers. I can't see a man who wants to be constantly around blood as any kind of decent individual. I'd rather pick up garbage. every dentist I have ever met has had thick wrists, black nazi hair on his arms and an ovaltine belly swarming with the hymns of rats. what lies are you trying to tell me? [* * *]

[To Steven Richmond]

Thanksgiving for what? [November 25,] 1965

[★ ★ ★] if you think f. franklyn's thing was rough on me, you ought to see what I did to my dear friend John William Corrington when the editor of *Steppenwolf* sent me his latest book of poems *Lines to the South* to read and review. I had praised Corrington's preceding book of poems but this collection became a complete reversal – automatic poetic poetry. I didn't know what to do. as you might know, Corrington wrote the foreword to my selection-collection of 8 years' worth of poetry, *It Catches My Heart in Its Hands*. he called me some pretty good things, and here I sat with his latest book of poems in my hands and it didn't have it, it didn't even try . . . I can forgive a lot of bad stuff if a man is swinging from his heels but he was making little cotton muffins. like George Washerbaby, I could not tell a lie. I had to let him have it. I never knew that such assassination lurked within my bowels. *Steppenwolf* will be out after Christmas with its bloody pages. yet really, I think you will find it different than the franklyn. I don't think it is snitty or below the belt. anyhow, hell. [★ ★ ★]

[To Veryl Blatt]

1.a. of course
thanksgiving
o lord you are so good to me you
Fucker!
[November 25,] 1965

veryl, you lovely baby of blue-eyed hurrah:

I have written Blaz for o.k. on intro and of course we'll get it. the most crazy thing on these letters, almost all of them drunken, is that most of the people have kept them. I don't write so many letters anymore and maybe that means that I am dying, and that's the way it works. but the letters where [*sic*] a BLAM! a typewriter somewhere, an electric light, something to drink . . . who needs more? anyhow, even I am curious as to what I pumped out into the vacant air. [★ ★ ★]

so listen, this Linda West c/o KRMG radio, I may have her other address, I think I do, but sure there is time, I am weary and drunk now and out of cigars and smoking these chickenshit little g.d. female cancer cigarettes. But Linda West only laughs anyhow, I doubt she saved anything. she read *It Catches* and here came this letter, so far as I can remember it:

'Dear Mr. Bukowski:

I have read *It Catches My Heart In Its Hands* and hear you have a new book out. I will gladly review your new book over the air here. I have always liked your poetry. I imagine the kind of man you are and I also enclose a few poems of my own that I thought you might be interested in.

(then more drivel talk)
(then)

I often wonder about you. are you tall and slim with burning eyes? or are you short and fat with a waddle and a slur out of the side of your mouth? are you cruel? do you live in a Villa? is your maidservant more o more beautiful than a cloud?'

and I answered her, as well as I can remember, only probably answered her better:

'Dear Linda West:

I am short and fat and oversexed and I live alone except with a female dog. I think that your poems are very beautiful and I can't see why anybody doesn't publish them. I am cruel by nature, almost vicious, although not quite. I don't have any education but I love to fuck fuck fuck, especially young girls who work at radio stations. I even like to fuck old girls who work at radio stations, who work anywhere and who would be willing to submit to my laying upon my ass and writing while they did whatever they had to keep their souls and more, importantly, my soul, alibe, and if not alive, alibe.

yours,
buk

look Veryl, that sheep may safely graze I better cut it off (ow, I mean, this letter)

[To William Wantling]

November 29, 1965

[* * *] maybe my last letter offended you? remember being drunk as usual but remember mentioning something about a desire to rape eleven year old girls. I said desire, not actuality. in other words, if you had an eleven year old daughter staying with me you might consider her pretty safe, at least a lot safer than with men who won't admit their desires even to themselves, or if to themselves, then not to the rest of the world. I am not saying that I am anything special but as I say that if you take offense at my naturalism, at that which nature has put into me, then, you are a damn fool. [* * *]

[To Douglas Blazek]

December 4, 1965

rec. *Ole* 3 and see you are still with hammer and sight and selectivity. I always await a downgrading from first issues of enthusiasm but you are only still more there. my thanks for the ads on various books. I am sure my starving, mad editors like them too . . . this is my next to last night off until Xmas and I must work eleven and twelve hours each night. hell, of course, sweet hell, but it's take it or quit the job or get fired and there is nothing in my brain working yet on the perfect escape. yet I have hustled my horse-race figures over and over and now the madman says (Buk), 'with my method of play, I can average $500 a week with a straight $10 flat bet on win.' I've put in hours and hours of work and on this thing and it would be some laugh if it were true! it's true on paper, at any rate, and almost frighteningly logical, and my job is to follow my scientific papers instead of emotion or hysteria or so forth. you get out there and some ass spills beer on your shirt, somebody steps on your shoes, you glance up and see a man staring at you with a mountain of immense hatred; you look around and here is some gal sitting on a bench with her skirt pulled up around her ass. you take a good swig from the flask Nash sent you, the one Hemingway drank out of, so it's good enough for me, maybe not good enough. anyhow, what I am trying to say is that a lot of things get in the way of pure paper theory, and it takes guts to continues to follow a straight central line, esp. when a losing streak occurs. and EXACTLY when you JUMP OFF, IT COMES IN AT VERY GOOD ODDS. I am going to stay on the line. listen, what has this got to do with the good *Ole*? I worked eleven hours last night, so make that an excuse. listening to a Rossini opera. I can see why they failed. all his operas sound like his overtures, and an over. and the meat of an opera *are* different things.

more beer. shit, maybe I will pick up. if you don't hear from me until after Xmas, please understand – the hours, and my health is bad; pain pain in throat back chest shoulders, sick stomach, weakness. sometimes I am working and I get faint. it is all I can do to keep from falling to the floor. it is very embarrassing. but after a while it passes. and after the tenth or eleventh hour you longer no longer give a shit. it is like being drunk, almost. you say *exactly* what you are thinking because you no longer care. senselessness. that most of my fellow workers seem to like their jobs and even like each extra call of overtime hours . . . is what?? disheartening, at least, when I think of the future of the human race. I was sitting next to a fairly sensible fellow the other night and when the screws weren't watching I said to him, 'You know, it would be nice if they let each man work the number of hours he had to in order to take care of his needs. you know, when you get tired of working, just get up and walk out.' 'It wouldn't work for you,' he told me, 'you'd starve to death.' like I said, he was a sensible fellow.

Frances and I have split. she and the little girl are over in a place on Carlton. it costs me something, but hell, I blow every paycheck anyhow, so what's the difference? I see the little girl every day so she'll remember me. I am soft in the head for her, Marina. the other day Frances brought her over and I was in bed asleep and she crawled on my chest and looked at my face and smiled smiled like crazy and then she kissed me on the mouth. little wench. and then she laughed. she's all full of this kind of love and she makes me remember somehow how it once was.

lighting up a Corona. fuck, I am a big money man. the boys on the opera on the radio laugh at me. [* * *]

Norse has not sent me his poems. I wrote him. now, Blaz, I just can't write this guy a blank check. I've got to see what you are printing. I realize that he is some sort of overlooked master craftsman with a master heart, but I've got to see the poems you are publishing or, I can't say a word towards or against him. he has an *instinctive* way with the word; he makes a man feel *good* reading him. the line is clear and specked with blood. I suppose what worries me about him is that he never throws the bomb or screams. but this is the danger point: it is hard to scream or bayonet and still retain the vindictive and cool Art-form. this was my trouble with *Crucifix*. everything was bothering me at once. I was stumbling all over the place and my blood was real, except for a few jokes, but the bull was making me look bad. it's best when you look good and say good. not rules, shit, no, but a way to do things like the wind or the trees or some gal at the track just showing you enough leg to make you forget God and his peashooter. fuck it.

Now you asked what I thought of *Ole 3*. please understand that, first of all, almost everything I read anywhere or anytime disgusts me. I mean – newspapers, billboards, poetry mags, poetry, poetry. . . . I mean, I just cannot hardly read anything anymore. I have backed up. choked off. whether this means ego or madness or stupidity or whatever, I don't know. so please, when I rate this stuff, understand my mind-state. this is important or else you are going to think I am telling you you print a lousy magazine and it isn't so. a new *Ole* is like new sun, only better because you can open its eyes and talk to it. I rate the littles in the following order:

1. *Ole* 2. *The Wormwood Review* 3. *The Outsider*

after that, there's a hell of a drop.

anyhow, if you have an *Ole* #3 there by you I'd like to go through it page by page with you and instead of doing a lot of talking I will simply rate the poems as they affect me. you see what this machinery and factories and all these x-wives have done to me? all right, for kicks, I will rate the stuff percentage-wise as it affected me, and remember – like I told you – my head is hard, the upper one. if you want more of a definition of the following ask me sometime, only now I am too tired, the bosses' goggling dry-sinking eye-of-skin death-faces monkey-swinging in my brain. over-time, over-time. now, they are playing WAGNER. good. there is a man who never wrote a bad note. what I mean is, it all came from the GUT. your heart can trick you but that little bit of underlay under the bellybutton sends it on home. all right. let's take it this way. 100 percent means the thing is immortal. zero means it is shit-death glued to paper. I will rate each piece, like some bigshot critic, on the following lines:

Style
Clarity
Meaning
Interest (force)
Originality

now I am the first to realize that these are just words and perhaps a further breakdown is needed but I am tired like I said and Wagner is dead. getting a bit drunk but that will help. [★ ★ ★]

[To Douglas Blazek]

December 31, 1965

have taken woman and child to their small place 8 or 10 blocks away and I wait to sweat out the New Year with the jackass horn blowers who will attempt to blow the snails out of their minds and butts, erect the skeleton of the the soul and try to make it dance make it sing make it do something . . . but it won't work. maybe not for any of us.

down at work they have worked me to the point of insanity. I have scratched both of my legs raw with my fingernail. and the damage to other parts is, of course, unrepairable. the schedule board still says WORK but I can't keep making it. they now have a new idea to work the cruds on holidays and give them 2 days pay. most of the cruds love this but I can't bear it. I don't need all kinds of money; I need time and just a small bit of money to keep me alive. but Christ, it either works one way or the other always – either I'm sleeping out in an alley without a job or I have a job and I work 7 days a week, 11 hours a day. both of these ways kill a man, finally. if I only had myself I could live on $20 a week, easily. just because I am 45 does not mean I don't like to pull the shades down and stay in bed 3 days and 3 nights like a slug like a maggot, and then to walk out into the sun, walk along the sidewalks, feel the whole city rocking and stinking like an old whore's ass. but I cry too much. each inch we get I guess we are lucky to get. a professional writer over today – I mean one who makes his living by writing. he left me his inscribed photograph in a picture frame. very nice, very nice. he talked about how everything fell into place for Hemingway. Hem had a nose for climbing up and he had the nose up, up Scott F., Sherwood A., G. Stein, various editors, others, and like a good American he dropped them when they were no longer of any use to him. he even got fired once from his newspaper and came back the next day like he hadn't heard. these are not admirable qualities. but all of us have holes. maybe he figured he had it and the only way to get through, finally, was to justify certain side actions? yet, how many millions of men think the same way today? well, balls. [* * *]

[To William Wantling]

December 31, 1965

[★ ★ ★] I understand there is going to be another article on capital punishment in *Spero* TOO, this time by somebody else. I must have a frozen soul for these cap punish articles are short-hairing me to a much earlier imbecility than I ever expected. I guess what I figure, mainly, is that almost the whole structure of everything is wrong so why pick at the parts? I mean, let's sink the whole ship. the ship of state, the ship of the world. A-Bomb? anyhow, what I mean is, take even jail. we don't need jails. we don't need morals. all we need is a common working sense and easiness and instinct. society kills more men than it saves. in fact, society kills everybody. none of us are truly alive. all we do is fight to save the last inch after we have given them 40 miles. religions senseless. morals senseless. so-called decency senseless. laws senseless. a fucking cop pulls me over because I am driving 80 miles an hour while drunk. the theory is that I don't know what I am doing and that I am endangering other members of society. bullshit. he doesn't know what he is doing. he is a wooden pigeon with a badge. WE CREATE AN ACTUAL *MONSTER* ON THE *THEORY* THAT WE *MIGHT* PREVENT A *POSSIBLE* MORAL AND SOCIAL WRONG. get it? you were jailed for getting caught using drugs. they were worried that you were getting something that they didn't have. it's a hell of a society when you are told it's wrong to use drugs but it's all right to kill yourself in a factory for a pitiful and demeaning wage. A FREE SOCIETY SHOULD ALLOW EVERYTHING THAT MAKES A MAN FEEL ALIVE AND GOOD. what then, you ask me, would you do with a man who rapes your little daughter whom you profess to love very much? well, the idea is, that under present conditions, this can happen anyway. the idea of a SOCIETY OF TRUST, not holy trust or church trust, but simple easy feeling, no jails, no war, no punishment . . . this man would come to THINK while walking down a sidewalk FREE that there was no necessity for his act, not in a sense of *taught* morals but simply in a sense of sense. things would take time to work free. I would say, don't even lock up the madmen, the perverts, the deerslayers, the sadists . . . shit, it's just now 12 a.m. happy new Year and my love to you both [★ ★ ★] what I mean is: we must *give* chance a chance. what the hell else. I can work out all the lack of rules. trust me. shit, I *must* be getting old. musing of a better world. I guess this capital punishment article thing caught a hair in the brain and started the sawmill going. well, we can't eliminate so much. the pain, the accident, the death. the tottering clay of us and our big mouths. your wife lost a kid. my first one did too. right in the crapper. afterbirth, afterbirth. an early fish flushed away like a turd. I was not much of a man. I was so insane that time, and years before that that I couldn't think of what to say, do. I don't blame my first wife for divorcing me. I was of very short stuff of soul. still am. I mean it. this is not theatrics. I am forever disgusted with myself. I am not even as good as my shit, my shit is better than I am. more man, more rose, more real. Barbara, I am sorry forever that my mind was tied-up with chickenshit nerves and dull crossword puzzles. [★ ★ ★]

Pound's x-girl friend Martinelli trying to cough up my whore-O-scope. stars, something. I suppose this puts me somewhere near the Master. just think, somebody Pound went to bed with is now writing me, has been for years. my, my. I know all about myself: I am the Original Hard-Luck Story of the Universe. Job only got tickled. [★ ★ ★] I can't make it into heaven now. burn this letter. maybe I can sneak past. could be I am in heaven now only I don't recognize it or could be I am in hell and I do. [★ ★ ★]

• 1966 •

[To Walter Lowenfels]

January 9, 1966

o Walter: thanks word on *Confessions*. no, nothing else like that have I written, and prob. won't. prose bit to shape up shit a bit and wonder where I've been. so that's that.

I understand Jon and Lou Webb have come across hard times – broken press and the like. I'd like to see them get into #4. a Patchen issue, but things are not working right.

well then. we all move on. flowers in the air. gaslight. drunken birds. paradise is a cold wet stocking dripping on the back unexpectedly. I get sicker and sicker. little men outside sharpening their spades. to hell with them: I have 5 bottles of beer left and a bottle of india ink that sits here and says on its side: TINTA CHINA A LA PERLA.

the world is very good. I am sure of it: I keep gaining weight.

[To Douglas Blazek]

January 9, 1966

[* * *] word in from Norse, damn fine letter, and perhaps he has more style and touch than any of us, young snip. anyhow, he has been laid up in some Greek hospital unable to stop shitting, which is a hell of a way to go, what? anyhow he is getting better and jumped out of bed in Hydra and escaped to Athens, where he is feebly typing up a batch of poems for me to look over to see if I think he can write or not write. for Norse – *Ole* issue. maybe I am being cruel? but I can't say anything about a man on 2 or 3 poems. the few things I have seen of his are clearly very good but I would like to see more for my own good and for his. I do not judge poems as a critic out of learning but as a human being out of my own experience which must nec. be limited but which

nevertheless contains truths and instincts and flowers and spiders and snakes and dreams and stinks which may apply to any man living anywhere, anytime. and sometimes the way the 'learned critics' talk about poetry and/or Art, I sometimes think I have even read MORE BOOKS and junked them down better. lot of ego to say this, yes, but you know as a man walks down a sidewalk or takes a piss or breaks an egg into a pan, strange thoughts enter the head and walk around, one of them being that the critics are my Aunt Sarah. [* * *]

[To Steven Richmond]

January 27, 1966

[* * *] still down with this flu or whatever it is and couldn't get to work again tonight. maybe keeping this flu is deliberate? do you think that going down to the liquor store in my bare feet is lengthening the case? or sitting up in that cold grandstand watching them run? I sit way in back by myself and they've got 40 sparrow ups there in the eaves, singing, chirping, shitting, but they have, so far, been very nice and have not shit on me. found a dead one on the pavement other day. didn't know what to do. couldn't touch it. couldn't move away. just sat there looking at the dead bird and feeling very sad for it, for everything, the works, and kept telling myself, you shouldn't you shouldn't, that's the mathematics of it, you ought to know by now. but that god damned bird hung in the center of my mind and I missed a couple of good plays. went down and had a couple of drinks, looked at some of the flaxy piss-dead women and drove on in. 25,000 people at the track and they had to show only me the sparrow. tough shit.

[To William Wantling]

January 28, 1966

[* * *] you know, baby, I think that the cleansers are the jails and the hospitals and the new whores, and without these Time seems to take it in the choppers – as waste. I think that unless a man is in constant realignment with himself he must die. the women might be good to us and actually love us as we trot off to our factories with our little gay lunch-buckets but that's because they are not dumb. they know that

we walk into and are chewed by the very teeth of death, for they see us when we leave and they see us WHEN WE COME BACK. a hot bath, a meal and good night's sleep, even a good fuck does not return everything. listen, don't put me down as against women – I'd hate to be one and I know that they have their own personal world of horror. but life keeps chewing us up and how often can we keep getting up off the deck, and what for? me, I've just gone limp all over and let them punch. down at the coffee break area they call me, HANK THE PLANK (my first name in Henry, middle name Charles), BIG TIME, MONEY!, etc., but they don't know that when I go home in the morning that I comb agony and poems out of my hair. but to hell with that. [★ ★ ★]

I like your photo and will send you one of mine if I can steal a WANTED ad from the local post office. you look like a rough baby, kid, and I'd hate to meet you coming down any dark (or light) alley. but actually, in the 50's and 60's a different type of poet has evolved through the dense brutality of our age. we've had to be tough enough to live and at the same time to save the soul. the university boys are merely soft and tricky and clever but they don't know even what a wall *looks* like or a cat or a fish or a landlord or a policeman or a blade of grass, unless they attempt to imagine these things and they do attempt, and, of course, the mockery of our age is that these safe and clever and dead men are published everywhere. this is why the audience for poetry is so small – the masses know that most of it is fake – has nothing to do with lives, their or anyone's, has nothing to do with Life. [★ ★ ★]

[To Steven Richmond]

February 2, 1966

[★ ★ ★] LSD, yeah, the big parade – everybody's doin' it now. take LSD, then you are a poet, an intellectual. what a sick mob. I am building a machine gun in my closet now to take out as many of them as I can before they get me. *All* the death does not lie lay ly with the academics or the poetry workshops or the pawnbrokers . . . [★ ★ ★]

[To Douglas Blazek]

February 3, 1966

[★ ★ ★] our boy MacNamara has quit his job and now I seem to get a letter a day from him. that's nice. nice and frightening. I don't know quite what to say, finally. I mean, the thing can get kind of religious. but whatdy you do when ya lose yore bible?

I guess I told you the woman and I split, she has the girl with her. finally it was her poetry workshop and church group that turned my gut. christ, you know I work nights, and after being pissed all over with the overtime bit, take me hours to fall asleep and then I'd be awakened by the shits giggling and making dull jokes in the other room. they just can't get together *enough* and talk talk talk, and, baby, complaint is bad, I guess, but if you could only see the *look* of them, the flat cardboard soul stink of them, maybe you'd know. if they had only had the decency to wait until I was at work . . . to discuss their freedom marches, peace marches, civil rights bits, poetry readings . . . how can you be made sick even by cardboard people who seem to want to do everything right? ah, christ, sometimes I think I *am* crazy! maybe it was simply that they were FORMULA people, even down in the shitpit where I dragged my ass to work I found a people more *real* and even they were nothing, but still a relief in comparison. there wasn't any argument; don't ever remember cussing her gang, although might have done so while drunk. now she has them and I have me and we can all die separately. [★ ★ ★]

but look here, how can you find things out, feel things, even have a chance to yawn or look at the wallpaper if your jaws are going all the time? I guess we all feel badly enough and I have felt plenty of times like going to bed and crying for a week (Hemingway is far from my ideal, or, at the other end, Camus either) but what I felt like crying about I was not certain – it could not be worded or spoken, not over a telephone or not even to myself exactly, and maybe that's the reasons for this fucking thing called Art, Creation, whatever, sometimes we hang it in *just* RIGHT – we get it all, the dizzy broads on the phones, the flunky fired from his shithouse job, the guys like me wanting to cry in bed, the cat run over, the empty beer cans, me writing a letter to you and me being 1/2 nuts with old airplanes running through my brain, ah. [★ ★ ★]

[To Steven Richmond]

February, 1966

[★ ★ ★] yes, the sickheads will think *Earth* is another dirty mag. they do not realize that the cuss word is used only as explosion of fury-agony when nothing else fits that space. but you are still a good enough human to tell a real poem from an unreal one, and I think that *Earth* one, #1, was right in there, right up there, alive and burning, as good as *Ole* and *Wormwood*, maybe better. you got rights to be proud of your baby, baby. and that damn cunt in Sacramento who wrote me that *Earth* was shit, she still writes me as if all were sweet. I have not answered. the *Promethean Lamp* made me heave and I threw it into the trash but I did not bother to get highly vindictive with the editors, to show them my hot prong because I figured they were dead anyway and that in the machinery of the human affair such things as the *Lamp* were expected in my nightmares. yet these sisters who sit at home in their gardens and piddle with poetry while their husbands are out there being chewed-up by the world, these piss-pure sisters have always got to let us *know* what they *think* they think from inside their sea-dead skulls. fuck em. I want to congratulate you sweetheart on putting out one of the most vibrant bouncing searing jumping living of the littles and I am honored and proud and scared and sick-dizzy that I had a poem or something for you that you could use. [★ ★ ★]

[To Jon and Louise Webb]

February 28, 1966

well, as zero hour approaches and the rat of death spins on the knife, I have bought myself 3 books today to read in there if read I am able – Camus: *Resistance, Rebellion and Death; The Fall & Exile and the Kingdom; Notebooks 1935–1942*, and now my radio gives me Brahms' First – apropos, for I was listening to this one when the F.B.I. walked in on me in Philly and threw me on in. I have told Frances I am feeling better but I am really not feeling so good, but shit. shit, yes. saw Marina almost all day today, she's a joy doll and when I leave them at their place and go to leave she screams, 'no! no! no!' and I hear her crying as I get into what's left of the car, as what is left of me gets into what is left of the car. hell of a life. got to take castor oil Tuesday night and then get up at 7 a.m. and give myself enemas –

shit is right – so he can probe through the tunnels for rot at 10 a.m., then I enter hospital at 3 p.m. that afternoon. god damn fuckers. started reading Camus tonight, a chapter called 'Create Dangerously' but I had read no more than 2 pages and he pissed me off, had me pissed off and disgusted. I too have been guilty of throwing statements around with abandon – whatever pleased my mind – whatever sounded right and strong and entertaining, but I hate to see a man like this building such cases, and then giving it at a lecture – University of Uppsala, Dec. 1957. [★ ★ ★]

in a sense, I feel it will be too bad if they cut my candle now. I have never told you but I always thought that my best writing would come after the age of 50. I have felt this slow fattening inside of me, the gradual thing, so gradual, a strange warm presence . . . well, shit, fuck the dramatics. [★ ★ ★]

About Henry Miller – print him if it will keep you afloat; he wants the wondrous Loujon format and you can't blame him. you'd like it yourself, for yourself, wouldn't you? Of course, Henry has slipped a few steps down, but he's still a good name and doubt he can ever *forget* how to write unless they kill him with a bomb or a stone or a hammer. Odd that I've read so little of him. in a bus station once in Texas, I think, and he too, like Camus, pissed me off. yet I realize that they both think, and write well, with force, I mean, there is just something in my brain that will hardly let me enjoy anything at all. I don't mean that I am an automatic crank or that I am bitter with the success of a Miller or a Camus; it's just that I'd rather not read. looking at the sun or a woman's legs or a horse race, this fills me; reading just fidgets and burns and flops across me . . . dead grease, print, the coffin-lid down. [★ ★ ★]

[To Douglas Blazek]

March 1, 1966

I enter the Queen of Angels hospital tomorrow. dear doctor wants to probe a bit more tomorrow a.m. to see if he can find anymore worse, but so far just surgery for hemorrhoids which have gotten so damned bad I can't function anymore. I am hoping, of course, that he doesn't find any dirty words like 'cancer.' anyhow, if you don't hear from me in some time you will know that I am sparring around a few rounds . . . and if you don't hear from me at all, finally, you'll know I lost the damn fight. This would be a time, I'd think, when I should be sitting down and pounding out immortal poems . . . anything I haven't said, anything that I should say. but I am disinterested. no desire at all. I believe Webb is pissed at me because I cannot make trip – I promised – to come down and cut more tape. But he gets so *tied* in his projects that he doesn't realize that things can happen to people. I mailed him 3 tapes yesterday, old ones, and now the machine is dead . . . the sea rolls in. [⋆ ⋆ ⋆]

[To Douglas Blazek]

March 8, 1966

back, still stupid with spinals, knives, shots, people, gowns, noise, stink, the o big ass load of pain, hurrah, I am sitting here (barely) on a fat red pillow trying to make my mind think down to the keys . . . not much luck. I feel rather upside-down. get up continually and go to can and there are little snake turds without eyes, cut somewhat like death, and each bowel movement about a childbirth, gripping elbows, saying, 'wwoowoo! sweet son of a bitch, mother, sing to me, sing to me!!' that shit sliding past the incisions of 15 years' worth of hemorrhoids and distorted intestine chopped loose. . . . when you think about poem, poems, or stories, about this time, all that doesn't make much sense. I'm afraid the poem has never quite come up to the actuality and certainly hasn't solved it, althought I don't suggest we throw our rusty guns away.

[⋆ ⋆ ⋆] managed to get out to old '57 Plymouth and start it last night, let it run, and so *that's* still alive. I was laying flat on my ass in the dark of night, moaning, my foot on the accelerator, charging the fucking thing. 2 old women came by and stared at me laying in there, they thought I was nuts, but strangely strangely I didn't even care what they thought. I stared at their moth-dry, white-pigment, chalky, room-for-rent, casket faces; their bodies like sticks of hardened shit, even the moonlight seeming to vomit away from them . . . it didn't matter, and they moved on creaking and chirping nothings of waste. to think, they might even once have been half-decent fucks, but now more stupid than armies, less clean than dirt. anyhow, I think the car is ready to go, and with a little time, I am going to be around some more, as indecent and imperfect and vulgar as ever. you think you can remove this old German-Polack like a bathtub ring? hah, they gotta rub me harder than that! [⋆ ⋆ ⋆]

[P.S.] [* * *] – have been reading Camus (off and on) . . . 3 books' worth that I haven't got to. stories not so hot, rather common and ordinary, standard. essays contain good brain matter and have quality but the *style* is so dull! why do they have to put us asleep to teach us?

[To Jon and Louise Webb]

March 8, 1966

back couple of days but first day I've had strength or guts to reach typer. I don't know how long it will take me to shape up. just about out of vacation time and sick leave shot. sad song. – hope you got package o.k. with mags and tapes. *keep tapes away from machinery or they will fade.* – each bowel movement here a real crucifixion; but operation I'm told was simply for removal of an extreme (15 year) hemorrhoid condition, plus, I believe removal of part of intestine pushed out of shape with strain. not very pretty what,??? nothing like a good clean heart attack – it seems so much more honorable, but, of course, it's not truly so. (Doc examined my innards with snake: what an invention!) would like to get a couple of new and fresh tapes to you but am simply in no shape to do so now. I do hope that we have a little more time. the $$$ situation looks bad; my pay will stop Monday and all operation will not be paid by my insurance. also have payments to Frances. various other things. but believe all will work out and I will be rolling again. god, it looks like we are all broke this time, TOGETHER!!

it's good, tho, to be alone again, out of the hospital, near the typer and the radio and Camus, and the sun and the sound of things flowing together. all will work, and easily, our luck is strong. health and love to you. Marina is so BEAUTIFUL!!!

[To William Wantling]

March 9, 1966

when you consider all the men born who are now dead, and when you consider the remaining living, these remaining living seem not only some miraculous mathematic, but also seem something to get *done* with: like a pruning or a picking or an ultimate roadend. would it be too precious to say that we live almost with a sense of shame, as if we were getting away with something? I would hardly regard my upcoming death as anything sorrowful or tragic – just the removal of garbage and a hacking voice that talks too much of too little.

– Bukowski, 3–9–66

[* * *]

[To Ann Menebroker]

March 11, 1966

'green,' new trend? 'green, green, I want you green!' – Lorca. the use of 'green' is now mostly an ultra-poetic Romanticism. of course, the word 'green' is not outlawed but it is generally used by the pretenders and most poetry is written by pretenders. the living are busy doing something else.

To give talks on Poetry it is best to have a captive audience. Get them where they can't walk out – say a hospital, a jail, an insane asylum . . . school auditoriums are not safe – those with guts will leave. you can't blame the masses for disregarding poetry – it is pretty dull stuff & obtuse & unreal in direct regard toward what is actually happening to them. In the Atomic Age they don't have Time to waste or to be wrong.

This letter was printed in Congdon's Magazine, *no. 3.*

[To Kirby Congdon]

[ca. mid-March, 1966]

if this letter is detached and punchy, understand, at least. I'm out of the hospital, and these couple of dark hollering rooms are mine to divide, to throw myself on the springs and wonder about how I keep getting it in the ass. (don't misinterpret . . . or do, who cares?) (which reminds me of a guy in a place I just worked, I mean used to work. he had this reducing machine which he put his girlfriend on and fucked her. 'we turn it on every night about 3 a.m. and it sounds like a washing machine. people wonder what I am doing washing my clothes at 3 a.m. but it's a great machine; you just lay there and it does all the work. you and I ought to try it?' 'you and I?' I asked. 'yeah,' he said. 'but who's gonna get on top?' 'what the hell *difference* does it make?' he answered.)

I have been vaguely unhappy, bored, disgusted with poetry for years, for centuries . . . I sometimes try to tell people why – not in the involute & secretive and vocabulary-deadened style of a Creeley or an Olson, but really, what the HELL *isn't* going on and what the *HOAX* is. Of course, the best way to point out is to *create*, but sometimes I can't resist a few beer-hall speeches. It is not so much in telling people how to DO things but in letting them know how the trusted kingpins have managed to slice an inch or two off the peckers of their souls and make them smile and say thanks. I'm 45 now; have only been in the game ten years but the way the body is falling apart I thought it would be best if I left some word. I hope I do not talk too much like a con-man. I'm sick of that; I've seen enough of that. anyhow, nothing.

the review on Corrington in *Steppenwolf* – the editor wrote me asking, 'if I send you Corrington's latest book, you mind reviewing it?' a free book is a free book. hell, no, I don't mind, I told him, send it on in. I thought it might be something along the lines of his last book, *The Anatomy of Love & Other Poems*, and that I could say a few good things and then go to the racetrack or the mill or the rack or wherever. however, *Lines to the South* didn't have it, and since I had stuck my neck out I had no other choice but than to chop Willie's off. (Corrington's). he hasn't sent the Klan up yet so I guess I can put this rusty luger back under the hotwater bottle. Corrington had me worried when I met him and Miller Williams down there. the talk was all University-power talk, intrigue; talk about degrees and all that very drab shit. evidently it didn't take long the for the talk to catch up with the poems. but if you think I just write adverse reviews like a vulture trying to strengthen his own flight with dead meat, see *evidence* number 9. I do a review entitled 'The Corybant of Wit,' a look through at Irving Layton's *The Laughing Rooster.* I am afraid that Irving L. writes very well. when I can read a man without lessening the electric charge within me, I know that man is a writer. to hell with iambic p.'s and spondees, I go on kilowatts!

I keep getting stuff in the mail from people about my review of Corrington. the odd thing being that they all agree with me, which worries me. there was some Roman ruler, I believe, who said: 'The people applauded. I must have said something wrong.' I know what he meant. then too, it tickles their twats that after Corrington be-friended me I jammed him. well, fuck it all. being a reviewer is too easy. I am afraid that if I reviewed my own stuff there would be blood all over the floor and walls. I know there would.

Corso? Ginsberg? maybe I am jealous of the big cats? they've got one thing I got – clarity of style, but they've got a little too much the sweet tooth for their own soul (soul-importance) and they suck up a lot of bait. Camus said we've got to be a part of History and get out with it, but I am not sure he meant on-stage bellowing to the idol-lovers. still, I am full of too much complaint, I guess, but I have turned down some offers to prance on stage for $$$, good place to sleep, food, drinks, fare, that bit. I'd have to be pretty hungry. (see Behan, see D. Thomas, see Christ.) the come-on is only a softener so they can rope you, kill you. I go with Jeffers – the best friend is a rock wall. (see Capone.) people do come to my door and I open it and treat them nicely, mostly because I don't have the guts to do otherwise, and also because they can easily have more than I. but then, too, these people are mostly *peekers* and the whole thing has nothing to do with CREATION or slamming the keys down, crackcrackcrack vapvap. I've got to be a loner because most of the time I am shoved into factories and places I don't want to be, and in order to get out of the spaghetti I have to crawl under the rug. I am not a snob and I am not precious and I am not playing genius; but where were these people when I was starving and freezing in a shack in Atlanta, when I was living in a cardboard shack without light, heat, water, food, toilet, hope, for a dollar and a quarter a week? where were these people when I was in jail, or on the park benches? where were these people when I turned the gas on one night and tried to kill myself? in Los Angeles? in hell? their sweet knocks, their quips, their stares . . . who wants them? if I fail to write any more poetry, they will be the *first* to say . . . 'he's lost it. he's finished.' I don't need their judgements. all I need is a sheet of paper, a typer, some food and some rent. win or lose, talent or no, age or death . . . I am, I was a human being. I never had a desire to look at a writer, to knock at his door, maybe because most writers never did me any good; maybe because I figured what they wrote was all they owed me, – if they owed me that. so, I'm just a crank who has had surgery of the asshole. fine, then.

bit of race rioting in Watts last night – not much – a Mexican and Negro killed, 25 injured. not much? I hear you laugh. I thought so. some writer, a guy who makes it professionally via the sex and nudey bit, phoned me last night. 'I've got my gun loaded! I'm ready!' he said. this guy doesn't even live in Los Angeles. highly sensitive sort. then his doorbell rang and he just about zeroed out. I think I heard the safety catch go off. 'gotta go,' he said. 'see you.' he probably shot a Western Union boy with a dark tan. [* * *]

[To Jon and Louise Webb]

March 21, 1966

[* * *] doorbell just rang and here was a little boy in the dark . . . 'Sir, I am working in competition with 5 other boys . . .' He has some magazines and newspapers there. I tell him as gently as possible that I cannot buy anything. god, they get to them EARLY!!! what? competition. a discouraging word. when I write a poem I don't think about shit competition. but christ I guess I am in competition with Ezra and Shake and Jeffers or, if not that, then with Judson Crews, Carl Larsen and Peter Orlovsky. yet, I am a hundred times more unhappy to see this kid this way, begging his papers under the lamplight. [* * *]

[To Douglas Blazek]

March 22, 1966

the dog poisoners are legion and slinky and seldom get caught, and we don't have enough death, they have to play dirt with the little we have left. I was supposed to go to WAR to save such creatures as these? the dog poisoners are usually members of long standing in the neighborhood, respected, churchly, own their own homes, and are often childless or their children have grown and tend not to see them anymore. the dog poisoners are usually between the ages of 55 and 70. most of them loved animals as children but American society and what it extracts from the body and the mind and the soul can grow very special monsters of its own. most of them are concerned with property and 'property rights' as they like to call them. and since they have nothing else to hold to, this becomes everything. not so long ago there was a doctor out here in one of the suburbs who clubbed a puppy to death with a pistol butt. it was not even a grown dog. and he did it in the open, on his lawn, with children and people watching. (I was not there.) but his excuse was that the puppy had no right on his property. being a doctor and fatted with the worship people tend to give doctors and fatted with $$$, he was simply bolder and more insane than his brethren dog-killers. the case came to court but I didn't hear how it came out. they didn't print it or I missed that edition. probably case dismissed or a fine, say $15. property, property. I had a beautiful hound once (half-wolf, half-collie; but gentle, gentle) and I was walking him down the street on a leash and he stopped to piss on a plant outside a real estate office on Beverly Blvd. I had him trained to crap in vacant lots. but he pissed on this bush and this real estator leaped out of his office, he screamed at me: 'HEY! GET THAT DOG OFF THAT BUSH! HEY! HEY! HEY! PISS IS POISON! HE PISSED ON MY BUSH!' you could hear this guy all the way to Bensenville, Illinois. I just looked at him, looked at his acid face and his eyes and his body dangling there. 'I can't control my dog's piss,' I told him quietly. 'Well, let him piss somewhere else! move him off!' I didn't move off. either the dog or I could have killed him if we had so chosen. 'Your chickenshit bush won't die,' I told him, 'and if it does, I'll pay you for it.' 'Get that dog outa here!' we stood there until he went back inside to count his blood chips of profit. sometimes I think that these people almost know that they are dead, ugly, wasted, and they don't want to see anything or anybody happy and careless and easy; they don't even want to see anybody unhappy in the way we tend to get unhappy – it has to be their way. my wolf-collie got killed by a car when I split with this woman. I had left the dog with her. pets seldom die of old age. how I hate the fucking world and their special ways and values! Blaz, you'll get over the dog (dogs) but you'll never get over what did it: The American flag. money. property. the dead citizens in cities of horror and madness and fear. christ, christ.

good that *All the Assholes and Mine* went. writing it so soon after, I didn't know if I was caught in the stream or could see it go by. and yet maybe too much objectiveness tends to let the air out of the tires. that's the trouble with most literature: everybody's so cool and superior to the action that it becomes a word-game, a chess game – and the King is asleep and the Queen wears kotex and the Knights and Castles stumble and the Pawns, well, they don't matter, do they? [⋆ ⋆ ⋆]

[To Veryl Blatt]

April 2, 1966

[⋆ ⋆ ⋆] listen, I know that the book of letters a long way away but if it ever happens, run what you wish. only there is something I'd wish to strike out in reference to Sheri Martinelli. I don't know if I did, but I might have mentioned her in other letters as 'Pound's x-whore.' she's a fine woman but don't think she'd understand. In a sense, I am a romantic; I mean when I call a woman a whore, I mean, in *my* language, a woman who loves *one* man and *one* man only and I use the term in fondness to depict faithfulness, and there is no derogatory intent involved. I know that this turns around the standard concept, but damn standard concepts. I also use 'whore' to mean 'death' which is also, in a sense, 'love' to me. so you see, I am mixed-up. yeah. anyhow this is all I would want struck from the letters [* * *]

[To Douglas Blazek]

April 4, 1966

[* * *] of course it would be sweet if you could get hold of a printing press; it would add to what is already there. *Ole* has so much more lifeblood than the others that it's . . . no contest, riot, runaway. I hope that a press will not delete the beautiful madness from your silly head. I don't think it will. as much as you hate it and know that it is killing you, that factory, without wanting to, is also keeping you alive – to this extent: that those few moments given to you – you realize that here the god damn sun gotta finally shine, no lies, no bullshit, words cutting into paper like flowers, like swords, like screams, like paint. your family too, as much as you love them, will sometimes think you are mad, think you are cruel, because you will want to cop some moments from them too. but they ought to know that without your writing and without your editing, without your crazy colored paper and your crazy debts, you would REALLY BE A TERRIBLE FATHER, you would be the average American citizen male breadwinner and he is a horror to behold, he is a sight to make one vomit blood and gut and hope all out, for even when he smiles even when he is kind even when he is a winner a lover a father a playboy a champ, he stinks he is rot, he is a flower without a head, a plant without a root, a slab of meat butchered and dressed in clothing. I've got a hunch your family senses some of this, senses your need to hold to walls, to cry at night, to go down in your basement and play with silly piles of papers. so, I'm not scared of you getting a press, I am not scared of you dying. I am scared of me dying. so many of my poems are coming back. one guy told me, 'I also rejected Allen

Ginsberg.' fine. but means little to me, for I have also rejected Allen Ginsberg. but worse, I read the poems, and it was true – they weren't any good. mainly because one line didn't even relate to the other. I'd say one thing, then jump right off into space with something else. and I wasn't even drunk. maybe that was the trouble. yet, it's good to fail. I don't say I had a belly laugh on myself but I did see that the way is curious, thorny and never clear. I am lucky too – to fail a lot. if you fail 40 times, 41 is not so bad. keeps the bowels loose, keeps you human enough to hope, and the miracle becomes mainly that you have typewriter and paper and that something *does* come out. umm, how I remember the hospital; operated on a Wednesday, didn't shit until sometime Sunday afternoon. shit is important too – as long as it's your own. what? [⋆ ⋆ ⋆]

[To Douglas Blazek]

April 6, 1966

you are like me, baby, the life and the way is killing you – it may come out in the chest or the asshole or the belly . . . something HOLLERS . . . Krist, I'd *like* to say the SOUL hollers?? ah ah, we are DeMop in the rowboat, orange huge muscles and mind and siff of the soul and nothing to cure it. ouch! you and I have seen enough factories and hunkies and beasts and straw bosses and layoffs and breadlines and unemployment lines and hangovers and hospitals and jails and rotten women to make anybody's stomach want to drop out and crawl off into a hairless hole to hide forever until the bomb until the whiskey god of love and easiness (DEATH) shows up. those chest pains of yours are from ugly work and nerves and senselessness; you have 2 clock hands drilling into your heart, and it's an ugly clock too, very. you need time more than the first 5,000 people you pass on the street and you know it. I do too. don't kid yourself – many people want SLAVERY, a job, 2 jobs, anything to keep them running in the cage. and when they call overtime night after night, sucking the last blood from our limp bravery, see them smile, smile their greasy overtime smiles, they love it. my god, they have a phrase for it down where I sometimes work. a word. 'PORKCHOPS!' they say and lick their greasy lips when the word roars down at us, as God shits on us from the speakers above that are turned as LOUD as the machinery allows:

'YOU ARE REQUIRED,' says God, 'TO WORK ONE HOUR OVERTIME!' that's the new word: required. then you make that hour and then God screams down, with just 2 minutes to go, that you are REQUIRED to work another. then, the same plan: another, another, until you get your lousy 12. all right, 12 and 8 hours for sleep, that's 20. hour lunch, that's 21. breakfast, dinner, travel, shit, shave, dress, undress, say something to your kid, look at the wall a minute, and all the odd things, haircut, buy shoes, get a tooth pulled, try to get the car started, kill a fly . . . that's 24, and you're back. more PORKCHOPS. you know all this. I thought I'd let you know that I know it too. and there's never any money. for it all, there's never any money. you have as much money working 40 hours a week as you do 72 or 32. strange, but it's true. you have a family, I have child support. we do not beg off. it is something we did and we run it through. I love my little girl ten thousand times 402. fine. all right. but we're crazy too. we'd like to walk down some beach with a knapsack and a cheap bottle of wine. we'd like to stare at the moon for 3 hours or just sit there and smell the stink of dead fish, of another death; we'd like to sit there and mug and tickle the shadow of China there across the waves, VVVASSSSH!! we'd like to do nothing for HOURS HOURS HOURS, gentle do-nothingness. filling like a sink with hot water. feeling our cotton brains up there. feeling mice between our ears. even wondering about Christ, wondering if there were 13 at the table, wondering if it ever happened, wondering if anybody spilled wine on their sleeve or farted. wondering all the easy things. comparing the sun to a lemon. falling in love with the color yellow like a big-assed whore. yellow, yellow, that's me, and it's my favorite color too. good. luckily I knew a lot of the traps from watching my father, from studying my father. I worked myself a lot of lay-around time in. I always lived with old drunken women, very OLD women because I didn't want children, I didn't want the trap. 'Bukowski,' the few guys I knew used to say, 'you can do better than THAT!' 'sshish!' I'd tell them, 'she's coming in with the wine.' I even used to amuse myself when I'd introduce my women. 'Hey, this is Mary.' 'Mary, this is Joe.' and I'd glim Joe's face as he took in the sagging bellied, wine-struck, age-struck Bukowski cow. I never alibied. actually most of my cows were pretty good women. I mean, all they wanted was me and something to drink. I figured that these were pretty endearing qualities. meanwhile, no babies, no marriage, no squeeze, and I didn't look so good either and I didn't feel so good either and I either felt equal to or inferior to many of my cows. sure, some of them were vicious sluts, dirty and hardened as 3 week old and unwashed dishtowels and so was I, straight, I felt too like cursing all the walls and landlords and fuzz and children and the stars and the queers and the money-grabbers and the stink of life. it was a good bargain: I knew where I belonged, I was clever. I slipped once, and out of compassion more than anything, found myself with a 23 year old wife. she neither had the bone, the wisdom, the chapters of life behind her. she was a snit, a snob . . . hypersensitive to the smallest criticism, but meanwhile taken in by the grand phonies, the liars, the movie-trained Romantics, the dead-souled pretenders of Grace. fine. but ridiculous. lucky for me, there was a miscarriage. that rather did it. her phonies moved in and told her what a beast I was, or rather, by pretending no-beast they showed the beast in me. which was there. which was truly there. of course. shit. so divorce. escape. I walked down to the beach and tried to read Faulkner again. I layed on the sand with all my clothes on in mid day so they couldn't see my scars. I've got these bloody hideous scars all over my back from some former hideous disease. show me something and I'll catch it. why I never got the siff or the gon, I'll never know. only the crabs. and I've screwed the filthiest lousiest stuff in bars from Coast to Coast. deliberately. did I tell you the time I picked up this young whore, around 19, 20 in this bar, a real fine piece as the boys would say, only the madam, some old hag around 55, insisted on coming along to see that I didn't spoil or mutilate her young fine meat income. o.k., I said. we sat up at my place and had a few drinks, more than a few, it was an old place up the hill by the Grand Central Market. I still thought I was a writer or something and was living on potatoes and boiled fishheads. everything went all right until I had another drink or so and then decided it was time for the great lover, Rupert Brooke Bukowski, to screw to fuck. by training and instinct, of course, I grabbed for the 55 year old hag instead of that fine 19 year old meat. training runs deep, pal. I'll always remember this hag with a face like a killer (I don't know if they wore a Green Beret) and she had one hand missing at the wrist and attached was an iron hand, very shiny and large and silver, with, I remember, one VERY LARGE HOOK protruding. and I mean protruding, baby! after the first grab at the hag, I think she was a lez to top it all, she backed off and swung the hook – S W I S H! – 'hey, this son of a bitch is NUTS!' she hollered. and I remember that hook swinging again and again and myself ducking, ducking around the room. meanwhile, the 19 year old meat very puzzled. me too. I ran out of the room and left them in there with my immortal short stories, to burn them if they wanted to, to fuck each other if they wanted to. . . . where was I? yeah? down at the beach reading Faulkner. trying him again. trying to convince myself that he wasn't a phoney to me. he'd won all the prizes. his photo even looked like a man. what was wrong? I felt like he was slipping me the smooth bologna. I am still puzzled. he can't write. he slicks it. he's celluloid. clever. cute. what's wrong with me? some monkeys were playing with a beachball and they'd bounce it near me, sand all over Faulkner, all over me, in my mouth, ears. I stayed on there, right in the middle of their game, right in the middle of Faulkner's game as my x-wife ran off with a cultured Turk with a purple stickpin and a cultured accent, a kind of Boyer, and he knew how, he owned a drive-in movie.

what am I talking about? mainly my extreme cleverness at staying out of the traps. so here I meet this woman. she is 42. I am 44. who needs to worry about children? responsibility? another good deal. by God, when Bukowski came along he must been in front of the line to get all those brains!

listen, Blaz, the day she told me she was pregnant, that moment, I do wish somebody could have photographed my face. it must have been a monument of disbelief, something say like a guy getting up in the morning and noticing that sometime while he slept somebody had clipped his balls off – I mean, that FIRST KNOWING, that FIRST LOOK, reaching down with the hand and finding nothing there. listen, kid, I *have* my balls, so far. even tho I wrote a poem about a guy who cut his off. I am just trying to give you the feeling, the look of it. 44 years of planned and deliberate cleverness. shot. bang. like that. over. I wish you could have had a photo of my face then because whenever you got the blues you could take this photo out and laugh for hours, you know. – anyhow, she's a beautiful little girl, a miracle, and glad she's here now, but jesus sweetheart, god or somebody pulled the switch on me, fast. well. think of all the young bodies I bypassed! arrrg! when bigger and better jackasses are born, Bukowski will still lead the parade. [★ ★ ★]

glad to hear *Assholes* will be a book. I dedicated the thing to Wantling not on the assumption of a book but merely to dedicate. last I heard he was working in a carwash for $1.25 an hour. this is kind of rough on near-genius. I don't mean that they should be spoon-fed and elevated a la Patchen, no matter what the misery. all men suffer, even those who *don't* write poetry, and if we're going to help Patchen with a bad back, we also gotta help Joe Brown with a bad back, or else this makes Patchen no good, you see? think you do. [★ ★ ★]

Webb, I dunno. he's blown thousands of dollars running around the country for a year looking for a new Taos, a new Carmel, a new something, meanwhile staying out of direct Atomic Warfare areas, according to the experts. well, that's his business. but he's running around in special trains with his wife, 2 dogs, the printing press, tons of cartons of paper, type, books, manuscripts. they had to get away from New Orleans, couldn't stand it – tourists, the Ku Klux Klan, thugs, bad weather for Lou's lungs. o.k. I get postcards from this city, then that: 'I believe this is it. everything fine.' then a week later, another card: 'oh, we can't stand it here!' and there goes the press and the dogs and the works somewhere else. Laredo, Santa Fe, Phoenix, Cleveland, Phoenix again. 'I feel El Paso will be the place. I can get paper. can walk across the border to whorehouses. real life. everything I need.' no, something went wrong in El Paso. too low? Santa Fe was too high, and other things. one place they rented a house (Phoenix), paid 2 months rent, $200. fine place, they wrote, plenty of room for dogs. then I hear it is too hot. air conditioners don't work or the blowers don't reach the crapper or something. 3 or 4 days. on the train again. the press, the dogs, the works. 200 dollar rent lost, but o.k. they learned something. Phoenix won't do. where now? now it's Tucson. $235 to get the press hooked up again. triple wiring like in all the other places. Tucson, o.k. have made down payment on a house. fine. low monthly payments. everything fine. fixing place up. there's even a bed for you. dogs love it. will have bookshop in front. send all your old books, paperbacks, little magazines. (I did.) well, fine I thought, they've settled. they went through the same thing a year ago, and finally came back to New Orleans. now, at least, they know New Orleans is not right for them. Los Angeles is in the Atomic area, Frisco is in the Atomic area, so forth. I had written them a long letter some time back trying to tell them that there weren't any cities, that shit spread wherever humanity lived. but they didn't seem to get the message, so when I got their notes from various cities, that 'this might be it,' I just wrote back fine, fine, good. now I just got a letter from Tucson, 'Lou misses New Orleans, wishes we were back. this is a lousy town. the busses stop running at 6 p.m. nothing but old, old people around, walking around. we haven't made any friends.' But they are going to stay, Jon says now, a year anyhow. a lot of work to do. the record Bukowski TALKING won't be out in April. *Chi. Lit Times* ad only pulled in about 20 sales so far. they just don't have the kind of $$$ to put it out now. October better. would take $600 at least to press the record. broke. might do the Henry Miller book submission first, that would give them enough money to get into #5, the Patchen issue, and then, in October, the record. I busted my ass, shooting mouth into a borrowed tape recorder, laying on the floor first on one side then the other because my ass was too sore to sit on, I got them fresh mad tapes for their April deadline, and now I find I had until October, maybe forever. it's Webb's $$$ and his right to travel but when he cries Wolf now, when he cries broke now, I really just do wonder who is crazy, me or him or the dogs or the press or the American cities and The Bomb or what? he gave me 2 great books, *Crucifix* and *It Catches*, I can't deny that. yet I wonder sometimes if I wouldn't have been better off coming out in cheap editions of one or 2 hundred copies? certainly the writing could have been judged as *writing*. it's difficult to hold down pages like that. I means *Crux* and *Catches*. automatically they are going to beanball you for coming out in a purple necktie. format, beautiful format! all right, fuck it, I wrote some poems one time, long ago, too. see the ungrateful wretch I am! [⋆ ⋆ ⋆]

Larsen's book is The Popular Mechanics Book of Poetry, *published by Blazek's Mimeo Press in 1966.*

[To Steven Richmond]

April 12, 1966

[⋆ ⋆ ⋆] got to agree with you on the Larsen book. humor is good when it stems from truth – in fact, truth alone is often humorous in itself, makes me laugh. but the humor of artifice – whose worst device is exaggeration – always makes me a little ill because it is just another con game. confined, my last days in the hospital, with some idiot with a t.v. set he never shut off, I was laid open to what the world considered comedy and at the expense of my dwindling sanity. how they made me ill with their obvious extremisms – lying there with my ass torn open, my beautiful walls taken from me. I suppose that the worst is Bob Hope with his flip little cute exaggerations. and his name droppings. I don't keep much up with the world and he drops these names I never heard of, all supposing to *mean* something. about the only lout I could stand was Jackie Gleason – at his best he showed some showmanship, at his worst he was like the rest. but Larsen, Larsen, no.

Bukowski wrote a foreword to Richmond's book, Hitler Painted Roses (*Santa Monica, 1966*).

[To Steven Richmond]

April 15, 1966

hang in there on *Hitler*, the more they holler the more you'll know you are getting closer to the bone. I remember when I was a kid, 16, 17, I was just beginning to play with short stories. came home one night and here were all my clothes thrown out on the front lawn – coats, shirts, shorts, stockings *and* short stories. the old man had dipped into a drawer, uninvited, and had become a literary critic. 'No son of mine is going to write stories LIKE THAT and live in MY HOUSE!' 'Come on out here,' I told him, 'and I'll beat the shit out of you.'

be glad *Hitler* curls their neckbones. you are there. [⋆ ⋆ ⋆]

[To William Wantling]

April 18, 1966

[⋆ ⋆ ⋆] dull letter. sorry. but have been writing a lot of poems, even a review of Artaud for local liberal rag. the libs too are a kind of jellyfish crowd. I want to see the poor man fed, sure. but don't make me love him. anyway, surprised they took the Artaud, I hung some strong salty lines in there, using the review as a crutch to slip across some of my own demented and boiling ideas. [⋆ ⋆ ⋆]

[Addressee Unknown]

Mid-April 1966

Randy, old kid,–

Frances and I separated now. turning your letter over to her. she is good at writing long (long) equivocal things. you'll probably get a 6 pager full of . . . wisdom.

I keep writing my poems and waiting, mainly, to die.

Sorry I am a little short of tonality and space here. All I can hand you is a brick. Love works like machinegun fire. I don't trust it.

You are a good young kid but you will be broken like the rest of them. Your first mistake was not to take the 5 years rap. It would not have killed you, not nearly as much as the 30 days you are doing now. But that's the way it works. It's very tricky. we are finally tricked out of the last of our wits. so be it. so says this drunken voice from the top of a syphilitic mountain.

Pappa Webb pissed at me now for various reasons. this is how it works. gangrene in the beef stew. so, they held me up to the sun and the sun shined on me. but whatever is left must go on, a while . . . huh?

If you want any advice from an old head, I'd havta say – try to hold off any real or desperate entanglement with women as long as possible. The problem is not so much in *losing* a woman, this is expected, but it is in seeing where they finally go . . . toward the rottenest death, toward the falsest of the false, toward the lie, toward the obvious lie forever. It's like a comedy, only you are the only one in the audience and they are on stage.

And look, pretty boy, I still don't get your movie-writing shit. are you, alone, going to turn the whole rot upside down and make truth of it? you couldn't take 5 years, how you gonna change a whole industry? I think that you are in some kind of dream-state. If you have the guts to wash dishes, surely you have the guts to know where you are. One doesn't work without the other. You confuse me because you have too many cards in your deck.

I talk to you straight because nobody else will and also because I have a little time now, having had my asshole sliced a bit, and unable to work. but actually, yes, I did meet more death in you the last time I met you than the first – you were more cosmopolitan, less human, more full of angles and ways. . . . Christ, I know the Romantic in us must die sometime, but must all *else* die too? But, this is the same old *horseshit!* – the old talking down to the young . . . I went through so much of it, and *all* their advice was bad. So, all ya gotta do, is turn everything I have said to you, turn it upside down and you've got the truth.

I told off some Catholic priest the other day. you think I'm turning into an old crank? enjoy your next piece of ass to your full capabilities, hahaha ha ha!

Joseph Conte was the editor of a racing journal called American Turf Monthly.

[To Joseph Conte]

Late April, 1966

sure if you can ram the #6 poem through, I'll take a year's subscription, I'm hooked on the horses but rather mathematically, playing with odds and systems, experiments. I've found that the further away you can get from a racing form the better chance you have. one system is based ENTIRELY UPON INDEX NUMBERS and shows continuous profit. the other is based entirely UPON THE ODDS LISTED IN THE RACING FORM AND THE ODDS ON THE TRACK PROGRAM. both systems work, in short, because they *reverse to an extreme* everything the public does or wants. the only problem is getting up your guts to play the things. [* * *]

[To Steven Richmond]

May 16, 1966

[* * *] by the way, somebody's stealing some of our fire – or borrowing it anyway. Frances showed me a copy of *Xenia* 2. she has a couple of poems in there and not bad ones at that. but what I mean is, baby, there are articles – attacks on Olson & *Poetry* Chicago, so forth. the problem being, with them, that the poetry they print does not attack the problem or rattle or burn or jump or exist. in other words, they know what's wrong but they can't dance. which still gives the edge to *Earth* – she dance, she know what's wrong & she know how. ya. [* * *]

if the universities ever read *Earth* they will burn their doors and books and walls. god damn, something in red just walked by. my pecker jumped like a worm in a sparrow's mouth. when they gonna let this old man rest? [* * *]

[To Steven Richmond]

[ca. June 1966]

[* * *] I composed this magazine in 20 minutes – from memory. I hope to *hell* you don't think I am serious! [* * *]

THE TOILET PAPER REVIEW

our motto is: we dón't give a shit

edited by
Charles Bukowksi

pirc
priceless

editorial

the only ones who can write is us. nobody else can write but us. we are the only ones who can write. I don't understand why other people can't write. send money. send your wife – for one night.
we do this for love.
we hate war. we like guitars. we paint. we swim.
we know everything. the world is evil. we are not evil.
send money. we send love. we send love everywhere.
send your girlfriend – for 2 nights. don't pay your income tax. blow up the troop trains. smoke pot. sell pot. write your president. write your gov. write your mother for money and send it to us. don't send your mother – at all. literature and the world are in bad shape. we are dying. legalize rape.
no payment for poetry.

yours, love,
Charles Bukowski

poem

o it says
vamma
?????
????//////
crutch
hold me
Hold me
o eternal motor
super heart
supermarket heart
sputtering
the night becomes me
and I die
– John Vance, Glendale

poem

it is only
me.
– Curly Eisten, Pasadena

poem

war is terrible. people get killed in wars.
I once killed a man. I will never kill
another man. bow to the sun. suck your own
cock. the stars come down like
RAIN. love, love
LOVE.

–Joe Esterlund, Cleveland

poem

o dear, the green of me, the green of me
is dying in the fountains
the green sun stops my breathing
mother asks me to get married
I can't teeth the world
or I am afraid
o my green my green is
going
in fountains
and the stars are
grey.

–Mary Jane Wicks, New York City

if you say you like poetry, this is another editorial, then god damn you, buy books, sned send me money, I am up on a pot charge. anybody who says they like poetry and doesn't send me money is a god damned fink.

editor

adv.

bring your case to me.
John Manse, attorney
3314 Tower Building

shoes repaired
Joe Coldone
111 E. 5th st.

note: all manus. must be acc. by stamped return envelope. not resp. for anything. no payment for material.

adv.

Dr. S. Rivers, psychiatrist
112 E. 5th st.

letters

yours is the best magazine ever. raw guts.
– Randy Page, Ohio.

your first issue knocked me out.
– Randy Page, Ohio.

I read it straight through.
– Randy Page, Jr.
Ohio

have been waiting a long time for something like you.
– R.P., Cleveland

how do you do it????
Randy Page –
poet

I was not pleased.
Rance Edwards, Eirie, Pa.

the police threw the cat out the window and found 4 lousy grains of coedine. I am going to enter Ohio State, take a major in Engo9sh oit. to hell with the spelling, the mispelling. if you don't like it too bad. this magazine is for fun and love, LOVE, LOVE. nobody will be send an issie until the write me a LONG LETTER asking for it. are you going to ask for it? send stamps, love, $$$$$. we don't have much money. paper costs money. and we need volutnteers to do the work. I've got the keep the lawns trim and have to collect rents from the bums in back. we hope to continue with this mag. but need your helop & love & money.
ed.

poem

the sky reaches for my intestine
and the kitten walks across the floor
and the door is the moon
and I am an iceberg
and want icecream and pussy
and my green is going
and I can hardly see the stars,
o my god,
the pain,
fuck you.
– Randy Page, Ohio

LOVE

LOVE

LOVE

AND THANKS TO ALL OUR FRIENDS.

[To Joseph Conte]

June 12, 1966

[★ ★ ★] got July issue and #6 poem, looks fine, and think it will fit some of your readers. but the horse-poems just don't come anymore – just the madness of the crowd, that whole body of many-legged, headed, cocked and cunted, wailing and greedy and angry animal. also suicidal. a hell of a gang. and the insiders shove it to them and collect – deliberate 5 pound overweights, first time starters, fillies against colts, bandages, bleeders, class jumps, the works. they jam it to them like bayonets and take away the money. whatever the crowd has learned changes and no longer becomes true – first they ruin the price and 2nd they are manipulated against. enough lecture. [★ ★ ★]

your magazine can help the stabbers, although it can't help me, I like to read it, sometimes to reverse the information and play the opposite, or ingrain it in my thought cells. I'm not knocking your mag; it's a way of making a living, and I like the photos – there is something in the photos working on me – not a method of play, but a fucking art process. I have made a painting of horse and jock, a bit obscure and heavy with color, perhaps comic, oil pastel, and maybe some day I get the bigheart or drunk or find something to mail it in and I mail it on to you. then, maybe not. I don't like to make tasks.

[★ ★ ★] tell Torregian I said to go to hell. I don't think he has read over 4 or 5 of my poems. If he thinks I am 'pragmatic and social conscious,' tell him to read my article in *Earth* 2: 'In Defense of a Certain Type of Poetry, a Certain Type of Life, a Certain Type of Blood-filled Creature Who Will Someday Die.' I do think that what he means in his criticism is:

> one: first, he hasn't been published enough; which is not a crime but which sometimes puts the blinkers on the open mind.
> two: I write too clearly, therefore there must be something the matter with me:
>
> > a: not sensitive
> > b: not poetic
> > c: not there.

this is age-old fallacy stuff and I can't be bothered with it.

[To William and Ruth Wantling]

June 20, 1966

shouldn't have told you about the Pulitzer nomination because it's useless and futile, no chance, but thought it might amuse you in a kind of obscene manner, you know, maybe here I am dying and I am nominated for a longshot shit medal. [★ ★ ★]

still weak but feeling better. must be short here now, haven't worked for a couple of weeks – doesn't help with $$$ but spirit she lifts like kite, color comes back in eye, skin begins to glow, no doubt fucking job is one-half of what is killing me. they kill me if I work, I starve if I don't. [★ ★ ★]

hello Ruthie:

o christ christ ya I'd ride a bicycle if not too many hills. I don't have a beard but I've grown me a little red goat. hell, thot it would look good in a casket if I get a casket. now now, don't lecture me. I know, dramatics. ya, I could put on shorts. old as I am I've got these huge mysterious muscular legs, don't know where they came from. I could see Bill and me now, bicycling, red goat and beard, legs and glazen eyes. . . . every gal in town would get it bad, my my, and we would pedal along singing Salvation Army hymns or old Wobbly songs. maybe some day we will, if Bill and I climb through our troubles. just never ask me to be happy, that makes me unhappy, or never ask me to be just, that makes me unjust. o.k. o.k. o.k. o.k.

[To Douglas Blazek]

June 25, 1966

[★ ★ ★] strange woman came to my door the other night, one a.m. 'yeah?' I said. she wanted to know if I were Charles Bukowski. I let her in. weeping face. good legs. I was sober, sitting there looking at the walls. soft pecker. I explained that I was ill, told her to look at my paintings on the walls. she looked and didn't say anything. Blaz, I will no longer fuck on demand or because it's there or because something has to be proved. that's called old age. I signed something and sent her on her way. now Hemingway would have had her all up and down the springs, flexing his soul muscles. I was glad when she left and fixed myself a glass of tea (see

T. S. Eliot) and then got down on my nubs and prayed for a good night's sleep. lately I can only get an hour, an hour and a half's sleep a day or night. if I get 3 I feel pretty good. keep leaping up imagining burglars, my brain going, going. or that somebody is planning to kill me. (that's an old one.) meanwhile Webb writes that I have been nominated for the Pulitzer Prize. Webb said they asked for a bio and photo. altho what a bio and photo have to do with a man's work, I dunno. [★ ★ ★] happened to mention to Wantling, and he and wife made a big thing of it, made me feel rather foolish. I liked better Frances' reaction. she came over with the kid and demanded 19 weeks child support in advance, she wanted to go to mountains or camp or somewhere with kid.

'god damn it,' I told her, 'don't you realize that I am dying? don't you realize that I am not working? I'm not a money tree, I am SICK SICK SICK SICK!'

'well, that's not Marina's fault, that's not *my* fault. I wanna go to camp, I wanna get outa the smog, I wanna get my baby outa the smog!'

that's when I thought it would be amusing to tell her. 'I've been nominated for the Pulitzer Prize,' I told her.

'yeah, the Foolitzer Prize,' she said.

that's what I like about these women. we can't fool them. they *know* us. [★ ★ ★]

[To Joseph Conte]

June 27, 1966

o o o o, listen, the poem by Lottie Adler is not for me, a rhymer and 'Life is Beautiful' type of thing. you'd be surprised how many of these I get in the mail – mostly from women. I guess it's the mother-instinct, wanting to save the no-good boy from the bottle, the jail, the alley, madness. also much of this comes from reading Keats, Shelley, a kind of wilted and *nice* romanticism, but they don't even need this. just the thought of what poetry *should* be, what they think it is, out of a movie or out of a highschool English course. the whole thing's basic and I don't mean to pick. the poem is lousy. the only way this woman can save me is to throw me some *pussy* and she isn't going to do that. tell her to read the *Artaud Anthology*, $3, c/o City Lights Books, 261 Columbus Ave., San Francisco, Calif. or at least send for my review of the book picked up and reprinted by Ferlinghetti out of local liberal rag. Artaud wrote the *iron* line, like reaming fire through cement. he's been dead since March 4th, 1948, so Lottie won't have to send him a poem.

Artaud one of the few writers I look up to. Artaud, Dostoevski, Celine . . . read Celine, Joe, this guy was laughing while they were killing him. *The Stranger* by Camus. there simply hasn't been a hell of a lot of good writing done – too much talking around corners, too much airy bullshit, too many lies. [★ ★ ★]

[To Joseph Conte]

July 18, 1966

ow, you ask an opinion and I cannot give you one because I would not want to be responsible for putting you into a jail cell or an army, either one. in a sense you are asking me whether it is better to eat hot shit or cold. your decision will have to be yours. in world war II (see *Confessions of a Man Insane Enough to Live with Beasts*) I lucked on through or insaned on through, one leg in jail, one arm out, ass in between, but whether I knew what I was doing subconsciously or whether I was all jacked-off in the head I'll never know, but it was probably a little bit of each. but for all I went through there is not much that I can say to help you. [★ ★ ★]

talk with your girl friend or close friends. most men figure that the easy way out is to go and hope that they don't have to kill anybody or be killed or mangled, but it doesn't always work this way. once they get hold of you they point you about the way they wish to. and a jail cell can seem pretty final; you would have to battle both the screws and your own mates in another type of power play. like I say, it's yours. my sympathy, but god damn if I can tell you anything.

[To Ann Menebroker]

Sunday in July, 1966

[★ ★ ★] the oddity . . . of continuing to write poetry as one *really* gets older – I'll be 46 in August, there is somehow a sense of shame as if one didn't belong, but I think this is an ingrained Americanism – that age is a crime and that poetry is for the young. my age is a miracle and poetry is for me, or, what I write, whatever that is, is for me. it's a clarification of issues and also some screaming and also some things which we don't know. it's Romantic, unromantic, useless and important. it's a way to go. I don't think that I can quit. I believe I will be writing little lines on my drooling bib in my senile crib. the pleasure of my madness. [* * *]

[To William and Ruth Wantling]

August 6, 1966

[* * *] Webb speaks of another book in late '67 or early '68, even tho I have told him I am feeling very bad. it is so strange people ignore me when I say this. Frances ignores it. everybody. it is not the sympathy bit I want; I just want a few people to know that I can't function so well anymore – the old warrior's got a flat tire. or maybe Webb speaks of the book to keep me going? I wouldn't want a book that way. I want my poems to leap through walls. not that the poems are important but if I am playing with poems I don't want wet sunflower seeds. well, shit, that's enough singing of the blues. [* * *]

[To Ann Menebroker]

August 13, 1966

yes, I'd say get a book together, out, never believe you write as badly as some of them would like you to think or never believe you write as well as some of those would like you to think, it's hash gabble, but the gathering is good for your health, the climate of your being. be there. and don't worry that maybe Pound has written better or Eliot (T. S.), or that your mother won't like them or that maybe Bukowski will or maybe Bukowski won't. to hell with Bukowski. so much of our world is comparison, competition, victory, defeat, scratching, climbing, burying, denying – champions, madmen, fools and apple pie. I am tired of their game. to an extent I am caught in their machine but I needn't swallow *all* the nuts, grease and oil. I wrote a poem in *Ole* about a poetry-writing doctor and this doctor read the poem (it was anti-him as the human being he posed) and wrote back telling me that I had 'slipped,' that he and his wife were very concerned about my 'decline' as an artist. I didn't answer. but actually, it is my FREEDOM TO DECLINE, to SLIP. I don't want to go on and on packing the dear old ARTIST-load anymore than I want to pack any other kind of load. we're all racing for the Moon of being Top Man. WHERE DO WE DIFFER AS WRITERS FROM USED CAR SALESMEN? this is why I hate to be called a 'writer,' and 'artist.' call me some other dirty name. think of some of this when you think about getting out a book. don't worry about some other 'finer' writer. think about getting a book out like taking a drink for yourself or scratching your toes. all that I am telling you here is THAT YOU DESERVE A BOOK FOR YOURSELF just like Pound deserves a book for himself or Bukowski deserves a hot bath on an August night of almost no moon. what I am trying to say here is perhaps not very clear – I have slipped, you see. there's a young man on the bench ready to take over my center field spot – bright eyes, strong arm, a way to go. I hope he enjoys the madness of the days.

well, enough speech-making. listening to something on the radio a bit dull and classical but with just enough bite to help me endure my landlord who rolls past this window mowing his lawn, bug bellied in no wind, hung to his proper string as the young girls walk by, and when a good one walks by, flowing like the magic of stuff stuck somewhere in me, old 46 gets up and walks to the window and looks out, sucking on his cigar, big green tears cascading down his face as he realizes all the years shot through the head, assassinated forever, wasted sure, drank senseless, hobbled and slugged in factories, bad dreams, 2nd rate jails, mouse and ghost-infested rooms across an America without a meaning. boy o boy.

sometimes when I don't write, please understand that something is happening – flat tires, overtime, illness, accident on freeway, bad horses or just the common white seethe of deadness taking hold inside. I am not hard; I would like to be harder – the days have too many teeth. I think you understand. if you've read my book *Confessions of a Man Insane Enough to Live with Beasts* you might prob. think me quite the cruel dog, but that is just the side I let them see – a cement thing with eyes poked in and mouth talking out the side. in this great land we have been taught not to be seen crying in the streets. we tabulate the works into a pillow at night in a room we think does not know.

[To William Wantling]

August 21, 1966

[★ ★ ★] But, actually, I don't know if I wd. like you with college education. You know what college ed. generally means? – security and *their* way of thinking. they run you thru the hoops and set you free – you think. there's something clean about washing cars. the kids – I know. layoffs, I know. no work, I know.

The game works in all different directions.

The trick is to work it enough in *their* directions to let you live, but enough in your direction to stay alive. the chickenshits call it 'compromise' – they mean give a mile to take a mile; I mean give an inch to take 400 miles. there's a difference. of course, the danger with my unbalanced education is that you sometimes end up standing on the razor blade. chop! [★ ★ ★]

Vagabond *no. 2 with the Bukowski material was published by John Bennett in Munich in 1966.* Klactoveedsedsteen (*named after a composition of Charlie Parker's) was published in Heidelberg and edited by Carl Weissner, who was to become a frequent correspondent and eventually Bukowski's literary agent in Germany.*

[To Ann Menebroker]

September [10], 1966

good to get call, seriously, tho I didn't know what to say, got lift. like old times, what, old girl? damn, how we carry on! I guess we often get the deep blues, both of us, and wonder what it all means – the people, the buildings, the day by day death things, the waste of time, of ourselves.

I've thought of phoning you at times but afraid your husband might answer and he'd think I was trying to break up your happy home, which I'm not.

very odd thing happened today. I got a letter from a street sweeper in Munich, Germany, and he showed a magazine (English-printed in Germany, the editor is a dishwasher) to a postcard seller on the street, an old man, and the old man read my long poem in the mag to a group of young people in the streets, translating from English to German as he went along. this is enough to chill hell out of me. I was originally born in

Germany and once spoke the language as a child but now can no longer speak or understand it. and here was this old postcard seller reading one of my poems in GERMAN, in the streets of the land I was born in. who says we don't return? who says that miracles never happen? unfortunately, the long poem is printed with a couple of pages reversed (*Vagabond* 2 is the mag), but the message still seems to get through, so what the hell? you've got to write pretty strangely to have your poem printed in any order, but, since, in this one I was talking of the old mysteries of the soul plus the good fight, it read almost sensibly. good.

meanwhile, another German magazine *Klacto* has taken a couple of my poems. the editor of this one is also very poor. what are all these poor men doing? what crazy souls they possess! it is good to have your own courage but it is also good to take hope and courage from the ways of others. this I haven't been able to do until lately. some very very strange people are arising, Ann. but mostly they are not arising in America. there is something about this land and its ways that kills almost everybody. there doesn't seem room or reason for the truly living creature.

but little miracles keep chipping in to keep me going. an unexpected phone call in the middle of the afternoon from Sacramento; a seller of dirty postcards reading my poetry to children in a foreign land; the *Lamp* taking a couple of my poems after I had accused them of belonging to the 'ladies sewing circle' – now my landlady shows at the door – 'come on down and have a beer.' and so I will go on down there and drink with her and her old man the rest of the night. they like me and I am glad. I am glad to be liked. corny? I am glad to be liked by the non-literary people, and the literary ones too. I am glad you are Ann Menebroker. I am glad you phoned. perhaps someday we will meet and it will be very embarrassing and dull, and we won't go to bed together, but no matter what you think or how odd you think I am, I will still be glad that you were, in many ways, a part of my life, and I especially remember you in the bad times of 3, 4 years ago when I was very close to suicide. it's been a long sweep of years and I think we are all stronger and better for it. when, often, I do not write or snap or seem the aged crank, do forgive this, for there are still times when the knife still gets close, very close, and things fall apart and I am not fair to people. I think, however, that you know all these things. and since you do, this letter is long enough.

Notes from Underground *(San Francisco) was a continuation of John Bryan's* Renaissance. *It ran for three issues from 1964 to 1969.*

[To William Wantling]

Mid September 1966

[★ ★ ★] *Notes from Underground* now out, you'll get your copy soon. I told Bryan yours was the best writing in there, und he agreed. glad you didn't insist on changes. it reads as a raw, original and sheer-pure work. if the rest of your novel is up to this level, some of your worries are over. everything fit, the conversation and the action. well, balls – before you swell out to python-size, nice to have known you. ya still gonna drop me a card after you're famous asshole? good.

actually, I am drying up on letters. it was a phase, maybe. big arguments along this row last night. I was not in it. everybody drunk around here, all these places. somebody in driveway couldn't drive. ramming into things. another drunk screaming at him. real loud bingo game. YA WANNA TRY ME? – THAT'S POSSIBLE TOO. I HAD AN ACCIDENT. – YEAH, WHO RAN INTO YOU??? NEVER MIND, WHAT YOU DOIN' LIVIN' IN A DUMP LIKE THAT? – I OWN THIS PLACE YOU LOUSY SHARECROPPER! this kind of dialogue. I am listening in the kitchen, drunk, smiling, broke, stupid, enjoying the flare from an electric light overhead. realizing that I am not the only man in the world who is insane. [★ ★ ★]

[To Douglas Blazek]

September 19, 1966

raining, something by Rossini, coffee here, just took Maria and Frances to their place – all day Sunday recovering from about a week's drunk, god o mighty, my timecard in hell looks like it's speckled with henspots – same old blackouts, dizzy spells, balls balls balls what a game! anyhow, rec. all the *Assholes*, und tanks, babe, your usual lively production, glad to be part of the team, and now *Assholes* is lined up with the others in the wobbly bookshelf and I kind of feel like a christmas tinsel Hemingway. [★ ★ ★]

I hope the foreword went [★ ★ ★] if you use the foreword, fine, it will be foreword #3 [★ ★ ★] Sherman, Richmond, Blazek . . . all odd-cat poets with warm and mad string of melody and punch and message. no regrets, shit, I stand back of these. [★ ★ ★]

I hope you and Norse mend it. I like to think that I understand both of you a little. we are all cut and hammered by so many things that do not always show in the poem directly. these things happen. our strings get out of tune. I know how you have to squeeze the faint and slipping and tired minute to get out one page of that mimeo and here I have an edge on Norse in knowing how it goes . . . the pains in the back, the neck, the chest, the fucking soul . . . the foreman's face again, and what a FACE! Norse, tho an excellent poet, is more the literary and leisurely type, and when coming across him try to remember his diving board is a little different. god, the sun just came up. see what these prayerful lectures of mine can do? but must get to sleep, or the sleep substitute. I'm going to need some moxie to handle them tonight, sick as I feel. I'm known as 'rough, tough Hank.' 'Hank the Crank.' 'Hank the Barber.' but you need fangs down there or they'll eat you up. I can't recite Keats to them. better the iron hand. [* * *]

[To Douglas Blazek]

Early October, 1966

[* * *] good, you'll use the foreword, even tho I guess part of it does not jive with your hives. I still hope we learn how to spell 'Polypolesian wars.' I am not for deliberate misspellings just for the hell of it. [* * *] I am not being straight-laced but why give them a chance for their dirty mudballs? [* * *]

[To Carl Weissner]

Early October 1966

thanks for M[anifesto] for Grey Generation, lively as hell, but don't know quite how much manifesto in there except life-um jump, which is o.k., of course, very little around. I have been on the drinking thing and very sick, but remember some tape myself, talking with big cat with beard who has run away from 2 wives, changed name and is now letting another woman support him. he has children somewhere, both poetry and in flesh. now new name. he didn't drink. took some stuff. I drank and took some stuff. most talk utter waste, of course, most of the time looking at electric light or wondering how stupid I am. and realizing I am much more unhappy than anybody I have met. I have a reputation for toughness, I don't know where it came from. I once tried to bust up a few heads and a guy's house, but, bah, that was sometime back. listening now to an opera that is putting me to sleep but that is all there is on my radio and I don't have sense enough to turn it off. [★ ★ ★]

you can talk about poetry and talk about poetry and all you end up with is an old rubber tire full of shit. I mean, we talked somewhat about poetry and it got dull. then I told stories about jail, drunks, whores, my father, and it got better. then maybe about the last 2 hours we found the recorder was not recording well. all that wisdom LOST! about a beancan full.

I can't seem to get straight around here. I have 15 or 20 poems I have scribbled into notebooks but can't seem to get them on typer, and a couple of editors asking for stuff and I can't even give them the joy of rejecting me. I think my chickenshit job has drilled a hole into me and the whole city is riding through me with dirty boots on and dripping condrum. [*sic*] – if I could get my hands on a good young piece of ASS!! ah. [★ ★ ★]

drunk outside staggering into hedge of thorns. I know that hedge of thorns. we are all drunk around here, all unhappy. we can't sleep. we are tired of talking. when we shit we sit on our ivory stools dumb-founded that something actually seems to be happening at last. we are proud of our shit. an act. our shit is as good as anybody's shit. old hollow god, try to ace us out here! [★ ★ ★]

god damn, it's ten o'clock. got to quit typing. the law, the law. the little drunken fists banging my rented walls!

[To Joseph Conte]

Early October, 1966

[★ ★ ★] I can't write any system articles, Joe. I wouldn't tip my hand on the good ones that I know. I know, I know, I am working for a living at an impossible job. if I know so much about the horses what am I doing cleaning the shithouse? I don't know, Joe, I don't know. maybe the Anita meet will get me over. I have developed what I think of as my 4-ply play; in other words, there are sometimes 4 bets in a race, but usually 3 fall on one horse and one on the other, or it goes 2 and 2. I'd like to think I've got the whole thing in a box and I think maybe I have: the horse the stable is shooting with; and the *logical* overlooked overlay, and my overlay may read 8 on a morning line of 8, or even 9/2 on a morning line of 5, because I use my own rating not the trackman's. I also have a weirdy called my overlay-underlay, plus one other juicer. the morning line fools most people and it's meant to; it is deliberately jacked out of line to draw the money in from players who take the line as God. sounds like madness, I know, but almost everything is, so why can't I join the crowd? [★ ★ ★]

[To Douglas Blazek]

October 14, 1966

[★ ★ ★] this time until Jan. is the overtime season and also I have to pass a rather diff. and searing time burning dull flaggelette exam to hold this job I hate, so it will seem Time done shitted all over me, but if you'd care for me to read some books and give you capsule digest with shark tooth, o.k., send me some books and I will submit wonderful reviews like nobody ever read top of spaghetti eating contest. it will give me excuses not to study chickenshit exam. but remember, I do not like very much poetry and I will have to say so. I DO NOT MEASURE BOOKS AGAINST OTHER BOOKS, I MEASURE BOOKS AGAINST MYSELF. further, I know I have plenty of blind angles but it is only by nursing and mother-nourishing my prejudices that I feel better, and the longer I nurse them the more they *seem* like truth, and I find that this being holy and kind and broad-minded toward others makes me unholy toward myself. I guess what pissed me most as a child was being 2 feet tall and having to take all that shit from those (parents) who were automatically in control of me through nature's and society's big dumb dragging asshole. now that I am six feet tall (minus 1/2 inch . . . why quibble . . . I am damn well covered with 220 pounds of beerfat and my feet and breath stink much of the time) the control is extended to other hands and other ways. [★ ★ ★]

Menebroker – all these letters through the years – enough to give a musty candle a hard-on. [★ ★ ★] now all this talk from dear Ann about offensive obscenity.

o b s c e n i t y

even the word THE WORD WANTS TO MAKE ME RAM MY DICK THROUGH A CEMENT WALL, and she – knows it. you follow? of course you do. this Tom Wolfe she talks about – *You Can't Go Home Again, Look Homeward Angel*, so forth –

completely bad writing, very bad writing, the worst, he drivels his jackedup juvenile romanticscockism all up and down the pages wearing you out like a cheap pair of stocking wear out. in the summer. of course, the first time you read him, if you're young enough and haven't been scraped too much by prune-picking machines, he really seems like the REAL THING. there are many writers only good the FIRST time you read them – Saroyan, the short stories of Chekhov, Upton Sinclair's lancing for a Utopia, Sinclair Lewis who seems to be writing from notes from his sleeve, Conrad, Jack London, Gogol, Gorky . . . but the second time around it is like reading a column on sports by a fattened and spoiled and stale columnist. calumny. cunt. crap. to hell with Tom Wolfe, I shit on his grave. [★ ★ ★]

Printed verbatim in its entirety. Holograph.

[To Joseph Conte]

Hey Conte!
Oct. 20, 1966

Fairly drunk.

3 fairly good days – $70 average – trotters & pacers, maybe luck, but fairly new-old insight. Fairly, fairly.

Kid, I consider myself a pretty good fucking horseplayer (poetry is like taking a shit) – horses are the Empire (like fucking) (see Frued's pupil) (but nothing that *simple*) Fruedy's are too obvious, much too much college mother-boys & unlived.

It seems like anything anybody *else* does that you *don't* do – then *that's* caused because you wore shoes a size too small and you wanted to fuck your mother. Right?

Actually, the so-called most well-balanced individual usually ends up in some useless & dry position such as President of the United States of America and ends up fucking (up) a lot of mothers & everybody else too.

The pyschiatrist (spell?) is the high-paid fuzz that makes up (lies) excuses for individuals who cannot understand a decadent & horrible & useless society (govt.) & a dec. & whore & useless life. He is paid to call these people crazy (insane) (physchotic – spell?) instead of the life & the way surrounding them.

The pyschiatrist is the pretty-boy liar of a stabilized hell.

As you must guess, I am drunk – but mean what I say.

Then too – the poet as preacher is a dishonest & copious extension of his normal function – see Pound, Ginsberg, so forth.

God damn . . . where am I? can you read this???

Answering your question – the newspaper bought by the largest % (percentage) of horseplayers entering local tracks (Santa A.) (Hollywood) (Del Mar) (Los Alomitos) (Pomona) is not an L.A. paper but The Independent (published in Pasadena). This is the one that 'moves', the horse-addicts suck them up. The *whole* front page is covered with horse-race bullshit information, so much so that one of their handicappers are squeezed over onto another page. The larger metro LA. papers (Times & Examiner) merely blow up the print on their one or 2 handicapers in an attempt to cover the page. In fact, the largest circ paper (the L.A. Times) does not even *bother* to reset type in order to blank out *SCRATCHES*!! except in the case of harness races where scratches are by *rule* not *morning* scratches but *overnight*, prob. before midnight???

The Independent advt. rates are undoubt. much lower, babe. So don't say old Buk never done your rag any good, what? But would prefer you check with some other horse in this area to make sure I am not bullshitting you. And so, Aunt Jeriamiah fucked a burning duck.

By the way, most of the articles in your mag *sound* good but are basically unsound as is most horse-info –

like most bologna –

A) horse must have had race within 14 days
B) 2 year old and maiden races are bad plays
C) handicap races are bad plays

and on & on.

The people who own & run horses take advantage of public information & education on horses to invert all possibilities for their own profit.

Furthermore, overlay & underlay winners are caused by 2 concepts:

A) public misconceptions, greed & fear.
B) the track handicapers's *deliberate* distortion of the line in order to confuse & bring in the most possible betting $$.

Hang in, kid,

Buk

[To Ann Menebroker]

October, 1966

[★ ★ ★] on obscenity, I don't know much about it except that it (the charge or talk about it) frightens and bothers so-called honest writers. to me there is nothing obscene about sex or bodily function (tho both become a mess sometimes); the only obscenity is *bad* writing on the subjects. good writing or pure Art is never obscene no matter what the subject, wordage, painted or sculpted matter. I don't think a hell of a lot more than that can be said. I suppose then it is only up to us to decide what is good, what is Art or what is not. and that's where roads and swords cross – Artistic moralities. what may be Art to me may not be Art to you and therefore obscene, or the other way around. and the line of demarcation is different in each of us. in other words we are never going to agree – you or I or anybody else, just what *is* obscene and what isn't. so no need for me to go on talking about it. [★ ★ ★]

[To Carl Weissner]

November 2, 1966

[★ ★ ★] they raided Richmond's bookshop in Santa Monica, Calif., taking around 2 dozen books, including some of mine, and also took a letter from the typewriter that Richmond was typing to me. 20 centuries of civilization, semi-Christian, and we haven't gotten anywhere. the publication of his newspaper the *Earth Rose* got their eyes stuck upon him. headline: FUCK HATE.

> Whereby, on this day we able minded creators do hereby tell you, the Establishment: FUCK YOU IN THE MOUTH. WE'VE HEARD ENOUGH OF YOUR BULLSHIT.

inside, poems by Bukowski, Richmond, Buckner.

4 arrests so far. Richmond out on bail.

[★ ★ ★] that hour I did sleep I had a terrible dream that a snake bit my cock. only I never saw the snake. only a kind of voice told me. and sure enough I looked down and there was this very clean ugly hole right on top of my cock (in the dream, babe) and when I awakened and saw that my string was o.k. I felt a little better. maybe it's the jug of table wine. so, then, enough. beware the hammerhead albatross.

Weissner eventually published extracts from Bukowski's letters to him in Klacto, *no. 23, Sept. 1967.*

[To Carl Weissner]

November what 18?, 1966

[★ ★ ★] by the way, you asked, should you like to run excerpts from any of my letters, please do. although I have an idea I have not written much. it is odd, but letters from you seem to calm me, give me some place . . . I do not quite stare at those rusty razor blades in the same dream-like stutter-stance. I do not mean that I need honeypie custard soothing, but statements of actual fact and torture of men within civilization make me realize that I am not the only man alive who has to fight himself to keep from driving an ice pick straight down his bellybutton. [★ ★ ★]

I get my limbo kicks with my drawings . . . like to draw people fucking each other, strangling each other, staring at walls, smoking cigars, lost among bottles under an electric light. once had a book of drawings due out but the guy just collected money on the ads and now sits on the drawings and no book, no response to inquiry, no return of drawings. a real shit. the world of the arts is full of shits too, both editors and writers, so beware, Karl. I was an editor once and I got some very nasty responses, espec. to my one or two page rejection slips which I used to write everybody. instead of soothing rejection this simply brought out the fangs, yellow ones, esp. from writers of reputation. 'who the hell are you? I've never seen *your* name on any of the little magazines? how can you tell me about *my* work?' so forth. or a simple little slip back saying 'SHIT.' it was true, I hadn't begun to write. I began at 35. but I knew whether I liked a poem or not. and why. and men don't write with their reputations; they write, most of them, with typewriters. each time you sit down reputation is gone with yesterday's sun; every man begins even again. right now, I am very glad I do not have a hotshot reputation – it keeps me clear with myself. [★ ★ ★]

good that Norse is mending. I can't say enough about his work. he is one of the few men whose work lifts me. some of the more famous leave me quite flat and empty, and angry with their dull tricks and empty kookoos. but Norse has this CLASSICAL SENSE OF REALITY. he can't write a bad line; I've never seen one. he uses the language perfectly. I don't. my work is full of stone, clipped little droppings out of the side of broken mouth. they have kicked too much shit out of me. I try to stammer out a phrase of fire but by the time I get it from my head-gut to the page it begins to look like an ad for a used car. my vocabulary dribbles down more and more to 30 or 40 words and there isn't anything I can do about it. Norse tells me how (in his work) but I can't follow him, I have to play with my own marbles. treat him well, he is one of the great ones of our rather strange times. [★ ★ ★]

Burroughs, Ginsberg . . . how does it feel to be communicating with the Lights of the Age, and also with me. B. and G. have disappointed me at times, but let's admit that they have done things, and that no man creates pure Art day after day. me, I get rejected enough and it's good for the asshole, it make my cock hard. the editor of *Illuminations* writes that Creeley attacked me at some place, he named some name, a club or reading place I'd suppose and the editor defended me. that Creeley searched me out for attack shows that I am functioning along the right trail. Creeley's type of writing has always disturbed me at being anti-life, scratched-out with snob and comfortable wire. that he has noticed the opposite of his writing and that it bothers him, that's fine. I do not say that sometimes Creeley does not create Art; he does not create my *kind* of Art. the years that I have worked in slaughterhouses and factories and gas stations and so forth, these years do not allow me to accept the well-turned word for the sake of the well-turned word. . . . there must be more for me or I am just another suicide in a cheap room or in the alley or in the sea of in the gas cloud. I do not treat my work as holy or necessary except to myself. the reason I send it out? to see if I am totally mad or not. I think. I think, but am not sure. there may be some ego there too. Charles Bukowski on a page. so that when I roll over in a drunk tank or am having my guts cut out or my ass cut out or my soul cut out, I feel like I've saved a fraction, a match stick. *save what you can under all conditions*, that's my motto, hurrah! it's only the man who gives it ALL away who is truly ugly, who does not deserve to walk under a tree and inherit the earth. [★ ★ ★]

got caught in a dentist's chair the other day, even tho I have no money and not too much courage. a French wench wiggling all over, with rich blue eyes like out of a paint tube came in and started cleaning my teeth, god I was ashamed, I am such a mess, but she leaned her flank upon me and scraped away, leaning there, talking to me, warm as bacon she was, great Jesus what joy, my gums bled and she said, 'I'm sorry,' and I said, 'it's not your fault, angel.' and she leaned the flank again and went into my ugly old mouth with her pick, and it was love again, the first time I have loved a women since 1952. I don't mean sex. Carl, I mean that kind of high-washed feeling where you *float*, where you can feel the love swarming out of you like a blue and white fountain of miracle. but I will never tell her, she will never know, for she already knows. she has been in America 7 years but she has not yet drowned. who in the hell expects to find these things in a dentist's chair. when that bastard comes in with his hairy arms and his pliers, then we'll have the moment of truth, eh?

[* * *] it is only when the Artist is dead that the masses enjoy his suffering and go to warm movies and eat popcorn and enjoy it. I was guilty of it myself. I remember when I was in the Village I went to see a movie about the life of Verdi. if I remember, there was a part there where he got a bag of nuts from an old woman in the street. he was starving. I like that. I have starved many times trying to cut some insignia into the cement. I shouldn't have liked it, the Verdi thing. but then when he came back famous with the beautiful woman at his side and he gave the old woman a batch of money for the bag of nuts that night, I didn't care for that too much. he was defaming her act, showing off to his broad. he should have taken the old woman to his place and fucked her and drank wine with her and asked her to talk to him across the kitchen table. but then Verdi was not perfect. I make some mistakes myself.

so I light another cigarette. have another beer. hold off the studying of the streets of los angeles that hangs over me like a mother ax. if I had any guts I would sit and write and paint for hours, for days, for months until I starved to death or until they came and got me. but I know that that is what would happen, one of those 2. I've been through it before. sometimes the police come or sometimes the landlady tell you you'll have to go. drinking, typing, painting, sleeping, that won't do. a man should leave at 7 in the morning and should come back at 7 at night, finished. church on Sunday. a handjob in the bathroom. no women unless you are married. this country is so soulless; no wonder they can't whip a handful of starving midget men and women and children in Vietnam. it's not Russian or Chinese aid that's holding it back. it's damn fool American fat boys who have lived like idiots, well-fed soulless idiots in and since the cradle. no wonder they torture the enemy; deep-in, somewhere, they know that they are lost, and inflicting atrocities upon a living and real people is their only way of getting back – like tearing flowers, burning butterflies, fucking and hating everything in sight. I have never quite heard of such a war; surely we have degenerated back to ages darker than the Dark Ages????

Omar the Tentmaker would have a lot to say about this.

too many people clear their consciousness with a hot fuck, but after the sperm is wiped away the world is more there than *ever* before.

how ya gonna keep 'em down on the farm?

now playing some Armenian or Turkish music on radio, from the Fez. a little cafe-like place down next to the Racing Form building. I went there one night, quite drunk really, they didn't want to let me in at first, but I was in one of my warm and gentle moods and they relented. I sat on a big pillow on the floor and some big warm wench kept bringing me all kinds of strange drinks but none of them knocked me out like continuous American whiskey would have and I felt warmer and warmer. there was plenty of alcohol in the drinks, I could taste it, the expert, but it only kept me CLEAR. people, men and women came around and sat on pillows and talked to me. I didn't want any ass. I just wanted to feel the people. and it was marvelous. and all the time, this strange music. I just kept laughing and enjoying, all sophistication all ego gone, burned-out. I don't think any man really wants to be a prick, really wants to hate, it is only pressures that make him hate. of course, I don't care for this THOU MUST LOVE, either. I don't like love as a command, as a search. it must come to you, like a hungry cat at the door. what? hearing this music reminds me of that good night. I am not always as hard as my poems. [⋆ ⋆ ⋆]

[To Ann Menebroker]

November 23, 1966

good on your acceptances, no surprise to me, you seem to be gaining on yourself, damn good sign; me, I'm showing slippage but little I can do . . . [⋆ ⋆ ⋆]

Xmas season is when the populace really becomes beastly. they cram and run and flurry wild and mama empty-eyed; me, *me, I* got! *we* got! my family! safe! goods! roof! food! a drink in hand! whoopee! – what sickening stuff. it's pressure and haste, a MUST. nothing easy or good about it.

then . . . HAPPY NEW YEAR. ugggg. [⋆ ⋆ ⋆]

William Hageman of Pasadena was the editor of The Willie, *published from 1967 by Manic Press, San Francisco.*

[To William Hageman]

November [?25], 1966

[★ ★ ★] when I said there were only 4 or 5 poets in the world who could put down a line or 2, I meant 4 or 5 poets who could DO ME ANY GOOD. the rest of them flatten my spirit, it's like swallowing sad sawdust, like being tricked again and again. the only way we are ever going to move the world a notch is through PURE ART, and baby, not much of it seems to be around, and I include myself. the best thing about mimeo is that it takes the pressure more and more away from THOU MUST SUCCEED IN ORDER TO PAY THE PRINTER. and it usually eliminated 8 or 10 hands in the pot, all printing their own stuff.

[To Douglas Blazek]

December 11, 1966

[★ ★ ★] somebody got me started on a novel and then got pissed at me because I tapped a rich friend of his for $150. I got drunk and had to get my car started, the old '57 was murdering me sitting at that curbing not moving, not moving, and also had to have 6 teeth pulled. how can we write novels with the extra poison from our teeth adding to the other poison? so now I gotta finish the novel, but not in too bad shape because I've heard from 2 outfits (small presses) that want to do a book of mine, and they seem trustworthy, but problem is they might have been thinking poem-book. this novel about 2 years I once lived in a faded green hotel, *The Way the Dead Love*. I guess I'll finish it. I screwed very nearly every woman in that hotel including the scrubwoman who was nearly 60. even screwed a guy in the ass by mistake one night. it ought to be a laugher. starvation, drink, madness and fuck. really all tragic and beautiful people including myself. the chapters will be short clipped action happenings, but no general plot, just a recording of the place. done like *Confessions* only much longer. I hope it doesn't pancake. I'll lose about 100 poems writing it. but shit, I've lost 100 poems, at least, in the mails. that fucker who lives with Warhol, I forget his name, won't return a batch, and in a recent issue of *Tish* I fuck recognized he stole one of my lines, used it as a last line to nail down a lousy poem: MY FEET TOUCH CHINA IN THE DREAM. those are *my* lines, babe. although accredited to . . . Malanga. giz christ, gossip. but true. and discouraging when weighed against my hopes for the human factor ever becoming clean.

they are going to play me a little Bruckner later my radio tells me, so I will feel better. you know that you are one of the few people I can talk straight to without worry that you might not catch on, or that you might be hurt. these are hard to find. sometimes I write a drunk letter to an editor after poems are accepted and the poems come back. this is kind of funny to me. somewhere in the letter I cross one of their precious gravy paths and they know that I am their enemy. in fact, I even throw in a few short chops to test them. these returns are mostly from people who only print 'name' writers. usually on expensive letter press. some of the poems they print are very good – not Ginsberg's or Duncan's or Bly's or Kelly's but say Paul Blackburn, so in a sense I lose something by flapping my drunken lip, but I do find the letter-form to be a very good exercise for limp-soul when the walls are running with blood (mine). you, I don't worry about. I kiss your ass not, BUT WHEN I CAN NO LONGER TELL A GOOD MAN HE IS GOOD AND IT MAKES A CERTAIN JOY RUN UP MY ARMS, WHEN I CAN NO LONGER DO THIS I WILL CASH IT IN. fuck you.

Bruckner. then there's Wagner without the words. and Mahler. there is the warm soup agony speaking, the wallpaper, the rooms, the roaches, the pimple moon. there are people with feet and hands and heads. it is all very something. I am not an Art or a music nut. I do not ream myself with sounds night and day over a fancy stereo that all the neighbors must hear too. but sometimes when I am very low low low and quiet shot, the job crashed through me like I am a tunnel, all *their* talk for hours: baseball, pro football, sex lies. the constant needle the American worker gives to the other American worker through shame and boredom and madness, and I have the best needle in the place – they do not call me HANK THE BARBER for nothing. 'that son of a bitch has a line for everything.' I even harass the supervisors to keep them off me so I can loaf more. I spend more time in the crapper than the janitor who cleans the place out. but I've had over 100 jobs from Miami to Frisco and I know how it works: I am only trying to save my life and they are only trying to kill me. my talent, if I have any, is the fight for the last inch which I will not give them. they've cut off my hands and arms and one ball and they face me with an m.g. but as the guy reloads his belt I spit in his eye. bravo. fuck the snob publications who only *think* that poetry talks about life. and I'm going to make the same fight with my poetry no matter if the mailbox comes all over the rented porch with rejects. Schumann's good too, you oughta listen to Schumann, just once. *once*. trust me. you'll know. you are probably a jazz cat. well, that's all right. I like that too when it seeps into my proper vein. but the dark long stuff hits the core. I don't trust Beethoven. he catches the ear with surface crash, and outside of the First Symphony, seldom a bad line. but I like more madness. I keep feeling like he's skimming on a giant mirror. yeah, I know he had his troubles. and I also know that if I had discovered him instead of the world discovering him I would like him better. shit perversity. jealousy? I do not know. I do not know my soul or lack of soul. I only know that I must be fair to myself also and that I must allow myself a judgement outside of the standard concepts. I've got to be kinder to myself. on the other hand, I only figure Faulkner as the giant fraud of the century. and using words myself, writing myself, I am on surer ground. even as a young man, a very young man, reading him on the beach while the other guys played football, myself being bigger and meaner and lousier than any of them, reading him on the beach there with the dandy sand being kicked in my face, not even knowing that I myself would someday try to write, I lay there, I laid there as I lay dying, and I thought, how can he get AWAY with this stuff? this obvious dull hack-trick shit? ah, babe, I was a very special critic from the moment I slid from the cunt and my father's face (naturally) was the first face I hated. but not the last.

thanks for the drawing, old boy. it always girds, grieves me a bit that they do not turn you loose all day to play with brushes and words, but like you realize, things that happen in that foundry come out in the paint and in the words, but still, I am not the one to believe in the SUFFERING OF THE ARTIST, or the suffering of anybody. including myself. every time I see a mouse caught in a trap or a photo of a lion shot dead, I am unhappy. unrealistic, they tell me. but to me Realism is only a condescending to the Actual and I believe that man has enough sunlight and god and luck within him to change the actual. when I let the mouse go and the lion eat me, if I am strong enough, perhaps the lion will finally not eat me, perhaps the mouse will sit down and listen to Bruckner with me. madness? shit, maybe. but where has world sanity led us? [* * *] listen, baby, you think my old mind is cracking? I drink drink after drink writing you, knowing that I must face that mob at 3 p.m. tomorrow afternoon. suffering from dizzy spells, weakness, may not make it, may fall to floor as they discuss the afternoon's pro football game. yet I feel that all I am saying here will *not* be wasted, you hear it anyhow. I know that you do. I give you lilt and go-on, do I not? and also myself. the strangest thing is, I cannot eliminate D. H. Lawrence from my consciousness, not the sex-appetite thing the public sunk its tooth into, but kind of the washing of feet and skin, the thin pin-point structured line. a very bitter man, somebody once wrote him off as. why not? he didn't accept the *outside* Realism, and I don't either. I go for the bloodflow stuff of the inner color. I remember a half page or so of his stuff about some taxi drivers (I think it was in Australia?) that is perhaps along with Dostoyevsky, some of the best writing I've ever seen. well, enough of that. [⋆ ⋆ ⋆]

christ, I am out of smokes but still something to DRINK. maybe just one good woman would cure me, licking her tongue around and round and around that thing, my soul stuck out into the air like a telescope. but here I sit, what, in a city of 4 million? hell, I don't know how many million and I sit alone. I've fucked my share but more and more as I grow older I know that I can no longer pay the price. what I mean is, the demeaning of self in order to get in or with. I have these problems. all the women in the world sucking my cock at once could not change what I now feel. which is, that I cannot kid myself into a generative love attitude AT THE EXPENSE OF SOMETHING ELSE. do you read? I am too far gone. I cannot faggot myself for the expense of a come. I refuse to make a million dollars to go to bed with a Veryl. I will stick my cock into the hollow of a tree and let lightning strike me dread dead before I ever funky myself again into that hollow and wonderful malicious hole that demands so much. will you write it off as old age and laugh? I don't think so. I trust you. I do think that you are the last man in the world that I do trust. don't die. on me. fucker.

Bruckner quite graciously good, and as I try to type my fingers have more and more trouble hitting keys properly, all right? good. you don't care? good. high heels going past window. fuck me, fuck me, they say. of course, Freud was wrong, sex is not the whole pie, and I knew this long before the detractors, but sex is part of the pie. exit goading impossibilities with come into cunt of lovely woman who has eyes of purple into her head. I've spent many a good night, and some bad ones. I've had some terrible fucks where the pussy spread from wall to wall, but even with this kind, a long night of talk and drinking, a warmness. – I've learned more from the women of the streets in rotting hotels than I ever have from Kant, Faulkner, Tolstoy, Balzac, Thorstein Veblen, G. B. Shaw, Karl Marx, Hitler. this is not talk shit, this is true.

I owe most of the heart of anything decent in me to the street-walkers of America.

don't get me wrong. there are a lot of savages out there. killers. shits. dopes. sub-normals. liars. but I mean you get hold of the one or 2 good women out there and Harvard is toilet paper, Blaz. I've been lucky. I only met one but she taught me where my arms were and my mind and my cock and my heart, q.t., wuz. I hope to write a novel about her someday but I don't think I am man enough to do it yet. I may never be able to do it. if I can live to be 60? I hope to call the book simply *Whore*. [★ ★ ★]

• 1967 •

[To Douglas Blazek]

January 2, 1967

the f.b.i.? what the hell? they really think we're porno? lot of other places they should (?) could go. must be something else that is bothering them and they use the porno as a left jab, as an excuse. what might be bothering them is that we are possibly creating life and nothing makes the dead more angry than this. that has to be it, sweetie. but relax, we are as clean as a desert bone. I guess you never thought your little mimeo machine could make J. E. Hoover twitch in his sleep. secretly you ought to be proud. of course, wives never understand such a thing – they feel it threatens their security, I mean the everyday things: supper, laundry, t.v., the funnies, the fuck, the picnic, the drive to Aunt Sarah's. but I know you can put her straight. [* * *]

The review mentioned in the next letter of Louis Zukofsky's A Test of Poetry *appeared in* Ole *no. 7 (May 1967).*

[To Douglas Blazek]

January 12, 1967

6 teeth pulled today, so stayed here tonight and wrote the review on Zukofsky. use it if you want to. I am bleeding like a river of shit and I guess I shouldn't get any beer, will swallow blood, haha, and cold beer will scream the holes in my jaw, old daddy getting there, there are only so many teeth to be pulled then I am FREE. ya. guy going to build me a bridge. will try to hold onto my remaining teeth a while. don't know how I will pay him but we never discuss this thing. very nice. I think he was drunk, he sang all the time he was working, and one tooth just didn't want to come out and he screamed STUPID THING, STUPID TOOTH! what's all this

talk about teeth? came out and smashed my tail light against a phone pole. poor old '57. I told those people I wouldn't eat any walnuts but maybe if I warm up the beer . . . ??? anyhow, Zukofsky in here, and hope you are making it through the days, you know like killing a bull every ten minutes or being put in a gunnysack with 14 monkeys. how do *we* last, old man? sometimes I think that we are braver than all the armies of history, and then I know that's stupid: the armies don't count, and we hardly do. except to the walls, a couple of faces and our own way of waiting. I am down to 4 codeine but that should get me through the night. knives, pliers, hospitals. watch out for spiders.

P.S. no arrival of F.B.I. rather disappointed.

[To Ann Menebroker]

January 19, 1967

[* * *] have been down, the old depressive hackdown, plus sickness, mine, Marina's and so forth, meanwhile working the hateful job, old stuff, but time all sliced to small sections of stumbling into a room and turning on a light and falling down. meanwhile there are a half dozen poems I wrote while drunk that I haven't yet lifted up off of paper. I mean, all I have to do is type them up but I can't get to that. no tragedy but a buzz in the dome. and down at work a foreman leans behind me and says, 'I want more work out of you, Bukowski, I want some production!' and I am dreaming of the lame bones under earth, the whole earth threaded with the bones of the dead – what a halloween. and then my little girl gets her foot caught in the rear spokes of a bicycle that her mother rides her around in in a little box in back, and I told the woman much earlier, 'I hate the god damned bike, it stinks of tragedy I wish you wouldn't ride her in the thing.' but no, she insists, but when all fucks up she runs to me with the mutilated kid. next it will be the whole stack of them in the middle of the street run over by a Falcon or something. but if you suggest that a woman should not do a certain thing she will insist upon doing it – thinking it proves that she has independence and a soul, but verily all it proves is that she is an asshole. well, let that be. but getting the kid to a doctor did get rid of an almost continuous cold, pen shots and liquid. but like I say.

so now, even as I write this it is time to go back to work. and even at work I am sliced with jackasses. I have a half hour to eat, I get a table by myself – a tough job. and here some nit catches my eye and brings over his tray: 'I just hate to see somebody sitting alone,' he smiles. 'I really don't mind at all,' I tell him. 'well, I'll sit down anyhow.' 'yes,' I say, 'tell me your troubles.' and he does. he tells me he was somewhere or other, babysitting or something, and somebody gave him 2 cans of beer and he got high right away, he fell asleep, and the next day Sunday he slept almost all day, those 2 cans of beer. this was the essence of his conversation. I grunted something and tried to eat during his cold turkey insanity. I finished and excused myself and went outside in the freezing cold in my shirtsleeves and stood out there for 5 minutes and then went inside, back to my foreman.

so then, I know you have your things too. it's not the large tragedies that moil us to pieces – we are fucking well ready for those. it's the little scratchings and drippings, the continuous stubbing of the toes and elbows, the car that won't start, the piece of tooth that breaks off as you are biting into a peach, dirty stockings, a sudden face in the market goring your peace like a bull, a ring in the bathtub, constipation, insomnia, a dirty newspaper, toothpaste too sweet, a fingernail flipping back and ripping from the finger . . . these things again and again, the similar small biting donnybrook continuous hail . . . these tear us to the final pieces. ah ha.

James Lowell was the proprietor of Asphodel Books, Cleveland, an important dealer in underground and little press items in the sixties. When he was prosecuted for dealing in obscenity, a large number of leading authors contributed to a collection A Tribute to Jim Lowell *(Cleveland, June 1967) to help raise funds for his defense.*

[To Carl Weissner]

January 27, 1967

[★ ★ ★] – yes, I wrote an essay in defense of Lowell, literature, art, us, we'uns. . . . the vise closes in. the F.B.I. questions Blazek, asks about me. Richmond out on bail, bookstore still open, and he's awaiting trial. yes, they picked up my *The Genius of the Crowd* at Lowell's. d.a. levy who published that, and other things now hiding from the police, warrant out for him. but the police have not knocked at my door (about *these* matters) because all they have on me is that I write in a very plain and simple style and don't even cuss too much – I am too god damned fucking mother fucking tired to cuss! [★ ★ ★]

I do not make it too well with the women because I refuse to throw them the smoke screen, and I really do not get enough good ass and I never will because if a woman's soul is a sack of shit I will not fail to tell them so, esp. when I am drunk. there are 2 new women on my horizon now, hungry-eyed, trying to act decently human but they are really not decently human. I don't mind that they are filled with snot and piss and shit and blood, with the newspaper print pasted above their eyebrows – it is the eventual explosive unfolding, the sharp claws stored in the coffee can. 'hey, son, I gave you some pussy, now kiss my ass, run my errands, listen to my harpy song.' oye, oye, oye. [★ ★ ★]

I am sure Marina will make me feel better tonight. we have a direct line going. everything is simple and clear and magic and even funny. – your daughter? on back of pic? the date? 1944? is this correct? how OLD ARE YOU, Abraham? [★ ★ ★] I have to go over and get Marina now; she looks almost *exactly* like the photo you enclosed, even has a hat like that. thanks the photo. it cheered me.

I don't know if I am glad I left Germany or not. I really think I would be dying wherever I was at. my formula remains the same – keep the last coal glowing long as possible. no sense in tossing in. make them come to us. we will throw the scabs, the guts, the pebbles in their faces, whatever they use for faces.

so now in the old car, the night streets, myself gagging in the love of their tranquil yawn, my los angeles non-people. Marina how do you live in this city? [★ ★ ★]

[To Carl Weissner]

[January 28, 1967]
the next day following earlier
letter (1967)

hello Carl:

this quick one, follow up, trying to fight off Marina who won't let me type long (competition), but I screwed up – the photo is evidently of you, and I called it your daughter – so now I've put a dent in your mulch –

sorry – but why in hell do they dress little boys like little girls and then hand the photo to a guy with a hangover? the 1944 makes sense to me now. should I consider you wounded forever? don't be. I wish I looked like my daughter. now she's making a train. I hold a conversation with her as I type: 'Are you making a train? ah, fine, hum hum. oh, did the train fall down?' Bukowski gone soft as poached eggs for ulcer patients. I always used whiskey for my stomach – I mean my ulcers – got rid of my stomach and my ulcers too.

heard from Greg who got the bundle of *Earth Rose* I slipped past the F.B.I. – Richmond busted for these – and now Dan is walking around hanging them in public places, like Spellman's crapper, so forth. a very energetic fellow. I always picture him with knife in bloody teeth, working upon the Fall and Decline of Empire, which ain't a bad idea. only I am lazy and mixed up with spondees and beer and bad health. all revolutionaries should be 6 feet 5, weight 380 pounds, look like young Gregory Peck with Heidelberg scars, and never be bothered with constipation, insomnia or the search for employment in the capitalistik nestegg. by the way, I hear that the Heidelberg scars are coming back. saw a perfectly bloody set in a mag, I mean photos of the faces directly afterwards, the faces of the lucky boy who collected his scar, and the hogfaces, the cementfaces, the lustfaces of the onlooking club members. you live in a hot town, old man. ACTION. the reason I am reading this mag which is a kind of sex-sadist outlay is that somebody sends it to me, regards an article, portion of which reads: 'It's possible that the New Bohemia stands on wobbly legs so far as terminology is concerned. It's possible that the New Bohemia is not avant-garde at all, but merely an appendage of beatism at best, and perhaps even the "rear guard" of that social phenomena. Take a look at the heroes of the beatniks of the sexy Sixties have chosen. They include Timothy Leary, Norman Mailer, William Burroughs, Jean Genet, Henry Miller, LeRoi Jones, Lawrence Ferlinghetti, Bob Dylan, Bertolt Brecht, John Cage, Eugene Ionesco, W. H. Auden, Anais Nin, Allen Ginsberg and Charles Bukowski, to name a few.' so there I am put in my place, but of the names mentioned I am only partially in tune with a few. (now they are going to give me Bruckner's 9th. and a bit of Hindemith.) Genet in portions when he doesn't creampuff out in love with his writing, Brecht in portions, and the very early Auden. and I doubt very much if I am any man's hero. as the mass goes down to a generalized and easy death there seem to be at the same time more and more individual people springing out of rosebushes with lushlife fire to make me wonder – 3 or 4 months ago I had not heard of either you or D[an] G[eorgakas], now my mailbox is on fire with loveletters from hell. not as an act of writing a letter – but as information from the center of the sky to keep me from cutting my throat. [* * *]

woman from Sacramento just phoned. she says she likes to hear my voice. wow wow. I'd sure like to help her. I'm told she's a looker. writes me 2 or 3 letters a week. she also writes poetry. god damn just dropped a cigar ash on my only good pair of pants and before I could get the damn thing up I burned a hole in the pants, and a hole in the leg. but the pants, that's what hurts. constant tragedy. ah, me. but these letters from Sacramento. little scrawls, tired: 'it rained today. I cleaned the house. 2 poems accepted by X. one of them is about you.' I keep this gal going in a kind of haywire way, and it's kind of sloppy and bites me in the back of the neck, but I try to remain the fuckedup human I am. everybody needs help and I like to help them: especially good-lookers with sexy voices who have read more than the morning paper. luckily for me, she's married, has children, and is probably disillusioned with her husband because he does not have fits, does not brood in the closet. a lot of guys marry these gals with poetic backgrounds because they think they are getting a chance at class, when all they are really getting is a pain in the ass. I have spoken. then too, these poetic bitches with looks always (almost always, I have found by *my* experiences) marry money-makers and then WONDER WHY MONEY-MAKERS ARE SUCH DULL STUPID PRICKS WHEN THEY ARE JUST SITTING AROUND *NOT* MAKING MONEY. so both sides are disillusioned, and the bitch sits around looking at her husband and ends up trying to write a novel on character-disintegration (*his*, of course!). in fact, I got a letter from my x-wife who writes me every Christmas, and she said she is going to write TWO novels on character-disintegration. mine, I suppose, and her present husband's. now, if she *could* write about *hers* . . . twice . . . she wouldn't have any classics, but maybe a couple of best sellers.

(this quick letter to tell you I am sorry I called you your daughter in 1944. in 1967.)

this has been a better week-end. last weekend there were about 12 different people here, and although I tried to treat them straight, easy, I might have been a bit weary, nasty and downright cruel, hahaha, and I haven't had all these people here this weekend, so I guess I know what I am doing. unless I can get at my piano (typewriter) an hour or so each day I am not worth a shit to anybody. not that I am creating anything immortal, although now and then I may slip over *that* line (?) but it is mostly the sound of the typer like ENGINE ////////// MY ENGINE MY ENGINE GOD DAMN IT, and when they shut my motor off I am no better than a hockshop owner. hey, *there's* a good beginning: suppose Dan G. and I went around assassinating all the hockshop owners, as many as we could until they got us? Dostoyevsky would say no. and it *wouldn't* change a beetle. and when I have been broke the hockshop owners always looked *good* to me even when they gave me almost nothing for something – because you see, nobody else *would*. it meant food or rent. to hell with the loss. so even vultures are sometimes useful. although I might agree with Dan that there *might* be a better way of helping the poor and the disowned. like say, a gun to begin with, and a gun to end with. the good thing about G. is that he is not just another standard faded commmie liberal pissedoff nuerotic anarchist, carbon copy like. he speaks from an ORIGINAL FRAMEWORK springing from the gut-soul of his breathing and wanting to breathe. he suggests that one of the reasons the F/B/Itch is fucking with me in the background is that I am corresponding with him. I consider that correspondence as a joy and an honor, sunlight and orange juice – it is Marina walking across the room bringing me a bottle of beer. about D., tho, I am afraid for him in the sense that he seems to feel the NEAR READINESS OF UPHEAVAL. things like Watts, so forth. the French Revolution. the Russian. me, I am not ready to mount the parrapets. I am a shit. I remember the 30's, the depression, the same talk – tho not as creatively sensible and warm as Dan's – and nothing happening. almost 40 years later and nothing happening. in fact, due to the ultra black Romanticism of the easily excited intellectuals (Camus to start with, Malcolm X to end with) the swing has gone way back to the RIGHT, and it is further away from them than ever. there are 2 very sad things to see in the world at least, and 2 of them are a very old queer and a very old revolutionary. man, hold, I have worked in the mills for their pennies, the fat capitalists, I have been drained drained and slugged and slugged and cheated, and Dan says bodies must go on the line and he means it, but we've first got to get enough bodies with stuffings, each with its own voice not somebody elses. YOU CAN ALWAYS PUT NEW GOVERNMENTS ON TOP OF MEN; WHAT WE NEED IS NEW MEN ON TOP OF GOVERNMENTS. the only way government (or no government) can work is through living men, and I am afraid we do not have enough of these around right now. this does not mean that I am for injustice against dead men, for even dead men have rights – mainly because they still feel pain, get hardons, have bellies.

[* * *] like any individual with individual experiences I have impaired

vision. the capitalist goes by his experiences and instincts. I am afraid I would make a *very* good rich man and I am AFRAID I would keep my money. I would build walls. I would create a Greecian Art from the souls of my slaves. I would fuck young girls until I got tired of fucking young girls. I would not worry about the lettuce pickers of Salinas. I would feel pretty good: I would feel pretty brainy; I might still even have a soul. THE WHOLE THING NEEDS TO BE CLEANED UP BY FUCKING WELL REALIZING EVERYBODY. you see, your boy Dan gets me to thinking about these things. I think of Norse standing up at a table when you walk in. I think of Norse sick sick dying cornered, I think of the good men everywhere being swallowed by the iron sky. and it just isn't government and capitalism and MAN BEING VICTIMIZED BY OTHER MEN, IT IS MEN BEING VICTIMIZED BECAUSE THEY WERE BORN TO DIE. all this is basic, all these things are basic – yet I have never read them anywhere. why? I suppose it is in the libraries somewhere, but IT IS SO DILUTED AND TRICKY AND ARTY that it flips off like a live fish out of the hands. truly, there has been very little good clear plain and true Art created within the life of Man. in Music, yes; in Painting yes – but in the written word, no no no NO! – the written word is till sucking its own tits, crying for mama, posing. let's take a case. Burroughs. all right. he is reaching, shuffling into a NEW DIMENSION. he is bored, mad, pissed with the ordinary product. rightfully so. any sane man is, any sane insane man. but Burroughs in mixed and mixing new paints, combos, finds flicks, colors, discoveries. . . . surcharged with butter and fire, much of it not bad Art. fine. but still he *is* sliding off the horizon. in trying to discover a New Reality he is losing the actual REALITY. this is his failure. let me illustrate – the only true forward-moving art is an art that discovers new form by still retaining actual reality – perhaps the best example of this is *Finnegans Wake* by Joyce. he moved the word out of the concept of the word but still gave us the actual world. the instance came not by *accident* but by the force of innards and the lonely madness of luck and the way. Burroughs pasteups of the clipped-up London *Daily Herald* or whatever, or standing on his knees upside down reading the bible through a film of boiling skimmed milk is often entertaining and REAL but more often a trick, a falling together of an insignificant world by tricks and a lot of glue. now it is possible to get a FREE WORLD WORD, a REAL SHOT FROM THE SKY BY WORKING THE TRICK, but down in us we know, finally, that the only way is to slug it down the river. not because our masters and schoolteachers taught us this but because the masters and schoolteachers must go, and Burroughs is only pasting their dry canine flicks upon our murdered brows IN DIFFERENT ORDER. not enough. we need new blood, new miracle – not the mixing of old soup. and now that I have killed Burroughs, enough of that.

god, enough of that. this is a short letter to explain that I did not mean to call you a girl. [* * *]

I am still listening to Bruckner 9th. do you think I am cultured, little girl? I like this stuff. if I weren't so poor I'd make a beautiful snob. even now I think I could be a music critic for the *New York Times* if they'd let me. but they wouldn't. before I was finished they'd burn the *Times* down or some music lover would assassinate me. let's get the pawnshop owners first. then, me. yes, I'd make a terrible snob. I just don't like most people's faces or the way they walk or the sound of their voices or anything they say. the people make me physically ill. shut me in a room with 5 people for 40 minutes and then ask me if I had a chance whether I'd save them or burn them. Dostoevsky wouldn't agree. somebody from some middle class mag was over to interview me last Friday night, no, the Friday before. but he just kept the tape going and I got drunker and drunker and I finally said, FOR CHRIST'S SAKE, MERCY, JUST ASK ME A DIRECT QUESTION AND I WILL GIVE YOU A DIRECT ANSWER. but he wouldn't. he was wiser than I. or more frightened. not both. there are very few, if any men, more wiser and more frightened than I am AT THE SAME TIME. I MEAN I FEEL TERROR CONTINUALLY. they have built me a little image shit thing of a brave and tough man. I will not buy it. I am a skunk thing, always turning, not knowing. I don't know where I am at. incomplete, nothing full. his friend, John Bryan, kept saying, 'Bukowski, you are a bitter old man!' and he meant it but I did not know what he meant. I am not bitter, nothing like that. I am mixed. I mean half the time I want to kill myself and the other half the time I am angry because I have almost no means of staying alive in a society that asks for turret lathe operators or experts on Space, the stock market, so forth. I don't know their game. I am these TWO HALVES AND NO HOLE. a good piece of ass would fix me for 3 or 4 nights but where is it?

I am now drunk beyond the meaning of my saying but go on. ??????

Kennedy was a half-man, hardly that, but a hero of the little punchy guy who wanted class and used K's seeming class to fill the hole. I'll always remember the day of Kennedy's assassination, how all the people seemed HOLLOW without impluse or guide. as if they had been scooped out. me, I felt the same. but I got this terrible feeling as if the beehive had been raided and the QUEEN BEER BEE taken out forever. even their faces had no anger. WITHOUT THEIR LEADER THEY COULD NOT EVEN GET ANGRY AT AN (seeming) INJUSTICE. this was the day I really read the human race down, realized that each man must be HIS OWN QUEEN BEER BEE. and that they could not ever be stuffed with the apple pie of political fairytales to save their dull asses. you can kill one man. it is a little more difficult (tho possible) to kill a worldful. let's try for a worldful. (Carl do you know any woman in los angeles who could come over and throw me a hot piece of ass? if so, tell her to wear high heels and a tight tight skirt, and my phone number is NO. 1–6385). oh shit, it's past ten p.m. and according to the rules I must stop typing. how can I make it? I am just getting warmed up. (Carl, do you know any woman in los angeles with a NOISELESS TYPEWRITER. if you do, tell her to bring it over. tell her to wear high heels and a tight tight skirt, and my phonenumber is the same.)

this is a short letter and I am sorry if you are a girl. wear high heels, etc. . . .

you know, it is amazing the ugly number of people in the lit. world hate me. no, don't send me to headshrinker. no complex. thing in present *The Smith*. AN INTERCEPTED LETTER FROM CHARLES BUK, something like that.* but really the parody does NOT WRITE LIKE I WRITE. impossible. maybe I do write too many letters. maybe I do write too many poems. but it is simply a matter of energizing into the INCOMPLETE ABSOLUTE, you follow? yes, you do. it may be a flowing of shit, and yet within all the turds I feel is some tiny flower. you might have to look pretty hard. I have had a lot of hard days . . . drunk days, days in jail, days of madness, days without cause or form, and the university boys take heed, they don't like to hear back alley talk. THE MAN IN THE BACK ALLEY IS SUPPOSED TO DAMN WELL KEEP QUIET! no, I ghostly damn well throw out the mangled butternut skulls of myself, the sucked-out flies, the cardboard faces of Jesus, Saroyan at Malibu, James Dean & Bob Dylan inflated Dylan Thomas inflated, the inflated fucking raft, Bogey the dull picture hero, myself spitting out my teeth and my life without a chance to breathe. they want the straight-lace picture. novels about the Civil War. novels about daring sexuality within the daring and lovely rich. the UNIVERSITY IS THE THUNDERHEAD OF DEFEAT. the young know this. so they get sucked away from this and they get sucked into other cesspools: Bukowski, Thomas, Dylan, Ginsberg – anything except by going into that lonely room and finding out WHO THEY ARE OR WHO THEY ARE NOT. it's too hard. and milked and slugged and smiled at by parents and grammar schools and high schools, they are already robbed by the time it

*Felix Pollak, "A Letter from Chuck Buck," *The Smith*, no. 7 (15 October 1966), pp. 40–47.

is ready for them to THINK. think becomes a dirty word. because they have been TAUGHT THAT THEY WERE THINKING ALL ALONG. not so, of course. but if a man can recover, if he has the bounceback, the miracle, he will find that the first 30 years were wasted in fighting off, regrouping before HE CAN BECOME EASY. THINKING OR LIVING IS NOT VERY HARD AT ALL; it is the other thing that they are doing that is killing them. [* * *]

[To William Wantling]

oily Febru 1967

[* * *] saw headline in paper: CONGRESS VOWS FIGHT ON CRIME. and I almost sat down and wrote a mother essay, 8 or 9 pages on what crime IS and what it APPEARS to be, how our whole social structure houses and pardons and builds laws for everyday sanctioned robbery and crime against each other, whereas a direct and HONEST CRIME is punished by police, judges, juries. the difference says our society is this: you can take a lot and give a little, but you can't take everything and give nothing. this is the essential difference between Capitalism and the Gun, and the reason why all judges, juries, cops are finks. the dope bit is all the same – it isn't the dope that matters to them; it's how you get it, who hands it to you. if it's in the doctor's handwriting it's all right, he is supposed to know whether you need dope or not, that's why he is so well-paid. but who knows better than I DO WHETHER I NEED DOPE OR NOT? who knows whether I need oranges or eggs or sex or sleep or dope? I do. Who knows whether I am sick or not? the doctor? who is more IMPORTANT? why is everything twisted backwards? but you know all this. [* * *]

well, now I need sleep, if I can only SLEEP! little girl slept with me last night and pissed all over me as usual. but she is a sweet box of candy. she is joy. I look at her and light goes all through me. I am soft, man, soft, and I don't mind a bit. to feel some kind of love after the jars and holes they've had me in, it's the neatest of miracles. [* * *]

[To Steven Richmond]

February, 1967

yes, the whores with one or more children will generally treat you more human to begin because their circumstances are more desperate but once they figure they have you hooked in against the pussy, lo, the more than trouble begins. there are about 3 women looming on my horizon, eager-eyed, trying to act like kool-true dolls, but I'll be damned if I think I am going to play buck-antler deer with a hard for them. I am tired of the whole gory scene and think I will remain a hermit of an old man behind pulled curtains – say, peeking at schoolgirls as they walk by, whistling through my broken teeth, then running for my paper and crayons and drawing the tower of Pisa, or the Eiffel.[* * *]

– yes, Georgakas strong stuff, not the usual textbook Marxist, neurosis-anarchist, Black Romanticist, bones-of-Trotsky, they-shot-Lorca, let's listen to a folk song type. he leaps from a kind of hammer forge energy purpose of his own invention, he does not hum the same old shit and is man enough to know where he is and where they are. and not introvert enough to let them overpower him with his *own* logic. he leaps like a wild and hungry monkey in a cage, but screams a seeming very good sense and livingness. if all his breed had the same living faculty, I'd throw in with them, start by setting Yorty's hotel on fire and so forth. but I am leery of his club membership, am afraid they are a bunch of hand-stamped farts, and so I sit at the typer, go down to the postoffice, go to the race track and write letters on windy afternoons to Steven Richmond.

THERE IS *ANOTHER* HIGHRISE APT. GOING UP DIRECTLY ACROSS THE STREET. I am now completely surrounded. I see all these beehives. I see people more and more living stacked on top of each other in a kind of demented high-priced luxury that they pay in a kind of fear and a kind of love of the stink of each other behind those shiny walls decorated with mass-produced art-work and sexfilm paint. luckily I can't afford to die in such voluptuous candyshit; I will end up in a cardboard box in the hills. I have discovered the last green hills in town – it is just before you hit Huntington Drive on the way to Santa Anita, a turn left off of North Main or North Broadway, I don't know which, anyhow the streets end there, and there it is: these slices of high green hills, tall, and nothing on them, no terrible houses, no terrible people, and I always feel like stopping the 57 and getting out and climbing up there, walking around in it, laying down in the weeds, but no guts, the city has me, the track calls me, but those hills ride inside me as I drive past, and looking at them, it's like vomiting up a whole sick metropolis and I feel better. there used to be a space like that on the way to Los Alomites but they found it, the developers, and they put their mass-produced houses there and the mass-produced people came running and leaped in and mortgaged their souls to somebody, banks, builders, could make 450 percent profit.

somebody when I get rich on the horses you and I will start a colony. there is still desert land somewhere. we put up these houses, rustics, made entirely of wood and unpainted. houses far apart, lots of sand between them. no police force. people can scream or drink or sing or take dope all night or all day or have lions in their backyards. only no rich, no literary pretenders, no Malibu, no Village, no Carmel. we interview those desiring to live there. 'lemmee see your paintings, your poems.' we look. we are snobs. we are pricks. we are selfish because we want to stay alive. 'no, no good, you can't live here.' of course, we take in a lot of stupid women because there aren't any other kind. then when it all gets *too* bad, we SELL . . . for 450 percent profit and LEAVE THEM THERE. (this is the way I talk after 2 good days at the track. last Friday and Saturday; when I lose I am much more humane and carry an etching of Karl Marx in my wallet.) [* * *]

2 p.m., 2:05 KFAC symphony now coming on, hope they give me something to lean against this highrise across the way . . . not bad, something offbrand by Haydn, who was a kind of a kool suckass in his time but managed to save some juice. there is much of him that I haven't heard – the masses, Mass in Time of War, so forth. but prefer Mahler, Bruckner, Wagner without words, Stravinsky, Shostakovich. shit, so what?

some guy at work met me on front steps, a small hard Negro with little cap pulled down over his ears. 'God damn, Hank, you're really full of BULLSHIT!' 'whatcha mean, Roy?' 'I saw that magazine.' 'what magazine?' 'I dunno the name of it, but I saw it. about you being a POET! what a bunch of BULLSHIT! and your photo with the little beard.' 'I don't know what you're talking about, Roy.' 'no, you KNOWS, you KNOWS WHAT EYE'S TALKING ABOUT, DON'T BULLSHIT ME!' It appears he saw a copy of *Dare* when he went to his local barbershop. this is the poem I got the $50 for writing. easy money but if it's going to get these jabberwockies on my back it isn't worth it. – some guy over other night to interview me for the *L. A. Times* magazine *West*. I was very drunk and think I insulted the guy on principle. he wouldn't even phone me for further details on article but phoned Frances. if this ever comes out in about a month or a month and a half they are really gong to try to rip the meat from me down at the bastille.

but I think I can handle them. they don't call me The Hammer and The Barber for nothing. all else aside, the fact remains that the only battle is to remain as alive as possible and to continue to create the poem or knit stockings or whatever you are doing or have been doing or want to do. anybody can go the way of Dylan Thomas, Ginsberg, Corso, Behan, Leary, Creeley, just sliding down that river of shit. the idea is Creation not Adulation; the idea is a man in a room alone hacking at a stone and not sucking at the tits of the crowd. [* * *]

Allen DeLoach edited Intrepid *magazine from Buffalo, N. Y. Bukowski was a contributor.*

[To Allen DeLoach]

February, 1967

[* * *] poetry is survival, sir. it throws some of the stink bombs out of my room. if it comes as rhythm fine or physic, fine, any old way. I think of it more as a loaf of bread, a long fat hot loaf, sliced in half down the middle, spread with pickles, onions, meats, garlic, chilies, old fingernails . . . add ice beer and a shot of scotch, ram it down under electric light, forget the mountains of faces and eyes and wrinkles and bombs and rent and graves, get it in, warm, smelling, filling, light a cigar, blow the whole room paint the whole room blue with smoke, play the radio, think of the bones of Chopin's left foot – that to me, is poetry, or zingplay, or the rays. [* * *]

Corrington's novel, The Upper Hand, *was published by Putnam's in 1967. The parody letter is 'A Letter from Chuck Buck' by Felix Pollak in* The Smith, *no 7 (15 October 1966), pp. 40–47.*

[To John William Corrington]

February 11, 1967

so you've done a moderne novel? May? good. now Putnams. you get around. slip me a free one, book I mean. I've got a whole bookcase full of free books, mostly poetry. I take much pride in my free books, most of them being vury good because the people wanted me to read them and felt I would see some light within the pages, and it works, easy like. [★ ★ ★]

I'll mail you the *Smith.* your name is mentioned in there. it is a parody of me, or whatever you call it. they pretend they have intercepted one of my letters. I write letters. by the way, I have never submitted anything to Ed Sanders. I wonder where they get that stuff? it doesn't matter; I think you might even call it a fun-piece except the satire is the sharp exaggeration bit, you know, and believe he detests my style and my guts – which is going to happen to all of us at one time, and it is part of the rocks in the shoes. [★ ★ ★]

as to the poetry writing, I am writing very good again after a kind of 2 years slump. which lasted from about Oct. 64 to Oct. 66. I do not mean that my poems were not being published, I mean that I did not care for them. now they come out full of butter and steel and my fingers hit the keys and it is easy. but my health shot. [★ ★ ★]

[To John William Corrington]

February 22, 1967

[★ ★ ★] I am not so worried about whether I am writing any good or not; I know I write a valley of bad stuff. but what gets me is that nobody is coming on that I can believe in or look up to. it's hell not to have a hero. it gets harder and harder not to have a hero. somebody to blow out the fire, knock out the goof, give you the word. my heroes are dead and the replacements seem very shoddy indeed. what can I do with Mailer, what can I do with Lowell? what can I do with anybody I can name? the thing is, when you first start the big boys have already been there a while. you look around. well, names. Dos Passos. Hemingway. Frost. Pound. Cummings. so forth, so forth. Jeffers. so forth. so you look round and let them go. they've been there. maybe you don't really like them but they are old boys in a picture book on the coffee table and it's kind of sad and kind of interesting. LeRoi Jones, Andy Warhol, D. DiPrima, Ray Bremser, you gotta be kidding! where's the big wooly guy with the diamond eyes and the cement lines? let me the HELL OUTA HERE! [★ ★ ★]

[To Jon and Louise Webb]

February 29, 1967 [?]

[* * *] here I seem to be going through AN INTERVIEW STAGE, kind of a silly treadmill but while going through it I try to talk as straight as possible but I suppose many men going through the same figure they are talking straight too. you never know quite when you're dying but you can get the feeling of it. I've felt quite a few death rays lately. [* * *] I'll send you copies unless you'd rather not see them; I mean they might make you sick: after all, I am a monster almost of your own creation. the Bukowski Vogue, one of them asked me, it's the Bukowski Vogue, what do you think of the Bukowski Vogue? I don't remember what I answered but I do hope my answer took some of the pin curlers out of his hair.

the idea remains the same. I am attempting to work with the poem; I am attempting to stay alive. I find it easier to work with the poem than to stay alive. all these interviews are beside the point. the typewriter is still there when I run a sheet of paper into it and I sit there and I begin again. there isn't any background. there isn't any cheap excuse. [* * *]

Marina growing growing and we are closer than the grass and the earth. it is a very good feeling, an easy feeling. no trouble, no strain. loose and free; creative without fanciness; real without flags. [* * *]

the novel *The Way the Dead Love* has stopped at chapter 5, but no problem. easy to write. about this skid row hotel I lived in for 2 years. it's just a recording of the people, and all the scenes come to me that I have forgotten, they all come up on the paper as I write. it's like being reborn, living it again. very strange. have been on gambling horse-binge which has eaten up my time. but no problem. a free day or so and I have 5 or 10 more chapters. chapters very short but filled with the distillation of the action. best this way. less yawns. [* * *]

[To Carl Weissner]

March 24, 1967

well, shit, a little high, nothing new. well, anyhow, John Thomas said he would airmail tape I did of my poetry – airmail – so you should have it by the time you get this, or very soon. friend, it is almost 2 hours to me reading my swillsteak business. not partkclary from any area, just what my hands reached or what was easy or consumable or felt like it. I didn't realize that I had read so long but had been drinking a bit and taking down these strange colored pills (not LSD), not really VERY high, only in a passable stage of FITS. I mean, time was a dishpan. it didn't matter. I read straight through, I *believe*, without a stop. most of the poems I had forgotten, didn't know the next line, intonation, connection, but feel really this was for the good rather than the bad because it stopped me FROM SETTING UP ONE LINE TO FIT THE NEXT. this is important, I believe. tho it may not be. I don't know. I know less and less – and feel much better for it. I think, tho, I am not sure – that the tape is on 4-track. you got a 4 tracker machine? I think this means you play the same reel through twice? anyhow, instructions are on box tape came in? aren't they? what drab stuff, this talk! only I always get mixed up on presumptions. I don't want to mix anybody up. I mean, people always presume that YOU KNOW WHAT THEY KNOW. YOU ASK THEM THE WAY TO THE NEAREST WHOREHOUSE. they say, 2 blocks left, one right, see this barbershop, ask for sam, he'll send you to clean cheap pussy. so what HAPPENS? YOU GET THERE and there are THREE barber-shops! and each barber is named SAM. you run back on in and get flogged across the asshole with a rusty windjammer rainbow clamstink frozen loaf of russian rye bread embedded with toy tots singing, 'somethin's happenin' and you don't know what it is, do you mista Jones???' [★ ★ ★]

by the way I have an idea of tape mutation intervolving thing but in an rear-area of my own gone gnome tot-process which is: tape mutation or word formage in symphonic or rhythmic breakthru. I have the patterns already processed on paper, the music notes, and hope that I have not [★ ★ ★] tipped my beerhand as I would like to try it first, and if I can explain to Thomas' thick head what I would like to do or change or forward or backward after listening to your Coleridge/Burroughs, Weissner tape, I think I could show you boys where you have missed a lot of chances and natural pluses. I don't want to hurt you Carl, you've done anything but put warts in my bloodstream and I want to thank you for the tape, which was very good in the first interfolding part, but you had too much help somewhere, you were too staid self-conscious arty too Burroughs really. all right, shit, I know he is a genius and I am ejalulative [*sic*] jealous, fine. what I mean is: both you genuine cats getting up too tight and kind of reading it off of paper, breathing tight, tight kitties, good kitties, but not letting loose with who you are as loaf of bread or something shitting; I don't MEAN THE ARTISTRY OF WHAT WAS SAID WAS BAD, THAT *WAS* ART, I mean the Artistry of DOING IT FAILED AS TOO TIGHT AND TOO HOLY. now the Gysin thing at the end was at the other extreme: too high-school and not enough holy Art. if you fuckers could only mix the 2 extremes you'd be in on target, and isn't that the only place to be? check with Norse on what I am saying. he won't lie to you even if it means the room rent. he's too inbred now. there's no out. ask him. but don't get pissed if he agrees with me. you won't. that's why I write to you. that's why I write to you straight. even tho we are all more sensitive – no matter how we act – than a female cat's asshole or pussy or wherever those ramrod hair ends scream into the NIGHT: Y O Y Y O W W W [★ ★ ★] my thanks, still, for tape. It was good, don't let me mix you up. My thanks. But would like to send you my mozart – cadillac intermix soon. don't be pissed. You won't be. [★ ★ ★]

oh, christ carl, it's good friday, my radio keeps playing these Mozart things when he was starving under shit church supported poverty and really throwing curve balls but the church only thot of it as bad music. it's like Blake, Blake was about as much a religious poet as some whore leaning down to suck purple dick for an extra dollar a mouthful. when the final breakthru is reached we are all writing about the same thing in different tonalities, and you know this, this is no great statement, we are tired of great statements. great statements are made by great liars. Christ had a big mouth and maybe a big ass. who know? if there were more paintings of Christ's ass (I don't know of any) than all these of His face, maybe I could go it. YOU SEE, THE FACE HAS LEARNED TO RECHRISTEN ITSELF IN THE FORM, SKIN, FEATURE, OUT-LAY AND APPEARANCE NECESSARY FOR IT TO SURVIVE. it is out front. a sign. not hidden, but certainly hazardous. MAN HAS NOT YET FOUND OUT HOW TO MASK HIS ASS. I am not being funny, Carl. what I mean is that I can follow any person a few feet (man or woman) and watch them walk, watch the balancing of the mounds – I know almost everything about them. AND WHEN THEY LEARN TO MASK THE ASS AND THE WALK I WILL GO TO THE LEFT ELBOW. you see? [★ ★ ★]

Tompkins Square Press was run by Tom McNamara. The book of letters was not published. The anticipated third visit to the Webbs, now in Tucson, took place at the end of June.

[To Jon and Louise Webb]

April 2, 1967

[★ ★ ★] I have ANOTHER NEW SYSTEM ON HORSES THAT I HAVE FIGURED OUT. this *may* be it, haha, ha. Frances and Marina gone someplace for a week. I miss M. guess that's why I got the blues. she lights things up for me and although she has not worked her way into many of my poems, she is still very much there, ya.

I think Tompkins Square going to do a book of my letters, the drunk ones, I guess. the drunk ones are best. anyway, I got a feeler from them. they say early 68. I'd like to read my damned letters. this is the only way I'll ever be able to do it. [★ ★ ★]

well, I've had 2 wild visits with you – the one in New Orleans and the one in Santa Fe, and if I can work this one out I hope that it goes smoother, to hell with dramatics. but Jon you are a tough guy to get along with, and what makes it worse is that I am a hard-head. I DON'T GET ALONG WITH ANYBODY. if I come down I think I will only stay a week, it will be about all I can afford – unless the horses are good to me. this is the weirdest system you ever heard of, yet it works like machinery – on paper. anyhow, if I come down I think it best if you let me look for my own room. I like a place where I can close a door. the New Orleans setup was all right except I was pretty jumpy. sick most of the time, and all those pages to sign. 3100 pages! jesus, you realize what a JOB that was? with silver ink? where's my boyscout medal? yeah, it's a shame Stuart doesn't know how to handle *Crucifix*. I'm real disappointed in his methods, but he did ship me $200.00 when I needed it bad, so I can't write that off. god, this time last year I was sitting on my bloody ass, right after the operation, and here we sit around now, all of us, still alive. [★ ★ ★]

[To Ann Menebroker]

April 7, 1967, 3:45 a.m.

Have been drunk for several many hours. trouble controlling pen. [* * *]

Your voice always sounds young as clear rivers crying clear things, no matter what you say, no matter what you say, I feel ice-joy cry in your voice.

But please don't feel sad. I think that *I am something that has just gotten into your head.* I am neither that way or that true.

if you could see me now, baggy-bellied in torn shorts, old, drunk, trying to answer a letter in the half-light of my life, then you would know.

there is hardly anything literary about me nor many either, so there you go.

writing poems is such a chickenshit game! if we were only more alive like they are more dead! then, sweets, we could *finally* write.

About this time Bukowski began his series of columns for Bryan's new underground paper, Open City, *under the series title 'Notes of a Dirty Old Man.'*

[To Carl Weissner]

April 28, [1967]

[* * *] right now I guess you are hurting worse than I am, but you we ARE ALL JUMPY, cool and tired and hardly caring but at the same time – AT THE EXACT SAME TIME – jumpy. I mean when I did not hear from you, I figured first that

a; you were sick

b; you had injured yourself

c; you had killed yourself

then I figured second that the tape was bad, that I had insulted you with the tape or that I had insulted you with some criticism of your tape, that I had TOUCHED SOME SPOT ON YOU AND THAT YOU WERE PISSED. the reason this type of thought-trend mangles me is through the experience that it has happened very often. so the brain cells say – 'oh, there it goes, it has happened again.' there were you with your head cracked like an ostrich egg with a sledgehammer and I am sitting around sticking false needles into my hairy ass ego. even in a long three page letter to Greg the Dan I explained how this so often happens to ME in this world. poor pure ivory me. like it even went on when I was a kid in school.

'WIPE THAT SHIT SNEER FROM YOUR FACE AND GO STAND IN THE HALL! DAMN RIGHT, AND FOR AN HOUR, NO LESS, NO MORE, YOU WILL STAND IN THE HALL!'

I never knew what those teachers were talking about. really. to me my face just felt a little blank. I was not much interested in what was being said most of the time, but who was? to be sent out into the hall because of something about my face made me feel monstrous, inferior, spat upon. excluded, and STUPID STUPID STUPID. and I would get up and walk out into the hall and all the faces would turn, all those good acceptable faces and they would watch me talk to the door, open the door, close the door and stand in the hall. that hall was always very dark and empty. and it didn't feel good. no, no. and it kept happening, through grade school, high school, those couple of years in college. of course, by college I had toughened up and when they layed on me I layed back and they soon found it was better to ignore me than have me slice them open with 5 or 6 words. but even in high school I was not ready. I remember once getting passing grades in this class, English, I think, and on the last day of class, in the middle of something else, the teacher, a female suddenly leaped up from her seat behind the desk and pointed at me and with tears on her face, actually sobbing and in some kind of rage, she said, 'Henry, I am going to FLUNK you!' (Henry is my first name, I use Charles my middle name when I try to write but that is another long story I might explain sometime.) and after class, after the others had left and I asked her what the reason was for flunking me, she wouldn't give a reason just that sobbing as if I had INSULTED her. I don't think it was love because I was a rather ugly fuck with a blank personality, and I still don't get it. I mean, these things keep happening and I am puzzled. I don't even want to talk about it anymore, only to say the letter to Dan never got mailed because there is a new newspaper starting here in town – OPEN CITY PRESS – and the editor wanted something of mine to print, essay, letter, so forth, and since I don't keep carbons I just handed him 2 or 3 letters I had written.

anyhow, I am glad YOU haven't turned . . . yet . . . but I am sorry it was your head in enfoldo smash that gave me time to pinprick my self-pity. forgive me, but understand that I am suffering from shell shock years. leave it up to me to fuck up everything. I am very good at it.

meanwhile, while you were jamming your head into wolfgang ersatz zero sludge I too was trying to kill myself but did not quite bring it off, maybe not kill myself but tinker with the limp edges of the thing a bit, a tendency I have when high, and maybe some day they will give me my gold star on head for being a good kiddy and bringing it off, but like now I am fucking that up too. I was up at Thomas' place and I am the only one drinking heavily, I have brought my own stuff and am slamming it down as fast as body will hold, sensing only electric light and faces, everybody else very calm and kool but I am going crazy quietly, my health has been bad very and there is a kind of delight in ramming it through with surfboards and elephant tusks, and everybody is so CONTENT they are like stems of flowers, not the flowers, just the stems, and finally it comes time to leave, I am with this editor (OPEN CITY PRESS; *Notes from Underground*) (John Bryan) and we go out to my 11 year old car and somebody walks through my side mirror to begin with and I get in with Bryan and I let the car roll, very steep down one lane two way street cars parked everywhere, and I think I ram something, Bryan very excited, 'Jesus, make it out, make it!' we are going again, down sliding, I have foot on gas for sound of engine trying to pull the strings up and together in me so I can hold and go, and then we are running along out of the hills at last, on the way out, and suddenly I turn left and we are heading steep UP into the hills again SOMEWHERE, very steep, and Bryan is hollering at me and I find a nice cliff, no houses too near and I take the car and run the 2 wheels along the edge of the cliff seeing how close I can get, I just hear Bryan's voice and ignore it, placing the wheels close to the edge and going at a good clip, and it seems a SENSIBLE thing for me to do, a very logical thing, a very good thing, really, but Bryan can't see it, and I pull off from the cliff to think of the next good thing to do but when I hit the street again he opens the door, leaps out and starts – running running away from me and the car. my first THOUGHT IS TO RUN HIM OVER, but I am rather disgusted with his lack of LOYALTY so I let him go. if he had been more loyal I probably would have run him over, but probably no German blood in him, poor chap. anyhow, I got home all right but of course don't remember driving there, and Bryan is still alive too. he walked all the way home, 5 or 6 miles at 4 a.m. in the morning. well, that's a nice time of the morning to walk – hardly any people you have to look at, no shock in belly as you pass the usual sucked-out corpses. [★ ★ ★]

it's raining and I think I'll walk up through the rain, drop this in box and buy one of those horrible newspapers. I enjoy the comic strips by inverting/*reversing* the meaning. and really, all you've got to do with almost any man's speech, thought, action, is reverse it entirely and you get some kind of truth. it comes out very clean. [* * *]

[To Carl Weissner]

May 13, 1967

[* * *] some collectors over last night thumbing through my bookshelf, took some of my early books which I am pretty much down on, plus a few other items, broadsides so forth, a painting I didn't want, and when the guy asked me what I thought – he had quite a bundle, 15 or so objects, I suggested $50 and he wrote me out a check for $100 – INTERNATIONAL BOOKFINDERS – and if the check doesn't bounce, it should finance my trip to Tucson, Arizona where Jon and Lou Webb are working on a record of mine – not poems – but talk mostly, drunk stories of my past. I'll try to mail you a record if it ever gets out. also handed the guy with the book collector a chapter from my novel, I am going slowly, chapter 7, I really don't *want* to write the thing but he keeps pressing me, and the novel may be good because I don't want to write it. it's like trying to run through cement, and I often wonder how people can think of themselves as *writers*? it is pretty near impossible to imagine oneself as a 'writer.' I can more easily think of myself as a rapist, a pisser of piss, a killer of spiders.

I am sorry for Norse in his suicide knot, and I have been in my little suicide knot off and on, off and on, and it's funny, if and when one does break out of the suicide knot, one feels stronger, better, a hell of a lot tougher, can take almost *anything*. the suicide thing may even be a process of growth – you fall back almost to zero, then lift back. it's a kind of rebirth process. I imagine it would even be good for flies. do flies think of suicide? just think how easy it would be for them to get their dirty work done for them. a nice little blood-sucking web with eyes and fangs and suck suck, held there, no backing out. all we've got is the tops of buildings for no-backout, and we change our mind 6 times on the way down and are insane by the time we hit the pavement. I like to work in more lively elements of variable choice and chance: sleeping pills, gas, the garrote. I tried gas once. turned on all the burners and laid down on the bed. it almost knocked me out, I was on the way, but something about breathing in all that gas, a kind of a grey-yellow feeling, and it gave me a headache, a terrible headache and the headache woke me up. and I got up laughing with the headache, YOU DAMN FOOL, YOU DON'T WANT TO DIE! and I kept laughing, it seemed very very funny to me and I walked in and turned off the oven and all the jets on top of the stove and I went out and bought myself a good bottle of whiskey and some very expensive cigars, and that night I ended up balling with a woman but I didn't tell her she was fucking an almost-dead man. these whores have a way of lecturing like a mama and it can get very boring. you really can never tell a woman anything – they will always reshape and distort the thing out of perspective because the woman is the babbler of rebirth and responsibility; they really love us, the best of them do, and they care, but their way of caring is somehow unsatisfactory, it's as if they want to cut the warts off of us instead of understanding the warts. they hope to clean us up to a big round zero, a kind of penitentiary happiness, a kind of in-jail happiness that cuts the balls quite off of clean feeling-being. a deballed smiling cuntsucker, that's what they want, and that's why I can't make it with any lady very long – I get this feeling that I am being stuffed into a drawer with the handkerchiefs, and they have such heinous ways of subjecting you to their love – like walking into the crapper while you are *shitting* and standing there humming, fixing their hair in the mirror, what hell, they love it, they love you, us, the stink of our turds, they are practicing the ultimate pain of childbirth and childrearing, it's tough and they must practice it, the cape movements, you can't blame them, but I wish they wouldn't practice on me, I wish they wouldn't make me the baby, the child, the blood, the screams, the bravery. I just want to be let alone; I just want to look at them awhile, their bodies walking across rooms or sitting in chairs, I want to notice the color of their dresses, the spikes on their shoes, I just want to eject a little semen, then forget it, hell. but they want to put me into their cage. fortunately, for me, I thrive on ISOLATION, hours days of being alone do fatten me. this sounds like bullshit to most. if I dared to tell them that I AM NEVER LONELY they would never believe me. I am a shit: I grow upon myself; I diminish in the company of others. I don't like to diminish. it's true that I have this fucking or non-fucking string between my legs that creates problems. this is why the true whore is my heroine. – she takes care of my string and leaves off. the harder the whore is, the more pleased am I. they will leave. then I can begin again. [★ ★ ★]

Jon Webb had probably solicited a tribute to Patchen to be published in the 'homage' section of Outsider *4/5 (1969).*

[To Jon and Louise Webb]

May 17, 1967

[★ ★ ★] On the Patchen thing, I don't know. you jumped me pretty hard once for a semi-direct statement on Patchen in the foreword to the Harold Norse *Ole* issue, but really, in a sense, the statement meant that *all* men with bad backs should be cared for; but P. seems to be a pretty delicate subject to discuss. I suppose it's easier to discuss Patchen than to be him. I suppose that if I were flat on my back I wouldn't be whistling *Hearts and Flowers* either. but still doesn't seem morally right to take the issue from you and suddenly go new directions. but how the hell did I get shooting my mouth on this? insomnia? that's no excuse.

[To Carl Weissner]

June ending 1967

I am on the edge of brain-hammer, that is, I have to pass this test in glass cage in order to hold chickenshit job that is killing me. have to memorize these little numbers exactly, know them off the top of my elbow, like tab: blackburn wlb 61, briggs 79, coolidge, rancho 22, griff 27, marV 31; san fernando rd.N., 1 linc., glass 5, Griff 47-West . . . so on, so on. pages and pages, and I wait wait wait and wait to study until the thing is upon me like a tiger. I read in while going down the escalator to the scheme room, I read it while I sleep, while I fuck, while I eat an orange, while I shit. it is a trick to eat the remainder of my brain and they know exactly what they are doing. but enough to that, just to let you know if I sound a bit strange, not quite like me – this is the reason.

book of poems coming, Black Sparrow Press, they are old poems that somebody found in a bag in a closet, to be called *At Terror Street and Agony Way*. editor coming over tonight, wants me to illustrate book but when in the hell can I illustrate book? – eastern-e.l.a., 1 n, haz 9 n, els 17n, Is-e.l.a ????? I have thousands of lost poems, lost books gather that never came out; these are just some that happened to show up. also may get grant to do my novel, if I am lucky and am able to fill out the papers by July and mail them in. I'll know by October. shit, it would be sweet to get paid to write! to just sit here and bang bang bang, and get paid to do what I have to do anyhow – like getting paid to shit or fuck, what? too much but worth a try. and prob. will not happen. just like the Pulitzer; I got nominated but they gave it to some woman. I got beat by a slit. well. what's all this prize and grant shit, anyhow? for the profs, for the goody-goodies. I ought to know better. [★ ★ ★]

John Martin, the publisher of Black Sparrow Press, was a Bukowski enthusiast from the start. The Press's first four publications were Bukowski broadsides, followed by two booklets, 2 Poems *and* The Curtains Are Waving . . ., *in 1967, and then in 1968 the full-length book* At Terror Street and Agony Way, *which was accompanied by a tape recording of the author reading from the book.*

[To Jon and Louise Webb]

Saturday night, June 24, 1967

dear Jon and Lou:

[★ ★ ★] got by scheme, 98 percent, but no pride there – only workhorse death. anyhow, now on my 4th beer, must fill out application on attempt at that grant tomorrow [★ ★ ★]

John Martin, BLACK SPARROW PRESS, just over [★ ★ ★] I don't care for Loewinson, nor the poet he is going to do after me, Robert Kelly, they are from the excellent school of snobs, I mean they are snobs but they seem to write well, almost real, certain shots of their writing lifting me, but then again it's all so well-worked and *seemingly* perfect that if you are not in too good a mood you get disgusted and throw the stuff in a corner. I guess that most of these boys are working centuries ahead, thinking how it might look in an English class, 2067 a.d., but they might get fooled – there might not be an English class then, or if there is those left might be able to sniff the strain of careful begging. I'm here now and the electric light is on over this typewriter and that's all I know. if some whore uncrosses her legs and has an orgasm 100 years from now over my stuff my bones won't light with neon. not where they are going to dump me anyhow. well, Mozart had a pauper's grave but he had some strange and glowing creatures at the handles. well, that's what counts: give me 4 good pall bearers carrying a cheesebox and let the president of U.S. Steel block traffic. [★ ★ ★]

[To William Wantling]

July 31, 1967

[* * *] I'll be 47 in August and maybe the same energy isn't there:

> Bukowski's old, Bukowski's old
> he wears the bottoms of his beercans
> rolled.

[* * *] some small press guy has been harassing me to write a novel. so in a moment of weakness, and after 4 or 5 beers, I shouted at him: ALL RIGHT, I'LL WRITE THE GOD DAMNED THING FOR YOU! I got the first 6 or 7 chapters done. title: *The Way the Dead Love*. then some prof who teaches at Loyola suggests I apply for a grant. I did. I turned the novel in and applied for a grant. I asked $6500 for a year's time to write the thing. that got me off. I won't get the grant but meanwhile I tell the small press guy that I am sitting around waiting for the grant and can't do the novel because then I'd have nothing to use the grant on. [* * *]

Louis Delpino was a fellow contributor to the little magazines. The Sparrow and the Cock *was a long poem that he typed up and bound as a booklet dedicated to Bukowski as a thank-you for a recent phone call. The projected book of tributes to poets recently arrested was edited by T. L. Kryss (who had edited the tribute to Jim Lowell of Asphodel Bookshop) with Delpino and Douglas Blazek. It was published as* Forever Worship the Second Coming (*San Francisco: Black Rabbit Press, 1968*).

[To Louis Delpino]

August 2, 1967

almost every day I get a piece of mail from somewhere from somebody saying, 'hey, fucker, how come you ain't answered my letter?': it's all right to be a good guy and to send 12 page drunken letters to 40 different people but after a while there just isn't enough Bukowski to go around any more. then too, like other people I've got my troubles – job eating me up, car that won't run, days of depression, sickness, so forth. have been real sick, job is hanging, I'm about finished there, and no trade, 47, no way to make it. not even writing poems anymore. meanwhile my little girl runs through here like all is sweet, climbing on the back of my neck and all that.

but not writing letters doesn't cure much. I mean, I walk around like say, thinking of that very good poem you sent me – it's in the bookcase now, somewhere, about madame somebody and that one fuck. one of the best poems I've read in 4 or 5 years, and I kept thinking I'll write Lou about it when I feel better but I've never felt better. then your letter this morning about Richmond so now I must answer. I wrote Kyrass telling him I can't do the Richmond. Cryass? Kryss? anyhow, I don't know Richmond. I mean, I've been drunk with him, seen him 4 or 5 times but I don't know him. there's nothing you can write about him. he holes up pretty much by himself, won't let people know where he lives. not that I give a damn, I'm a loner myself. but others complain that when they do find him, show at his door, he tells them, 'go away, I'm busy.' and he is, and that's his business. he usually has some bitch in there that has wandered into his bookstore, or whatever it has now turned out to be. he is covered with hair, fucks a lot, and I believe he is on the acid. also has dollars from family. told me once he is coming into a million or half million when he is 25. he was drunk, so I don't know. anyway, the thing with Richmond is that very few people know him; I'm one that doesn't. I wrote a foreword to a book of his poems, and that's about it. Richmond is just a certain type. I don't believe he wants anything written about himself, nor would he want me to write it. I did the foreword to his poems and that's about as far as I want to go. book called *Hitler Painted Roses*.

frankly, I get a little tired of the Kryss books on these poet cats who get busted. I take it that this one is to be the 3rd. shit, a lot of people get busted who aren't poets, or when they do they don't think the bust is so special. plus too many of the bust-poets can't write a cat turd. or when they do write, it's all about busts, the nazi-state, so forth so forth. they become neurotic and closed-in. at least Behan, Genet, those, made a logical literacy form out of their incarcerations. these other boys cry too much in mama's hanky.

like I say, I haven't been feeling good. maybe cranky, maybe cancer, maybe insanity. only God knows and He's jacking off. but no Richmond. o.k.? fine. and thanks for the very good poem about Madame somebody.

[To Carl Weissner]

August 8, 1967

[★ ★ ★] christ, shit, broken stick – I will be 47 on the 16th and it won't be long before they are dumping me, and it's not death flapping down like that, it's just that I haven't been able to BREATHE properly. it has been like living inside a sardine can and then somebody comes along and hits me with a hammer. no fair. although, granted, I've helped them kill me, done almost everything possible to hurry along the process; and given a choice of walking through a gateway or ramming a wall, I have always seemed to ram the wall. but it's not entirely stupidity. there's a lot of sensible well-worked disgust resting within me too. why walk through the gateway when there's a guy on the other side waiting with an ax? and these carbonated waterlumps who are my fellow man, how did they get here?

I haven't written a poem in 4 or 5 months but I refuse to worry. it is not my idea to walk down the streets with poems glued to my forehead. the concern of the poem is to form itself – too many fellows pull them out with ganglia attached, no eyes, no feet; just dull puss and putty put-together. I have done it myself – worried about shadows and axes and the human face. something on paper – a bit of snot – it appears to help but it does not. now sometimes I just climb in bed and waste the few good hours – listen to sounds – the burbling turds of the city – the lost cunts – the flash false happiness flowers – what a machine we've built! this way I can work it out pretty good, in a kind of black cave of my mind, making little quiet measurements like a tailor. it is when I get drunk and then drunk and then drunk, and then the dank screeching hangover in steel collar and chains and dementia, worst kind of chickenshit fears, real, but chickenshit anyhow. my whole bedroom walls are glued with quiet experimental screams. I have them framed in blue and grey and green and red and yellow and whatever, and even when the dive bombers come and the city shakes and the electric light blinks on and off and the cat puffs up in anger under the palm tree, even then the screams hold their places, like places on a map yes, like tatoos. [★ ★ ★]

Delpino worked in the Philadelphia post office. He had recently had part of his drum set stolen.

[To Louis Delpino]

August 12, 1967

jesus, I sure as hell don't want to start any tedious correspondence but I am down to my last beer, and thot I'd drop this is the box on the way up to the liquor store. I've just beat out my weekly column for *Open City*. something about bullfights on t.v. and Ernie H. [* * *]

I pity your ass in the post office. I've been there 10 years. each night is more hell than the preceding one. they put in an air-conditioner that doesn't work. we can't breathe. people fall off their stools. the supervisors are hatchet-men, hand-picked. everything is graced with fear and stupidity. there and everywhere. try to get your drums back, for christ's sake!, they'll murder you.

hot hot here. the beer the beer, that's all there is. all of me is a big fat mound of beer. awakened several times in the night with nightmares. I don't know where I am going.

Neeli Cherry by. I showed him *The Sparrow and the Cock*.

'god damn, this is good writing!'

'yes, it is.'

'who is he?'

'just somebody who lives in Philadelphia.'

well, man, I am down to the bottom of my beerbottle and there is no keeping me in here. sorry on the Richmond. just got a special delivery from Kryss who says he doesn't believe I can't do some writing on Richmond. well, it just isn't there. you can't set up a bank shot unless the run is proper.

be good to your wife. she probably thinks you are crazy.

Kryss writes that he is going to do a book of poems by WILLIE. that's more like it.

like you, the mousy little mag scene is beginning to become less and less with me. I think because it is manned mostly by the very young, who then fade and some more very young replace them. which is all right in a way but in another way neither grows bones or heart. the poetry has this blithe lively sameness, the newness of sex, the terribleness of evil and so forth. all right for a while. then as it keeps being said you begin to yawn and yawn and yawn and YAWN. what's new for the new is old for the old, and what is needed is darker earth and an almost plausible way. I am not speaking of religion; I am speaking of a movement forward from the same old crap. and I don't think we are going to get it. *The Sparrow and the Cock* was pure literature. I am tired of propaganda. now I've got to get me some more beer. [* * *]

Michael Forrest was the first author other than Bukowski that Black Sparrow Press published.

[To Michael Forrest]

Sunday August 20, 1967

forgive me for not answering sooner. I have been in a real fucked-up state. still am. health gone again. dizzy spells. fever. hours, nights, days, years of DEPRESSION. dark gauze stuff. no sense. just a haning [*sic*] hanging there. I make up words. why not? I am fucked. tried work tonight, the spells came over me, worked 3 hours, could go on longer no longer aye, grabbed side of case to keep from falling. and all around me, those FACES (faces? *feces*!) looking. no air. I left. they have been counseling me that I miss too many days. I get warnings, warnings. they think that I am faking it. the doctor thinks that I am faking it. 'there's nothing wrong with you, Bukowski! next patient, send in the next patient, please nurse.' I walk out and make it down the steps and the whole area of the boulevard is like a roller coaster. I can't see. everything is sunlight. then shade, like dropping right into hell and being kissed by a smelly face like a toaster. like that. not exactly. something. I guess a man has to go to hell 90 times to see heaven once. for me, they can forget heaven, and hell too.

o, shit, it's hot, the fever, the heat. I have this fan on. no good. I am afraid to drink. and the refrigerator is frozen solid into a block of ice. I have the door open and the ice won't melt. I touch the ice and it isn't even cold. it's like marble, like porcelain. the radio will barely play. some kind of opera scratching. somebody is in agony. I smile just a little. The Comedy of Agony.

meanwhile, I have not written, have not answered letters, have not written poems. [* * *]

John [Martin] probably will do my book of new poems – if I am here – next Spring. I think Webb and I have fallen out. I wrote a column for OPEN CITY PRESS about my visit to Tucson and I think he saw it. I no longer hear. that's o.k. I don't think it was a dirty column. only factual. I have been doing a weekly column for *Open City* and if you want to see some, let me know and I'll ship you a few. they let me write anything I wish. might stop doing the damn things soon. poems first, or living first, hell yes. [★ ★ ★] applied some months back for a grant from the Humanities Foundation. submitted what I have done of my novel, *The Way We Dead Love*. say they, I will hear in October. I asked for a year's worth of money – $6,500 to live on while I go the damn thing. it's true, I probably won't get it, but what hell of a hell of a shot of life that would be; it would add 20 years to my life!

well, I am feeling a little better now. I guess it's the sound of the typer. it's the sound in my blood. what a way to get hooked! 'Doctor, sir, I am sick. please let me type.' [★ ★ ★]

Blazek moved from Illinois to San Francisco in 1967 and en route stopped to meet Bukowski. The mutual readjustment of mental images produced by their exchange of letters was apparently disillusioning for both correspondents: afterwards, 'there was no lasting warmth between the two men,' reports Neeli Cherkovski (Hank, *p. 172*).

[To Douglas Blazek]

September 5, 1967

ah shit, what a birthday caaard! I am taken. great, old man. thanks.

I suppose the days of long letters, the long-letter days are quits between us, but they did their work; both reading them and writing them was beef and roses and wine and clean socks, good things.

Landlord and landlady standing out there, gibbering gibbering gibbering, I can't think. the fuckers stand around and shoot mouth night and day.

dogs barking through the gibbering. why don't they go in the back? they live in the back. everybody gotta stand around Bukowski's window, make his nuts jump and whirl in agony, ah. reminds me, book coming out, working now, Black Sparrow Press, *At Terror Street and Agony Way*. that's where I live. a friend, a kind of friend I have in the hills says the title is corny. well, it's corny if it's not happening to you but if it's happening to you, then it's not corny. too many people are afraid to say the obvious, or they have to be just a bit cute and in the shadows, playing it out. see Creeley's latest title: *Words*. now there's a man who has never considered a butcher knife. well, for all that, editor asked me if I would do 50 original colored drawings for 50 editions plus 5 inch tape for some of the editions, and I said yes, and so my ass still up in work, not just the common drag work that kills, but working with the minutes I have left when I am not at the track when I am not drunk when I am not playing with Marina when I am not sick when I am not crazy, anyhow have done 12 drawings so far and that's part of the way there. anyhow, he pays pretty fair royalties, and Evergreen took one of my poems, so maybe I will not be swept under the rug – $28 drunken phone bill, gas, lights, car breakdown, dentist bill, doctor bill for sickness of the 3 of us – hell, you know the act. it's like a war. you sit in a room and outside there – there are all these factors working gearing sharpening to chop you down. all god's children got troubles, what? I can't even renew my driver's license. can't read god damned book, dull, may need glasses. mental block. all god's children . . . my hemorrhoids are back. coming back. coming back. all that operation. finger up the bloody ass. hems coming back. must get off the beer for a couple of months, if I can. also same old dizzy spells, fits of depression, missed days at work, broke, clothes shot, same old shoes. . . . everything crazy and lumbersome and getting worse. shit, shit. then I go into work, make it, the LONG LONG LONG HOURS, people just sitting there WORKING, pissing their life-hours away and not feeling a thing, even feeling comfortable. oh, captain, let's blow my fucking brains out and be done with it. [★ ★ ★]

Penguin Books published selections by Bukowski, Norse, and Lamantia in their Penguin Modern Poets series (no. 13), but the book did not appear until 1969.

[To Carl Weissner]

September 26, 1967

hello, Karl: god damn it, I mean, hello, Carl Carl *Carl*:

[★ ★ ★] heard from Nikos Stangos, PENGUIN BOOKS, I think it is some of Norse's dirty work. anyhow it appears Norse und myself and one other, maybe Lamantia, will possibly appear in their next poet's series of 3-in-a-book. which would feel very strange to me. now I am trying to put Stangos on Al Purdy. I consider Purdy and Norse the two best living poets, and it would make me feel strange, good, godly, golden to run in a book with these 2 magicians. Stangos is a new editor and he's had his fill of the run – Olson, Creeley, Dorn, Whalen, Snyder, so forth, who, for me, are too architechial [*sic*] and mathematic. but, shit, it could probably fall through, and I am ready for that too. or maybe not, because hearing from Stangos he feels very warm and real and ready to take the flyer. he does not appear to be the backout type. I sense that he ready for the gamble. Norse and I have been in the underground cobwebs for so long that I feel that any type of good luck will not now destroy us or make us careful writers – that is not too careful to keep taking shots in the dark dark dark. I think we are now too old to think of anything but the days as they are, with us hanging there, drawing these things, and waiting. no school, ho, no politic, just the typer and the walls. [* * *]

[To John Martin]

October 18, 1967

been meaning to write. your special delivery royalty check bounced me out of bed at 7:30 a.m. Sunday morning. almost didn't answer door. but the enclosure was well worth it. people who have seen the *Curtains* drool over it. I mean, the printing, layout, so forth. [* * *]

[To Thomas Livingstone]

October 18, 1967

have been fucked-up, drinking, so forth, general decline of the psyche, so forth, and so late answer. yes, I liked your writing in *Nothing Doing in London*, they just sent me your pages. the part with the guy in the phone booth, the whole phone booth bit was an immense and startling piece of writing. the pages sent me had laid around on my battered coffee table for a couple of weeks, and finally one day in a fit of depression, I though I was going cuckoo, real deep blues and no way out except all the way, and then I picked up your work. when I got to the phone booth I started laughing. real good writing makes me laugh; if not out loud, then kind of inside, but yours had me laughing outside too. I'm crazy this way. let me say that your writing saved the day for me. that day, anyhow. what luck. what's going to save the future days, if anything, I don't know.

on books. frankly, Purdy's last book was not as good, and maybe the one before that not as good . . . I mean, if you're going to get Purdy, try to get *Poems for All the Annettes.* 2$. the publisher is CONTACT PRESS, 28 Mayfield Ave., Toronto is the address listed and I think Toronto is in Ontario, Canada. the book may be sold out, tho. might be better to write Purdy [★ ★ ★]

my own stuff is out of print and I am out of copies, so hell. but have just corrected first proofs on something to be called *At Terror Street and Agony Way*. a bunch of poems somebody had handed to somebody and somebody had stuffed in their closet and then later somebody had put them on tape, and there I heard them in a place up in Silverlake hills, and I said I wrote those poems and the guy said hell yes, John gave them to me when he was running his magazine, and I said, so that's what happened to them. meanwhile a guy bugging me to do a book, so I took the lost poems to him, threw in 4 or 5 new ones and he had, we had, the book. I've got about 500 poems out there missing. I mean people don't return them. I never see them again. fuckers. real shits. so well. a book of *new* poems will be out early next year, no title yet, but *this* book *At Terror Street and Agony Way* will be out *soon*, like I say, at printer's. publisher wants $4 for the mother, Black Sparrow Press, p.o. box 25603, Los Angeles, Calif. 90025.

I hope some of this helps you out. now the clock hands dig into my back. how's that for corn? anyhow, time running out, game must go on, all that shit. so, here I go. [★ ★ ★]

[To Douglas Blazek]

October 30, 1967

[★ ★ ★] yeah I'm still writing columns most of the time for *Open City* and I'd clip and mail some of these to you but I am tired, TIME TIME TIME slugs me up the side of the head, saying old man, you got nerve. lay down.

give it up.

admit you're dying

so if I get out the scissors and start clipping the things I'll feel pretty damned silly, like I am being watched.

[* * *] your problem is the same as mine – difficult to transmit the living juice from gut to outside speech, almost impossible. and not to pat our broken backs, but I think that's the way the good guys fail. watch the fluid-speech, interesting boys – they have coconut brains. anyhow, you ever hit town, mother, phone. I will never forget the old long letter days, the days of *Confessions* and *Assholes*. them was good daze, babe. you in your factory. me where I am now. both being burned alive and not a fucking thing to do about it. bung-holed, axed, knifed, smeared in our own bloodshit and then told by an eyeless rat with a tin badge that we were not doing well enough, missing too many mondays and spitting out blood into the urinals. your letters got me through some days. it was a time. [* * *]

[To Douglas Blazek]

November 3, 1967

[* * *] on the dick-print thing I thought it over and I can't help you. at first I thought SENSATIONAL, why not? like Hedy Lamar strung to a cross at any age. but later I got to thinking – no, dad, you're too OLD to print your cock across a cover. leave it to some hairy young cat. I am not crying the old-age blues, Blaz, I mean it just doesn't work to have some old beggar like me print his cock. it shuffles over into the area of madness that way, which is o.k., only I am mad enough crazy now. I hope you understand and do not think me chickenshit. I go on instinct, and for me the thing does not seem spiritually sound. o.k. I let you down.

[To Louis Delpino]

November 7, 1967

I've kind of dropped out of the letter-writing phrase [*sic*] in order to batch up enough glue to hold myself together a bit longer. the letter-writing thing can become a trap – I started by writing one or 2, then it got to three or four, then it got to 13 or 14, and all I was doing was writing letters. now, if this were my prime purpose, fine enough, but there are other things to do along the way too – like taking a good crap or inking out a sketch or catching a few winners at the track, or just staring at walls.

wondering about toes and your waste, and what the game was about. there are TIMES TO DO NOTHING. very important times. hard to get between women and jobs and sickness and and and . . . so, the writing of too many letters to too many people can get to be like carrying 50 pound rocks back and forth during your few moments of leisure. but people will get pissed; they will think you're up tight or writing President Johnson or essays for the *Atlantic.* me, I'm hanging onto the slippery walls.

Bukowski's 'Notes of a Dirty Old Man' column in Open City *(July 14–20, 1967) gave a sardonic account of his trip to Tucson. In it, Jon Webb is transparently disguised as 'the great editor.'*

[To John William Corrington]

November [?15], 1967

thanks for return of *The Smith.* being attacked by men of no talent is only a bit enjoyable for me, to me. also somebody, a gash, attacks me in what she conceives to be my poetic style in the latest issue of what? what? oh, *The Sixties.* they seem to be worried green shit about me, and that's all right. I don't worry about 'em.

yes, it's sad about Jon Webb and me, kid. he gave me two great books and was publishing and pushing me when hardly anybody else was. I can't forget these things. but I did write the column in *Open City*, but I hardly think it's a hate-column or unjust or dirty; I just told a story of a few things that happened on some very hot Tucson days. column enclosed, and if you think I am a fink or disloyal, well, shit, then it can't be helped. Tucson was hell, kid, I stayed at Univ. of Ariz. cottage and it was between 100 and 110 degrees every day, and I was the only one who could drink, except Lou's old father, and I quaffed a few with him. but it was a rough trip. Jon kept trying to get me into an argument about the hippies. and I stayed out. he wanted me to write something attacking the hippies and I didn't quite feel like doing it. I am neither pro or anti-hip. I just watch. I mean, like I am neither pro or anti-milkman or pro or anti-tree, and I am not even sure about the war. the black–white war, the Vietnam war or any other war. then they wanted to play cards. so we played cards for hours, for dimes, and they seemed to enjoy it. I'd win the money most of the time and give it back. they have this gambling bug. which is their business but

I am not bitten this way except with horses. so they keep running off to Vegas. where Lou plays the slot machines – the biggest percentage gyp evoked against the gambler, the worst play you can make. they told me that the ladies get a free pair of stockings for each FOUR jackpots they hit. they told me that Lou had won either 14 or 16 pair of stockings the last time they went, and Lou doesn't use stockings. their business, but I view it as a type of madness, especially when they are crying broke most of the time. naturally I didn't put this crap in the column and I only tell it to you because I consider you a friend and figure I can talk straight with you, and want you to get the FEELING of what occurred while I was down there. ah, plus I looked at old Jon a bit oddly for couple of days – he'd dyed that beautiful double wisp of white hair RED. god. and all day long it was, 'Lou, have I taken my pill yet?' and there'd be a long discussion on whether Jon had taken his pill, and then Lou had this bad lung thing and couldn't breathe and that was sad, but she still snuck her smokes. and some kids came by and they both ran in back and I had to talk to the kids. I showed them some of the books and I showed them the press. very nice young kids, clean, quiet. they left. then Lou hollered out, 'Jon, you can come out, they're gone now!' and out came Jon, with quivering and quavering voice saying to me, 'WHAT'D YOU SHOW THE *PRESS* FOR?' I didn't answer him. I didn't know what to answer. dirty gossip? Jon *is* hard to get along with, kid. he's always got the sword out, slashing at something. then he'd try to bait me on the hippies again. and it was hot and Lou couldn't breathe and then the cards came out; none of this in column, and no man's perfect, not me, not you, not Jon, and this ain't news, kid, I get attacked plenty myself – the other day a poem-letter knocking my life and ways in local underground paper. it wasn't even a good poem. but back to Jon and Lou, they are bookmakers supreme and good people too, but sometimes I write and I wrote this column which I enclose. I sent the column to a reporter of the Tucson paper who interviewed (bigshot) me, and told him not to give the column to Jon until he felt that Lou was feeling better, but I did want Jon to see it; I don't like to hide or sneak punch. evidently he eventually saw it because when I wrote him he didn't answer and so I knew. Jon is a very sensitive cat, not a sloppy hardened beerhead like me, but I guess he figured it as a kind of disloyalty, just like people figured I was being disloyal to you when I attacked one of your books of poetry. but it isn't disloyalty; I would be the first to come up with blackjack and snub-nosed automatic to blast a hole in some human wall or inhuman wall if you were in a jam and needed to get on through. there's still some German in me. which means loyalty, honor, all those old-fashioned words, and I half expected both you and Jon to understand this, but sometimes maybe I don't think or figure too good. well, enough of all that. [★ ★ ★]

so here I am, 47 years old, hanging from the same old rotting limb, Jon pissed, you half-pissed, and my little 3 year old daughter more beautiful than ever, a perfectly formed body jumping with life, gold-red hair, she loves me. and the other way around. if we were both standing at the edge of a cliff and somebody said, 'o.k., one of you will have to jump.' I wouldn't hesitate – I'd push her right off. no, kidding now, man, *I* would go. and I've never been that way before. but I have some of that feeling for you and Jon, even tho I don't show it too much, and now the old gang is fucked up and torn to shit. which shows you what a dangerous instrument the typewriter is. [★ ★ ★]

jesus, what a gloomy letter! but I am badly hungover and all horrors magnified, I guess. so now that I've cheered up your day I'll let you go. [★ ★ ★]

[To Allen DeLoach]

Late November, 1967

[★ ★ ★] I've been writing so long and failing so long that there is hardly anything anybody can do to my balls now. I was always a very slow starter, and even in my early twenties, laying around drunk and jobless in N.Y., Atlanta, Philly, New Orleans, Miami, St. Louis, San Fran, I always had the thought: 'Bukowski, if you can ONLY LIVE TO BE FIFTY, you will be there.' I am 47, and I *might* make it. with me, it is this strange thing filling up inside of me, day by day, year by year, I can feel it happening through all the women and drunks and fails and sleepless nights and suicide days, I feel this FILLING THING working down inside of me. deaht, of course, I meant to say DEATH but doesn't it spell nice 'deaht' – deaht is always there, but the filling thing functions on merrily and without any help from me. I've got some kind of LUNCH stewing up inside and it's nice to have, I mean while walking down the street or shitting or fucking or breaking your leg, it's there. how sweet can the gods get when and while they are ripping you to pieces? [★ ★ ★]

[To Douglas Blazek]

December 16, 1967

hello virile captain slugger of the gross elephants:

no, not going with the overtime, too sick, really, washed-out, parts broken, and you might be walking down Haight any day now and somebody will come up to you and say, 'hey, Blaz, you remember this Bukowski guy?' 'yeh.' 'well, he died.' even Bukowski can die. Hemingway did, and they say, Christ. well, christ, christ, so I am hanging on, barely. (I will write you a letter some day when I am 70. from the fountains of hell.)

hope to enclose last column of Dirty Old Man. I can't enclose them all. *Open City* has moved over to a fairly respectable boulevard, near City College, and I hadn't been over until today, and some of my fears were true. I mean as soon as the publications begin moving up a little, they begin to operate like he dear madam's exclusive fly suckoff parlor, extra phone, new hustlers and con-men, take-over chaps, and the volunteers get younger with tight dressers and cool pussies of snobbery. it wasn't too bad today but I did detect a bit of it, and I foretold to a buddy of mine who used to write for them but no more – 'as soon as we help them make it they will have no use for us. bad writers will take over, the pages will be 3/4 ads, and the rest will be unreadable.' I'm not saying they've gotten to that yet but swinging in the door here was this receptionist and she gave me this look like, 'if you're the trashman, he's already been here,' but I busted right past her cool cunt and hollered 'Bryan Bryan where ya at?' I saw him nailing a board to the wall and he said, 'Hey, Bukowski!' and the cool cunt musta read the paper because when she heard 'Bukowski' she hiked her skirt 4 inches, spread her legs and her pussy started to hiss Yankee Doodle Dandy thru her bargain basement panties. but maybe they won't get up too high down there, I hope not, anyhow, one column a week is almost too much for a dying man and maybe I am looking for an excuse to quit. quitter, quitter; dirty dying old man. all right, all right. [★ ★ ★]

sure, man, run some of my letters, would like to see, for whole thing becoming covered with a kind of moss and I feel dead already & would like to see that I did gabble about in my palmier days – when I jacked off with both hands, crosshand stroke, underhand and back up around the ass. would really like to see it; would revive some of my mimes. right now, as far as the writing goes it goes slowly. I wait on myself, feeling badly, feeling the Notre Dame worms crawling in my bellyhairs, I still wait, wait for the poem to come out – butter and tacks and a lady with a limp and beautiful knees going by my window. my window my window my window ah my window. [* * *]

[To Jon and Louise Webb]

[December 27, 1967]

want to thank you for the o.k. to PENGUIN on reprint of some of *It Catches* stuff for the *Penguin Poetry Series*. it won't be out until Xmas '68, and the royalties are not astounding but if I am around by then whatever bit it is might save me from the pit, the pit of madness, sickness, the row, whatever pit there is, each inch helps save what's left, so thanks, surely, the o.k., esp. since you are evidently down on me – a column, a Shermanism, whatever the hell, I don't know, but that's the way it works. I know that you were very unhappy and worried in Tucson and both not feeling well, and it was a bad time for me to be there. so it goes, but still you were good enough to give the PENGUIN O.k., so you do not play small and bitter games and crash a man down because of dislikes. that's good moxie, and all I can say is 'thanks,' which doesn't seem like very much.

I hope that wherever you are now that things are easier.

I didn't get the grant. just a form-letter. so it's try to hang onto the horror of the post office; if it weren't for Marina I think I'd just go out and lay down in the gutter. everybody I know has either gotten a grant or been offered one, so I guess Bukowski is just shit with the govt. agency, and so I sit and peck at the typer while my toenails bite at my feet. in same mail – a few weeks back – a letter from W. C[orrington] telling me, in essence, that I could dish it out but not take it.

the dog-pack is really after my aging ass.

did have some luck with *Evergreen*. poem in Dec. issue and they have accepted a rather long one on bullfighting for a future issue.

so the horses began again Tuesday and maybe a little action can help me forget the whole damn poetry scene. it's good to drink a hot coffee out there, the ice wind from those snow mountains north chilling your god damn shorts as you work out the winner of the first race. that's as good as anything. we don't ask much of the gods. just that they keep quiet for a while.

all right, then. punchy, I shape up to stick more letters. in my neat little shit-cage. and remember the good days past. there were some.

• 1968 •

[To John William Corrington]

January 3, 1968

ah, balls. listen, everybody writes me, 'why haven't you answered my letter?' [* * *] listen, I have this large blue coffee can on the shelf and it is full of unanswered letters. this neither means that I like or dislike the people who have written them; it means that I am drunk or playing horses or sick or non-electric, can't do, you know. no snob, just no time; I'd like to be a snob but I'd rather have the time. here, let me show you – I reach into this can and I pull out these and find that I OWE letters of response to: one: Jack Micheline (c/o Cohen); a Steven Osterlund – who wrote last August asking where he could get holden a some of my pukes; a Willie who calls himself the 'manic'; an x-horse magazine editor called Conte who is now in Augusta (postmark says Sept. 25); a Douglas Blazek; a William Stetson (his postmark, Aug. 22, unanswered); a Bassett at the William Morris Agency – 1350 Ave. of the Americas – postmark, June 12, '67; a Larouche of Albuquerque; a William Wantling; a Marcus Verily Grapes who writes very drippy letters; a Jim Roman (his dated 6–26–67); a Heinrich Fett of Andernach, Germany, 547 Andernach, Privat Str 1, my 79 year old uncle who says 'I don't understand why you haven't written. Are you well?'; an A. W. Purdy, 137 Waverley St., Apt. 3, Ottawa, Canada (his mark: Oct. 11); an Ann Menenbroker of Sacramento, who I ask to please RELENT but the letters arrive, one two three a week; my x-wife, one Barbara Hayakawa of Aniak, Alaska; one Scott Reed of Edwards, Mississippi; a Hale Chatfield of Hiram, Ohio; one Stuart McCarrell of Chi (his mark: March 19, 1967); one Dan Georgakas, a most interesting and violent anarchist; one H. Norse of 23 St. Marks Crescent, London; a Boatright; a DeLoach; a Charles Potts, Listade Ciereaex or something, L, no Jalisco, Mexico; a Richmond, Steve, of Santa Monica, Calif; a Bob Peters, dept. of English; a Fox, dept. of English; a Winski, writer of lurid sex tales; a Sherman, writer of lurid sex tales; a John and Susan Cornillion who promise to visit 'this summer, if we may'; a Ben Tibbs, who always sends me a dollar for Christmas; and more and more, Christ, there are others that I have simply thrown into a big closet box and have closed the door on forever, I simply throw my dirty sox on top of them. shit, meaning what?

I guess that each of these people does not realize that there are other people writing me, and sending their little signed books of poetry. all right, I'm not Henry Miller. I've not made it as one writing. I work the post office. my ass is bloody. I went to the track today and lost $100. what do I have to do with anything? I can't keep up, I can't keep up with all these people. me, I write Jon Webb but he doesn't answer. well, that's dirty laundry and a kind of joke but I guess you know I am hurting, drinking beer, and it's vaudeville, good show, not snot. I think you read. I really think that you do; otherwise I wouldn't fuck with you, or visa versa – as the Spaniards yoused to say. oh yes, I like your IBM. send me one in the mail, right away. I want my little girl to know what they look like because I will be punching one, I mean she will be punching one all day for some greasy pinching slob because I don't have money enough to send her to college let alone buy her pretty candies and ribbons, tho she is beautiful without, they will prb. kill that. like the sparrow is on the eye of god and he better start cleaning out HIS bunghole.

back to letter-writing. belles lettres. yah. and your, our same old argument about Faulkner and tons of falcon stream of conci. dirty-boy italics. ah, let's not get on THAT again. oh boy. only, I mean, I just CAN'T answer all these damn letters, and I'm not even famous or even decently bearable to the sky, I mean I can walk down any street and bow wow, nobody will even sperm-like separate me from the pebbles, which is good, I am lucky to live and flow into the tons of open areas waiting, see, you know; so, I mean, I still can't answer ALL THESE LETTERS BECAUSE IF I DID I WOULD DIE BECAUSE SO MUCH CLAIMS A MAN, FINALLY, IN ONE WAY OR ANOTHER THAT HE HAS TO MAKE CHOICES. if he makes the wrong choices he is dead before his time – war, women, horses, friends, literature, whiskey, the way he points his head when he sleeps . . .

(I owe a letter to Carl Weissner) (a good boy, a good German boy. a shepherd.)

so, with the letters, feel good. I eliminate or they eliminate me. I must answer: William Corrington, Douglas Blazek, Harold Norse, Carl W., Jack Micheline. the others may be good boys, and so was *Guys and Dolls* a good musical, so is *Marat/Sade* – the Nuts, also good.

but. of course, I am pissed. you inferred, as they say, in your last, that I could dish it out but could not take it. mother, I have been taking it for a long long time. in the factories. from the whores, from the goslin bosses. from goldy goldy lox. from Amos and Andy, the 3 Stooges, Bob Hope, Santa Claus. all the shits. I have for a long time held still for a literature and a culture that pretended to be life and talk about life but I will no longer do that. [★ ★ ★]

I mean, babe, I *have* been taking it. and so have you. and when these college profs rip my doorbell, I do not hate them. they bring me whiskey. they've heard some tale. and they have a class in the morning. so they sit and listen to me talk and wonder where it comes from, where the hell the wonderful SECRET IS IT MUST BE SOMEWHERE, EH? *they* look so much better, talk too much better, have more, feel fucking ass more, – how come their words don't come out . . . o.k.???? me, *I* can't tell them. only maybe they got too much butter in their ass, maybe they aren't old enough or burned enough or the ass comes too easy or looks too good and when the nails come up through the shoes you don't beat them down with a hammer, you buy 3 new pair.

looking down, if I may, it seems that hardness kills, the tough boys kill each other, I have seldom seen a living man in a factory, and looking up, it seems, if I may, that softness kills, I have seldom seen a living man teaching a class in English Lit. I. and so when they come around and bring me whisky and I get drunk and cuss them, there are later little letters in the mail that they still love me and understand me. this is their training and not their passion. in a sense, it *is* their passion, like ham and eggs for Sunday breakfast, but it is NOT their blood-passion, and the sooner they learn their blood-passion, the sooner they are going to have trouble where they work, and the less they will need me. who am an old man, drinking beer. [★ ★ ★]

books? *Terror Street* holding up because I've got to do this tape and 34 more drawings. could have done the whole bastard thing while I was losing $100 to the horses. but it's not always like that. sometimes I win. one meet I won $3,000 and took off 3 months and slept in different motels along the coast between L.A. and Mexico, while still keeping my apartment (with shack-job) and fucking every whore and some non-whores in between, feeling good, looking at the ocean while drunk in the moonlight, lifting the bastard coronet of that bottle, knowing that it would *never* be that good again, like that, I mean, now, maybe it's even better, there's the little girl, Marina, walking through it all, but I am sure she wouldn't have been a shit to either of us (me and her) if she hadn't appeared through the spectrum of the other. like that. – I mean, I have fairly-well worked-out a kind of battle palsma [?plan] to face, death, you know, take it good like that, easy, rather like I do now, only she, Marina, has brought me a kind of holiness, a kind of teaching and I do not laugh as much or hate as much, the other people, she tells me that they are something other than I think, and I accept *some* of this. we have long talks in the dark, before sleep, this 3 years old girl and I, and since her picture is clear, unlearned, unburned, but clear, still, I pick up, I back up, and I don't *use* her – she simply fills me. Or, so I think.

all I need now is 60 days in jail or 10 years, and my whole thought processes will be realigned. everything happens for the best and the worst. like when Marina was first born, the line popped into my head, 'she will probably be fucked by a sailor who never read Walter De La Mare.' that was then. now, I think, so what? what could be more beautiful? only that, if she wants a sexual fulfillment, let it be hers, and let it be as near the man she likes as is holy possible. the problem of the poor being that they just usually submit; the problem of the rich being that they never know what they are loved for. [★ ★ ★]

[To Douglas Blazek]

January 15, 1968

[★ ★ ★] Heard from Penguin & Webb relented, said o.k., so it'll be Norse, Bukowski, Lamantia, Dec. '68.

The problem with being a poet is that by the time you get well-known you can't write anymore. or, at least, not as well. but, still, being young & unknown isn't the answer either. a lot of them grin out machine-made shit that they think is very real only because *they* like it. then, they quit. to become a good writer takes time & luck & moxie & no special *desire* to *be* a good writer. [★ ★ ★]

[To Jon and Louise Webb]

February 25, 1968

[★ ★ ★] don't know if I told you but I have been twice interviewed by the big boys in the post office who don't quite like the idea of me writing this column 'Notes of a Dirty Old Man.' that column has cost me plenty of woe, as you might know. also somebody wrote in to them saying that I was not married to the mother of my child and that we lived separately. the same person also mailed them a batch of 'Notes' with certain passages outlined in ink. they didn't care too much for something I wrote about the post office, plus a thing on sodomy. I told them that I would have to continue writing 'Notes,' no matter the result. 'Are we to consider the postal officials as the new critics of literature?' I asked them. I also mentioned the ACLU. they said that they were not sure of what to do with me because they hadn't had 'a case like this in ten years.' ten years? I wonder who the other guy was? anyhow, I am told that the whole business must be taken up higher for review. I was sitting in a large dark room at the end of a long table with just this little lamp there and these 2 people looking at me. I'll probably be machine-gunned someday as I walk out this door. joke, of course. or, is it? they asked me if I were going to write anything more about the post office. I told them, probably not. so it might be a truce or they might be waiting for me to really expose myself where they could more easily strap me to the cross.

'have you ever had any books published?' they asked me.

'yes.'

'how many?'

'I don't know. 4, 5, 6, 7 . . . I don't know.'

'how much did you PAY these people to publish your work?' ummm, ummm, umm.

[* * *] have really been in very strange mind state lately. seem to be frozen. can't move or write. 25 or 30 unanswered letters in big coffee can on shelf. Harold Norse seems to be in this same deep freeze – the inability to do anything. shot to shit, sick, weak. it might only be a refueling period. or maybe we're both finished. difficult to tell. strange that we should both be in the fix at the same time. I consider Hal a much better writer and person than I am, more human, and getting a letter from him is always a big event to me. I hear Anais Nin is trying to get him a grant so he can come here to Capistrano Beach, where he thinks there is a doctor who can cure him. that's a place down about halfway to San Diego. it would be good to see him. no need to talk. we could just sit around the same room for a couple of days and look out the window, or walk along the beach, say about 6 p.m. among the insane and wild-eyed gulls, we walking along wondering wondering what went wrong with the machinery of everything. [* * *]

met Neal Cassady before he died, up at *Open City* one night. I had some beer with me. have one, I said. he drank the thing like water. 'have another,'

I said. he was crazier than I was. it was beginning to rain and we all got into the car, Bryan, myself and Cassady. we got one of the famous Cassady rides on the rain-slick streets. then we ate together at J.B.'s and had a few more drinks. Neal was the hero of Jack Kerouac's novel *On the Road*. about a week after I met Neal they found him dead along some railroad tracks in Mexico. he'd mixed too much booze with nembutal. deliberately, perhaps. [★ ★ ★]

[To Thomas Livingstone]

February 26, 1968

well, Mahler's 10th on and I'm hungover and climbing out, climbing back in again. I read your fuck-piece and that boy is a master-fucker, man; I guess every man wants to be a master-fucker and that every woman wants to be fucked by one, and maybe a few men too. well, I have never been a master-fucker; I am usually too drunk or disinterested or cold-hot; a task, you know. and fucking often turns out to be a dirty task, a trick to do. and, in a sense, I think any man's crazy who does it with real Art. 2 dogs fucking outdo anybody. so, still, yes, enjoyed your piece.

uh, Stuart still has *Crucifix*. he doesn't know how to move them, nobody knows he *has* them. [★ ★ ★] *Terror Street* out soon. also a tape to be issued of Bukowski reading from some of the poems in book. $10. too high, of course. but John Martin (Black Sparrow) knows his collectors. so he's only issuing 50 tapes. he knows how to make money printing the poets. his royalties, per issue printed, I think he is the highest in the business. he's printing everybody now – Creeley, Olson, dozens of names like that, pays them in front upon publication and still makes good $$$$. but he realizes the market is limited – really, you know – so he runs only issues of 150 to 250 books, but he gets rid of them. me, he's going to do first, he said, 500 then 750 because so many whores taxi drivers sex freaks circus brakers and Fuller Brush salesmen read me. I am easy to understand even when I don't understand myself.

also have had an old book picked up that has gone from hand to hand, not bad poems really but each person who has touched them has been kissed-off by bad luck, so now I hope Potts don't eat poison or something. but he's gone to work on getting Darrell of Glendale to work up the book with his new press, and Charlie completely off screw, he intends to publish, what was it 1,000 copies or 2,000? but sensible enough to charge only one dollar. he also wants to lay money and 150 copies on me, but I tell him, take it easy, kid. he writes poetry, and I met him down here once, we got a little high here at my place. real quiet guy. not much talk. I liked him. I am not much talk either. so we just sat around without strain. anyhow, book called *Poems Written Before Leaping from an 8 Story Window*. c/o Charles Potts, 6433 Telegraph Ave., Oakland, Calif. 94609. Apt. #J. one dollah. I intend to agree with him. I think the fucking thing will sell out. it's the next poem that counts, we know. it's the way we walk across the floor. but it would still be well to see things working good all around. we've had some coming – good pussy and good luck. I'll take the latter.

listen, Tommy, the next time an old lady very active in church work leaves fleas and lice behind, you tell the man. you missed a perfect shot. I been kicked out of too many rooms for being a drunk and a madman, a bringer-in of ladies of the street. kafka would have spilled the beans on her; me too. if a church lady has fleas and lice the church is fucking her up. sometimes I think twice before killing a fly, but I always end up killing it if I can. all that stupid flesh recognizes is shit. in a pigpen you wouldn't stand a chance of getting a piece of ass. let us know where we are, then we can be kind when kind is sensible. when kind is insensible we are only adding to error. we've got enough help with that. end of lecture.

I have written 40 or 45 weekly columns for the local underground newspaper *Open City*. column called 'Notes of a Dirty Old Man.' some smut-peddler in North Hollywood who thinks that I am dirty instead of literary wants to run columns in book-form. hinted $500 to $1000 advance. but I am so fucked-up, job killing me, health bad, sucking on beer bottle, smoking smoking, I get on phone now and then and talk to the guy, hard to reach, must get past his fucking switchboard, 'this is Charles Bukowski,' I say, 'I'd like to speak to Mr. X.'

'Charles Bukowski? are you one of our distributors? your name sounds familiar.'

'no, baby, the only thing I distribute is the end of my cock into wet and throbbing pussies.'

she gasps and connects me with Mr. Big.

'ah, Bukowski!' he says. 'what is it?'

'ummm, ummm,' I say.

'what is it?'

'I'm tied up. can't get out to see you. must get things in order. tremendous fucking job.'

'I know. yes. well, Charles, line it up. can you call me Tuesday?'

'I think so.'

'o.k., you call me Tuesday.'

Tuesday comes. she gasps and connects me.

'listen, Mr. X, I got fucked-up. I don't know, you know.'

'I don't understand.'

'ummm, ummm.'

'what?'

'how about next week? I should have all the stuff lined-up by then. hell, I gotta buy some kind of artist's portfolio to haul the crap down in and I hate to go into Art stores, everybody is fake as hell and it takes ten years off my psyche.'

'o.k., call me Wednesday next week, line it up, and then phone me.'

'o.k.'

I think I've had 5 or 6 conversations with this guy but I haven't moved an inch. I kind of know what Harold is bothered with over in England: THE FROZEN MAN IN THE BARGAIN BASEMENT OF HELL. I can't *move*. it doesn't matter. after all, who really wants fame or money or pussy or anything you have to STRAIN at or WORK for?

lay back, wait for the Junkman to come get you. it seems the only sensible thing. world-renown means world-error. there's never a way out. sit and wait for the ax to fall. just try not to be shocked by its fall. your head, my head. balls.

all right, man, they are beating on the walls.

I am not much good at constant correspondence. just felt like writing tonight. and your letter was down there on the floor. you were the target.

all right, another beer, another smoke, then to bed, waiting for ye Ax, ah.

[To Carl Weissner]

February 27, 1968

yes, I too have 35 or 40 unanswered letters, but now entirely beyond me to answer them; I can't keep up; for each answer to a letter, 3 more come in. I am not in the letter-writing business. I am in a stricken-down stage now, anyhow, bad health, can barely make it about, hand on. I've just decided to let people think I'm a shit; it's easier than answering all those letters. [★ ★ ★]

rumors on town hall reading of Bukowski, Corso, Micheline . . . impossible. didn't you know I have made it known for years that I don't read publicly? I am a shit, Carl. just turned down a reading, with fee, at Univ. of Southern Calif. Festival of the Arts. I've never read in public, don't intend to unless it means the difference between starving in the gutter and starving in a closet. I prefer to starve in a closet. have turned down fees of from $200 and $700 and told them to go screw. I believe that if the pricks get a man on stage they get a man jumping through *their* hoop, they make a jerk out of him. I am not an actor, I am a creator, I hope. I do read on tape because this still leaves an area of solitude and peace, but actually I've done very little reading on tape and any professional actor could read my stuff better. for a general audience, that is.[★ ★ ★]

meanwhile Postoffice has found out I do this weekly column 'Notes of a Dirty Old Man' for the local underground paper *Open City* and they look upon it most darkly, they seem to think that some of the work is *dirty* and really not up to what a postal clerk should be doing in his spare time. I have had 2 long interviews with the big boys in long dark rooms and we have sparred back and forth, quietly, neither side giving ground. but, meanwhile, I am still employed and I still continue to write the column. which some smut peddler in North Hollywood wants to put out in book form but I just can't seem to get out to see him – although Bryan says he is good for $1,000 advance, I am still FROZEN. I get smut-peddlar on phone, we talk, I say, 'soon soon,' and he says, 'fine, fine,' but I just can't seem to get out there. really FROZEN, Carl. can you understand? it's crazy. people want to do good by me and I won't let them. I guess I'm just tired. too much going on. and I look down at floor as I type this to you and here is this package, *still there*, looking up at me with its eyeless face, waiting to be mailed to England. ah, England, my England! oh yes, and PENGUIN wants to send me advance royalty check on the Lamantia-Norse-Bukowski thing but they also send these *papers* that must be filled out FIRST, something about the United Kingdom, I must declare that I am not a member of the United Kingdom or something, 2 or 3 pages, horrible, I can't get a pen to damned page, and when I do I have to find a Notary Public, some dame will hike her skirt and I will get a hard-on and she will charge me $5 and place a red seal upon the last page of the blue paper if I EVER FILL IT OUT! paper, papers, I've lost my social security card, can't get my new registration card into folder on steering wheel of my 57 Plymouth, have lost my state income tax card, new papers to be filled out for govt. partly-sponsored life insurance on job they are trying to kick me out of, 8 or 10 pages, the landlady wants to come in here and put up new curtains, I say, 'wait, wait, there are dead bodies in there, I don't want you to see all the dead bodies.' she laughs, but even she and her husband fuck me up; I just about get straight and she comes on down here and knocks on the door and gets me to come down and they both get me drunk, we sit up all nights singing very silly songs, and I can't get anywhere. [* * *]

[To Jon and Louise Webb]

March 18, 1968

[* * *] and, I'm having problems with the Penguin royalty dept. god damn. first the guy writes and says you must fill out enclosed forms before we can begin to process your check. he doesn't *enclose* the forms. a few weeks go by and I write him, 'you didn't enclose the forms.' he sends the forms. 2 months go by. I finally get myself to fill the god damned things out. go to a notary public. all that shit. drop letter with forms into mail. the other day I got another letter from royalty dept. 'sorry, but we sent improper forms. would you mind filling out the enclosed forms?' now I sit around and look at them. if I fill *them* out, it works like this: I mail them to the Dept. of Internal Revenue U.S.A. there are 2 copies. then the Dept. of Internal Revenue is supposed to mail one of the copies to the United Kingdom Income Tax dept. and then I don't know *what* they do. inform Penguin that I am in the clear or something? it looks like a process that will take months or a year. I don't suppose this would bother anybody but me. I can imagine a guy like Corrington blithely filling out the forms with hardly a thought, and even feeling good about it. [* * *]

Statement *was a pamphlet/manifesto by Robert Kelly, published by Black Sparrow Press in April, 1968.*

[To John Martin]

Monday in [April?] 1968

thanks for mailing *Statement* but I can't understand this kind of writing, but granted, it *does* take talent to write 8 or 10 pages and say absolutely nothing, and it's safe too. At first I thought it was Robert Creeley but, no, I see Robert Kelly. I'm afraid you've been sucked in by the poetry nestlings who pluck each other's feathers. but if you can make money off them, fine.[* * *]

[To Carl Weissner]

Early May 1968

[* * *] god yes! would you do the selections and (I hope) translations on my poems for Verlag kiepenheuer & witsch? got a good letter from R. R. Rygulla. if you could do the dirty work for me, it would help. I am up to my ass. take any poems you wish. I needn't even know. tell Rygulla I said o.k. you don't know how much I appreciate. like I say, up to my ass. just now, I have been doing paintings in the kitchen. this bird, Martin, wants 75 small paintings which will be mounted in the backs of special hardbound copies of *Terror Street.* I've made around 60 paintings up to now he wants 20 more. give me 20 more, he says, and I'll pick them up Monday. I've done 6. these editors just don't realize that paintings just can't be made up, oh splash splash the merry brush – each painting must come from the balls like a fuck. few men can fuck 6 times a night. 20 is just impossible. [* * *]

[To Jon and Louise Webb]

May 16, 1968

[* * *] I have been writing 6 columns a month, 4 for Bryan and 2 for The Underground Review (New York). I am going to tell each of these guy 'one a month' and if they don't want that, let them shove it. mostly I am disgusted with the contents of their papers. very high school stuff. plus 6 columns a month gives me no time to fiddle with my precious poems, esp. feeling as weak and down as I do now. [* * *]

[To John Martin]

May 29, 1968

rec. your beautiful check and the 20 copies *Terror Street.* hey, boss, no royalties on the tape? but we workers always complaining! check much more than I expected, and I hope you don't get stuck with a closetful of *Terror Streets*.

yes, would like to do another book with you – the new poems – will keep carbons of all the shit I write from now on. plus, there is *plenty* of back work. I must somehow shake Webb, who's a good man and has done well by my work, but the no royalties thing is the setback – I'm only human, after all, my friend. but let's let him bring out the poems he has in the present Patchen *Outsider* before I tell him. I don't have copies of the poems but believe they are rather good ones, so best to let the *Outsider* run them so we can get our hands on them. I don't want Webb to have an emotional disturbance.

drop me a note now and then telling me how things are going. I believe that you have published more poets in a shorter time than anybody in history – and have done it neatly. most of us now running around with our little Black Sparrow tatoos. the action is good and the money ain't bad. tanks, kid. [* * *]

[To Carl Weissner]

sometime May 1968

[* * *] the Bukowski/Richmond LP not so hot, except I think I managed to get off the poem 'Experience' o.k. the Martin tape is the *one* – all else compared to it is nothing. you will SEE, hear, if you EVER get it out of Martin. I even like it myself, brother, caught myself on a good night, no poetic bullshit, just a natural speak-piece. try to get his tape; you will punch your balls out against some side cupboards. I promise. but try to get the full tape, instead of the selected retail tape. the full one is a 7 inch spool both sides, 3 and 3/4s I think. Martin left out some good ones, 'The Body' being the main omission and the best reading on tape. beast reading, rather. [* * *]

[To Jon and Louise Webb]

June 4, 1968

[* * *] got $460 royalties from John Martin for *Terror Street* and it just about saved me from going under. my checks from god damn p.o.

have been very small due to sickness – I owed *them* 192 hours sick leave. now Martin wants to do my next book of new poetry and I think I'll have to let him. the money may damn well keep me off the row or out of the cemetery. I hope you understand. I know that your plans for another book were rather indefinite. you've done more to promote my work than anybody, of course, now I hope you'll be kind enough to understand that the body needs help too. I mean this sickness thing. so let's let Martin do my next book, o.k.? and I hope that you don't get pissed and we have to go into one of our long dark silences. as crappy as I feel that wouldn't help much. [⋆ ⋆ ⋆]

[To Jon and Louise Webb]

June 15, 1968

[⋆ ⋆ ⋆] guy wrote me the other day about an old review Rexroth did of me. I never saw it. something like, 'Bukowski a great writer? nope. a pretty book . . .' he drags in Hemingway on me and then says that as a bum I know my business but that Ernie mingled with Artists and writers of his time, kicked around the continents . . . maybe you saw it and never showed it to me. a pretty book? why, that sunken-jawed subnormal! it would have been a GREAT book with Rexy in it, what? these boys can really get catty and jealous as old maids. as for being a Hemingway, I don't want to be a Hemingway. and to mix with the writers and artists of my Time, uhhh uh. leave me alone. I'm crazy enough already. and if I am a bum and not literary then thank all the purple and green and golden Christs of my
Valhalla. [⋆ ⋆ ⋆]

I am at work the other day, hungover, beat, tired, sick, numb, dirty, done. this kid walks up to me. 'Pardon me, sir.'

'yeah?'

'are you Charles Bukowski?'

'yeah.'

'we're studying you in American Literature at college.'

'umm.'

'I recognized you from your photo. it was in our school paper.'

'oh yeah?'

'I've tried to get some of your books at the library but you're rather . . . restricted.'

I laughed. '"restricted." that's a nice word.'

I got rid of him. ridiculous. everything is ridiculous. I am dying. he came back a week later. 'hello, Charles.'

'hello, kid.'

'what do you think of the Kennedy assassination?'

'I wrote something for this week's *Open City*. fifteen cents will get you the lowdown.'

'all right.'

. . . I am drinking a coffee. as I get up to walk away I hear him tell his young buddies – 'see that guy? he's a great writer . . .'

'aw, come *on*, Bob!'

'yes, yes, it's TRUE!' . . .

well, you see now, all I have to do is lean back and take the applause. life is getting easier all the time. [★ ★ ★]

I've got a whole potful of poems to send out but can't get to them. I mean, those you've returned. in my old age, I do re-work. I mean, I knock out bad lines, throw in one or 2 new ones and sometimes I've got a poem. I don't think it's cheating. it's more an instinctive thing. I just can't bear some of those lines anymore. [★ ★ ★]

[To Jim Roman]

June 20, 1968

long time & sorry, but been going through same type fire & death all men go thru & it has sawed me off a bit.

I see same results with fellow-poets who have not made it $$-wise or fame-wise

& results are terrible:

crack-brain

bitter men

raving –

me, I have rested quietly (if you can call 8 or 10 hours a day sticking their fucking letters, as such . . .) and simply waiting on the word –

of course, all the time, wonder if death should come at my call or its call. umm.

Our Corrington now teaching at Berk., U.C., and don't give up on him. His warmth is 2-bit whore but his style is classic & history bugs his brain. still I like him. [★ ★ ★]

[To William Hageman]

June 21, 1968

[★ ★ ★] write-up on Ginsberg meeting Pound in current *Evergreen*. Ginsberg comes on poetic and phoney. Pound talks straight English without the lacy bullshit. Pound I think has found out he had *style* but the content was educational, a kind of structural flow that took care of itself, sounding well but not ever really ever *saying*. too much of anything. that's what always pleased the college boys – the whole thing was a very stylish yawn – which takes some *doing*, don't get me wrong. Pound was worthy. but I think he knows now that he was just making a good pudding instead of hellfire. esp. now that everybody is bullshitting him on how great he is; a kind of ass-kissing before a death that must be very near. for us, too, maybe. but he's older, surely. [★ ★ ★]

by the way, certain things I don't like – that is, the new boys coming up and thinking that they are changing the language. I've been watching this since 1932: '&' instead of 'and.' 'laffing' instead of 'laughing.' I don't even want to go into it. it becomes boring. not that it might be wrong, only that the boys hu r duing it thinks its sompin gnew . . . not their fault that they are not as old as me and the woodwork. (by the way, when you see an '&' in one of my poems it is put there by some damned editor.) [★ ★ ★]

[To Frances Smith]

July 1968

I know you worked hard with these god damned things, maybe too hard, and a lot of aces seem to go down each time we fail, or fail for somebody, but since I am playing God-editor and have been rejected more than accepted –

> 'a little rejection is good for the soul;
> total rejections can kill a man . . .'
>
> bukowski over a beer at the midnight
> sun, Albuquerque, 1945 . . .

I think I had better tell you
since nobody at the Bridge is really going to tell you
the Truth is only my Truth
and I know you are touchy, very . . .
but I think you would have been more hurt if I had handed these back with some cliché and a wave of paper –
well, shit, nothing's easy and poems are the hardest
but poems can be easiest too if we start conning ourselves, and
there is little doubt that most people
probably including myself
would have made better Presbyterian preachers,
so that's a lock and rock
so now listen
since the Bridge ain't gona tell you
maybe I got to save your buttersoft ass, ha,
stop twitching, bitch,
I've seen that hair and tooth too much too long over
too many breakfast tables
through my hangover skull, and believe me,
I'd rather see you write an immortal poem than strike out;
I am not your enemy but neither can I feed you bullshit . . .
[★ ★ ★]

[To Steven Richmond]

July 23, 1968

[★ ★ ★] by the way, Bryan wants me to edit the next literary insert (Renaissance) of *Open City* and I said, 'all right.' I can see why he didn't want the job. he had a bucketful of half-ass submissions. so now I am in the process of writing various people in order to get good stuff. because if I am going to edit a section it is going to be stone-pure hard, but I've found out the difference between wanting to print good stuff and printing it. [★ ★ ★] I'd much rather *accept* than reject, but once you accept one bad piece because you drank a beer with a guy or you liked his stuff in the old *Ole*, what the hell, you are going to accept more and more bad stuff until it's all bad, what I mean by bad stuff is, bad *for* me. that's all I judge by. [★ ★ ★]

[To Steven Richmond]

July 25, 1968

hookay, kid, you made it with three [* * *] which is more poems than I have accepted from anybody yet. [* * *]

got a couple of bitchy little notes in mail today. the boys don't like to be rejected, especially after I ask to see their work. I find, tho, that this is the danger of these guys printing each other in their little mimeos and reading to each other before the lesbians and homos: they get deluded into thinking that they are *doing* something. are something. it's only a sucking-out of each other's assholes. guys like D. R. Wagner, Ritch Kretch, Charles Potts, so forth, can't write but they go on and on writing so long as the mimeo machines can get ink and paper. I pick up the average little and just yawn myself into hopelessness – there are exceptions like *Wormwood, Klacto, Outsider*, but for each of these there are a dozen others, half-heartedly done, self-important and about as real and interesting as Brenda Starr in the *L. A. Times*.

I don't write too much anymore but when I do I get rejected enough and when I get rejected I *usually* find, after reading the poem, that the editor in one way or another was right. and instead of writing a solemn and bitchy note I sit down and carve me out another poem. [* * *]

[To Douglas Blazek]

July 1968

[* * *] your stuff is still warm toast with butter and the children sitting quietly by the window and the first HOT coffee against the hangover; you've got this spilled-over and unpretentious earnestness in a way that none of the other poets have . . . a Blazek is a Blazek. but after saying all that, I am only taking 2 poems because I look forward to a definite space limitation with this damned thing, and so even with the stuff I like I have to keep it down to the bone; which, in a sense is good because it forces me to choose the finest from among the fine. so, therefore, the other poems back . . . no 2 and 1/2 year hold. [* * *]

but I still like poetry, any gathering of poetry, hung in between a bit of prose and prose shouting – the prose like kind of lumps of crazy mountain and the poems like m.g. shots vip vip vip vip!!! and I'm going to have more of a problem getting the prose I want. why don't you write me a kind of essay on poetics, what's wrong with poetics, generally, and what a man really NEEDS . . . you know, when he comes home after they've clubbed him to death, after he comes home with his 3 or 4 greasy pennies of pay and there is the old lady with hair uncombed, yellow teeth, on the phone, running up the phone bill with insane and unreal woman talk; the kids glad to see you – but just for a moment – like a new toy – and you know you ain't you, you're just a dirty dishrag or gum under the seat, you're just stale piss clubbed with a flyswatter. then *tell* what KIND of poetry is needed and why Creeley, so forth, are the palest and most tortuous of atrocities. something like that. would be good. [★ ★ ★]

[To Steven Richmond]

[Fall, 1968]

the 100 pager isn't doing. I'm frozen at 28 poems. can't find another in the universe [★ ★ ★]

poems printed in Ren. all selected by me, except the DiPrima's, which are bad writing. D.P. can't write. maybe that's why she gets a yearly grant from the HUMANITIES (govt. sponsored). Bryan slipped the DiPrims in on me. and didn't run all the poems I had accepted. [★ ★ ★]

[To Douglas Blazek]

September 23, 1968

some university is offering me $$$$$ for a collection of my materials, and the more I can give them, natch, the more I will be able to make.

my thought was that collection of letters you (and Veryl) had gathered. I wonder if there is any chance of getting hold of these, preferably in the original but also photoed if not in the original? the better I offer these boys the more they are going to give me and it might help me get out of the bloody post office at last, what with the PENGUIN book coming up and a few other things. [★ ★ ★]

[To Carl Weissner]

[October 14, 1968]

well, I have some dribbling shit for you, it may make you unhappy, it has made me unhappy the way it has worked – let me get this untwisted here. some univ. library, with the stuff I have on hand – notebooks, typescripts, extra books of my poetry, my paintings, all that gobble, well, I am getting a nice offer from them – enough money to set me free for one or two years, just to write and lay in the sun – and I get an idea if I get this shot my luck will continue – just got the first advance on a book of prose *Notes of a Dirty Old Man* – but the univ. library thing also hinges on my getting quite a few letters, plenty of them BACK from people I have written to.

it looks the way I expected Carl. the literary are a cold and inhuman bunch. I have been writing to the wrong people. they may talk life and humanity in their *work* but when it comes time to *doing* it, you might as well ask a goldfish to change a tire because you've got a broken arm.

most of them simply don't *answer.* others answer but just give me literary jive, kind of essay junk, not even really speaking to me, and not mentioning a damn thing about the letters. one sent a letter of reason explaining why he *couldn't* return the letters and his letter was the saddest of them all; I mean the reasoning of it – I've been talking to an imbecile, a high school boy, a little jealousy tink.

I will say this – if *anybody* asked me for their letters back under the same conditions, my only thought would be, what size envelope should I use? or how many.

now it's your turn at bat. I want to ask Norse when he gets here. and there are 2 others. I hope you can help me, Carl. that post office is tearing me to pieces like a tiger in a cage and the people stand outside watching taking notes or looking the other way. well, let me know.

[* * *] jesus jesus Carl PLEASE SEND LETTERS! I have a chance to breathe, to see LIGHT, god oh mighty! don't put the lid on my grave. someday it may be my chance to help you. now must eat and go to POST OFFICE. eleven years. eleven years down there. going babe. let me hear.

The third correspondent mentioned below was Douglas Blazek, who later did in fact return Bukowski's many letters to him. Corrington apparently never did so.

[To John William Corrington]

October 15, 1968

Well, how to begin? I wrote you a lot of letters one time and NOW I want them back. now, wait wait. a certain Univ. is offering me quite a bit for my little mags, notebooks, paintings, books and *letters* that I have written to others. a lot hinges on the latter. the letters. there would be enough money for me to take a year or two off and simply write instead of dying on that post office stool where I have been for ELEVEN YEARS. often nights down there I've felt like I'm actually going CRAZY. or I get these dizzy spells where I hold to the case as everything spins. the old soul is simply saying, no, no, no, no more please! I do need more time to write [* * *] I need the letters to get free, break into the open and get some downfield blocking. I'm 48; I've played the tough drunk who spits blood out of the side of his mouth long enough. I need a little breather. o.k.

yeah, o.k. so I have written these various poets, 2 or 3, so far that I have written letters to. one, no answer. the second just sent me back a kind of literary essay, badly written, with no mention of my request for letters. the 3rd just sent me a kind of juvenile bit about how he rather kept those letters under his soul's pillow and how they saved his life when he had to put in those 6 tough years at the foundry. he just *can't* part with them now! oh, no no no, ask me ANYTHING but that! his wife now works while he pounds out reams of poetry that is getting duller and duller.

so, it all works out. I've said for 3 decades that the poets were shits and they keep proving me right. and if I *ever* write any fucking memoirs I'm going to name names and shits. it's about time we bombed the stinkers out of their closets. anyhow, there are 3 or 4 more to write to, one or two women, say 6 more all told. if I get completely shut out I don't ever want to hear the word POET in the same room I am sitting in. I have explained to all these people, will explain, have written a couple again who didn't seem to hear well the first time – I've explained exactly what this will *mean* to me. these fuckers write about LIFE but it's all shuck. that's why some of them write so badly. they'd rather kill life than live it – mine or theirs.

so, Willie, for Christ's sake mail me the letters, set me free. I remember returning all yours upon request one time when I lived at 1623 N. Mariposa. lining the things up on the rug and trying to get them in order of date before sticking them in the envelope. I'm not playing angel, Willie, but when you asked for your letters back it never *occurred* to me to say 'no.' it wouldn't make sense. that's just the way my head works. I hope yours works the same way. [* * *]

well, man, curve ball or straight?

[To Frances Smith and Marina Bukowski]

October 16, 1968

I haven't heard from you and hope all is all right. I mailed a $5 some time back. it wasn't much but hope you got it. with all the thievery going on, no telling what might happen to your mail.

so far I have tried two poets who have my letters, letters that I have written to them, explaining that some univ. will pay me enough for a year or two of freedom if I can give them my letters plus the other stuff I have on hand here – paintings, mags, books, notebooks, so forth. so far one poet has said 'no.' the other sent me back a kind of literary essay letter, not mentioning anything about the letters.

the poets are shits. I have always said so.

so I am writing 4 or 5 more and keeping a scorecard. it wouldn't surprise me if I came up with a blank.

throat still a little sore but improving. missed 4 days work. they still won't fire me. it's the busy season now.

pleas let me know if Marina is all right.

and take care of yourself.

Hank

[*enclosed with preceding*]

hello Marina:

I went to the store today and I was thinking of you and I bought a red light, a blue light and a yellow light. these fit into the lamps. someday when you get here again we will put them into the lamps and see how they look

I had a very sore throat and had to see Dr. Voegel. I am somewhat better now and I am not drinking any beer at all right now because I think that is what is making my throat sore. so now the police can't get me and throat will get better, so don't you worry about me, I will be all right. and I hope you are all right too. your paintings are still on the wall and they make me feel good when I look at them.

I have to go to work now. please try to be happy. I am sorry your last visit was so short; it seemed you'd hardly gotten here and then you were gone. and I was sleepy all the time. but I love you very much. stay healthy and happy and have a good time.

[To Carl Weissner]

[October 23, 1968]

yes, the New York letters. . . . yes, the Heidelberg letters, January, when you get there. very important. my thanks, sure, straight off the cuff, not many coming through – Wm Wantling is one who *is* – but certain others offer silence or send literary essays; one just sends me a lot of verbal shit about his tough life – his wife works to support him while he writes and *she* doesn't earn very much. anyhow, there are a few others who I must write; the ones who said NO are the ones I expected to say NO; those who have said YES, likewise. I know that these fuckers can prob. sell these letters after I die and make a few bucks, but I've tried to tell them it is more important that I live NOW, that I get out of the post office for a year, out of everything just sit and hit the typer and stare at the walls; after that, I don't care what happens. one year of FREEDOM, babe. the letters *are* their PROPERTY as they so sternly state. all I'm asking for IS THEIR property so I will not go nuts. ah ha. you are a good one you understand this thing. I have personally prepared a SHIT LIST OF THE SHITS which I will publish in my deathbed memoirs. the chicken shits will not get away with anything. they will be exposed and burned and wiped and whipped and tarred and feathered before the city gates under a full moon. and the good guys will be listed, although the list will not be very long, that's the way it goes.

most of the poets are shits. they only WRITE about LIFE. and then not very well. and those who howl the loudest about injustice and pain, lo, all that, those are the ones who dish it out to others. terrible terrible little shits, the bunch of them.

Karl, I gotta thank you plenty for coming through [* * *] all I can offer the good guys is further lifetime communication, and I will not *always* be bothering them for letters back. the shits, (editors and poets) no more communion, poem or letter or word or beer or sound. and although this may not sound like a very big threat, it is sure a fine thing to get those pains in the ass out of my soul, and that in this way, I have been warned against them. I'm not playing saint, Carl, just cleaning out the dirty dresser drawers. so? [★ ★ ★]

Notes of a Dirty Old Man to be issued in book form by porny publisher. they think I am dirty. but they publish good stuff too. *Happiness Bastard*, Kirby Doyle. Essex House. good advance. I have written about 70 columns in 70 weeks so they have a lot to pick from. not too much, either. I threw out a hell of a lot of it. luckily, most of remainder is in typescript. I gave Bryan 20 bucks to have some Negro he knows type up the rest. Bryan paid the BLACK IN FRONT. Negro did a few, faded. Bryan says he will find him, get him going on the rest. gave Bryan 10 percent for setting up deal with Essex house, and he deserves it, I never woulda thought of it. but if we don't get the typescripts in by Dec. 14 we gotta give the money back. a cool grand. fuck. get 4 percent retail sales up to 150,000, 6 percent after . . .

[To John William Corrington]

November 2, 1968

Dear Mr. Corrington:

I see you did not answer my request to return my letters. Silence is the tool used by superiors to their inferiors. It is possible that you *are* my superior. I have noticed a marked divergence between us since you made your trip to England and poked at the corpse of J.J. for that extra dangler they give you in college. I have nothing against explorations and education except that I have very little of it and so must work from instinct like any slaughterhouse, workhouse, street animal. I recall meeting you in New Orleans. I recall that you didn't bring your wife. I recall other things. This is not a crank letter, this is a letter to explain you to me and the only way I have to do this is to write it down.

It was poking at J.J. in England that first dehumanized you, then it was getting paid good money for a bad novel, no, not a bad novel at all, a medium novel, a wooly jockstrap of fatal reference and day-dreaming, plus a few fine passages. But like money turns a whore's head, money turns a man's head also. After all, there is a hell of a lot of difference between being printed in *Epos* by a Commie who lives with a mulatto (mulatto? u, should know), then getting a bit on fine stationary from an editor in N.Y. with circulation push and that thin but fat check placed within. This makes you a pro. Although some thinks this makes you a prick. Some think Mailer is a prick. But he is mostly a pro. But pros seem to turn to pricks, finally. See Mailer, Genet, Burroughs, Ginsberg, who the hell else? showing at the Chicago Yippie thing. As giants of Humanity? Bullshit. As Giants of Publicity. Still, all these were at one time pros. and some pro remains within them. It is difficult to destroy a truly good man even tho he makes many foolish mistakes against his soul. I ain't no Saint. I drink myself sick and play horses and love my child only and work like a coward on a job that has destroyed me for eleven years.

But I want you to know that I still do not consider you my superior, even tho I am a postal clerk and you are a Dr. of Literature. To put it bluntly, I think that I am the better writer and the better man and that your refusal to answer my letter was chickenshit and chickenfeathers and chickenfat. My dear Southern Gentleman. of course, I am drunk, what other way is there to be? And I'm even fond of you for Christ's sake, no *form* what? Anyway, I am sorry that home in New Orleans is swallowing all your money like a slot machine. ah, life can get HARD, can't it? especially in Berkeley. – DON'T TELL ME THOSE ACID-CATS CAN'T UNDERSTAND FINNEGANS WAKE? tell them that's it's just like music or singing or talking, you say and feel what you want, but don't INVENT majestics that are not THERE like you people do, also with POUND's Cantos which are nothing but dry and hard work with little joy, and Art is the Joy of Telling the Truth, bastard, just like I am telling you the truth now.

Since I last met you (New Orleans) the gods have for some reason put upon me to meet many college profs and some few men of fame. they all fell short in naturalness – they are shits and goofs. and so, at last, I see the game. the pretty facade. everybody hiding. what TERRIBLE WORD-SLINGERS they ALL are! what little inventiveness or easiness they have! shits, a worldful of shits in some disguise or other.

You said you would send me your last novel. You never did. Did you steal it from my letters? You have failed to answer a request upon last letter mailed to you. Southern Gentleman. My dear Southern Gentleman,

I'd sure as hell *hate* to meet a Southern boor. I won't bother you any more, professor, you are the pro.

[To John William Corrington]

November [?28], 1968

all right, I am a shit and of the breed, but at least you had class enough to say you'd send the letters, so fine, it means a lot, a break, I've got this collector-editor working with the univ. library, and he's a good boy, I mean he knows how to *talk* to these librarians, I *don't*, so I leave it in his hands, and he's doing the whole thing without fee, the guy simply likes me, but of course it means giving up many things I have: tapes, paintings, notebooks, magazines, books, typescripts – really cleaning out the closet, and I'll prob. feel better after everything's gone – like a bad woman you think you needed, ya know. so, *do* send the letters. it's fine of you, and will prob. help me get a year or so off from the grind, and much going on now, I need the TIME – [★ ★ ★]

p.s. – oh yes, also, if you could send your own letters back, the ones you wrote to me, *that* would help too. think of it, man, it's almost like being dead – the scholars pawing over us, and it wasn't so long ago that I was running errands from the corner bar stool for sandwiches and newspapers. don't return this letter. it's for the bathroom wall. yours. and listen, thanks again for all.

• 1969 •

Hugh Fox, then teaching at Loyola University, Los Angeles, wrote Charles Bukowski: A Critical and Bibliographical Study *(Los Angeles: Abyss Publications, 1969), a mimeographed book on his work. Gerard Dombrowski was editor of* Abyss.

[To Gerard Dombrowski]

January 3, 1969

[★ ★ ★] Well, you asked me about the Fox book on me. You want it straight? It was dull, straight, academic and uncourageous. It was textbook frogs hopping their dull lilypad hops. Dull; I said it twice; I'll say it thrice: dull, dull, dull. THE POEM-MESSAGE or FORCE was completely overlooked in the mamataught thing of this belongs here and that belongs there – : this is this school, and that is that school. Fuck that. I used to g.d. have to fight the bullies all the way home from grammar school to college, and they used to follow me, mocking me, daring me, but there was always more than one, and I was one, and they knew I had something packed in me somewhere. They hated it; still do.

Very well mum, you printed the Fox book on me. In a sense, it was congratulatory, but as a man who has lived in the worst circumstances of life, often not eating and not caring to; often wanting to eat and not being able to; often living for a month behind pulled shades and eating green potatoes and listening to the works of Bach and the footsteps of my landlady – knowing that almost everything was impossible and sickening – getting drunk on rotgut wine; being drunk at 12 noon and laying in alleys behind bars hoping trucks would run the life out of my body; being poked in the back with sticks by small black children as I lay senseless like some dying piece of meat; while working the factories, the slaughterhouses of the world, while being kicked off the back-end of tomato-picking trucks by those who sensed that I did not belong there; while traveling with the railroad track gangs from New Orleans to Sacramento and having to fight them one-on-fifty; while living in a scorpion-filled paper shack in Atlanta, while all the things I could go on and on with – do you REALLY THINK that I could accept the soft-Fox fucking dissertation on when I was an Existentialist or a Burroughs or an immortalist or a whatever??? I have your book around the corner, and I'm sure almost that he called me none of these – but what I mean is – he pasted his chicken-shit labels all over me. This poem is this. This poem is that.

How the hell can Fox know what a poem is? He is/was taught what a poem was/is.

I am a poem.

There is no way out.

I doubt that I can match Dr. Fox's degrees. But his poems begin to sound more and more like mine. But there's a catch – ability plus experience can never match a shadow, and that's what Fox is – a SHADOW of Buk. It just ain't gonna work, no matter how hard he works. Or they. All the Bukowski copyists. Every time I get a free copy of a little in the mails, I open it and it all sounds like Bukowski – very bad Bukowski.

That's their problem.

But I do hope that some other bellowing, water-mouthed prick comes along to take the heat off of me so that I may/can go about and do what I have to do. [★ ★ ★]

[To Jon and Louise Webb]

February 5, 1969

got the Patchen *Outsider* 4/5, and the old magic is still there; I could recognize the angelic beatificness of a LOUJON book even while being slugged while drunk. . . . enclosed a sixer for hardcover edition.

every man's life has its particular misery, but I would like to see you both write a book, yes a BOOK about THE ADVENTURES OF LOUJON IN A LOW-DOWN CLIME, or something like that. all the times the press went in and out the window, sometimes the same window, out, in, out again. the time of the attempted robbery. the time Bukowski tried to gas you. the bed up in the air. the bathtub filled with pages. that ugly and cold Santa Fe scene. the crazy and dull visitors. the madmen. the gangsters who push their bad work almost with threat. the pests. the sickness again and again. flood, fire. old papa with his beer. Bukowski vomiting in the University trash can. the old hand press. the madness and agony of everything. all the things I do not know. Lou on the corner trying to sell paintings. the deaf and dumb guy in the bar. city after city. all the odd benefactors with strings attached. the whole crazy wild story. I'm sure that there has never been a press and a time like yours, and I think that it would be a shame and an error if it were not recorded, because someday somebody is going to do it and they'll get it all WRONG. well, it's a thought anyhow. [* * *]

also *Penguin Poetry* 13 out. but won't be printed in U.S. until June 26, this year. Bukowski-Norse-Lamantia. but we are already in trouble. the slick-poetry academy boys and critics are already after our asses. Sinclair Beiles wrote a good review of *Penguin* 13, said it was the best of the series, but *London Magazine* refused to print the review and Beiles sent it to a South African paper which also refused to print the bit. Beiles wrote Norse that he thought Hal and I were the best living writers using the English language. which is neither here nor there, but the battle's on, and Hal suggested that we fight back instead of taking it as we have all these years. so, again, I come to you two . . . Nikos Stangos, the editor, has review copies which he can mail out. and I wonder if you might know anybody who could possibly give us a favorable review, or if not favorable at least unbiased and unprejudiced before the reviewer sits down? all my work is taken from *It Catches* and from *Crucifix*. and Hal's is all good. Lamantia weak here and there. but I've agreed with Hal to enter battle. so if you know of any reviewer who might not be stricken with Creeley-itis, please let me have their addresses . . . and many many thanks. I know I've laid a lot down on you here. now must rush out. [* * *]

[To Jim Roman]

February 25, 1969

REMEMBER THE STARVING WRITER!

how's that for an opening line? anyhow, sent you a good month or so ago, upon request, a signed copy of *The Curtains Are Waving*. you mentioned a bit of remuneration. it was my next-to-last copy. did you receive it?

I hope that you haven't caught 'Corringtonitis'*!

(* a refusal to acknowledge receipt of mail and refusal to answer inquiry. a disease which befalls one usually after a trip to England, say the University of Sussex at Brighton for one's Ph.D.**)

(★★ an over-exaggerated accomplishment which is attained more through drudgery than skill. i.e., a 'lickboot,' a 'chilblain,' a gatherer of calloused candlewick; i.e., a terrible bit of wading through shit.)

Notes of a Dirty Old Man is out, – paperback. a gathering of filthy stories and inane ravings. $1.95. you can probably located one in Fort L., Jim, at your local book or liquor store, but look in the porny section. *I* don't think the stories are dirty. when they lean to sex, and many of them do, I believe that sex is a very tragic and a very laughable matter. – see Boccaccio, *The Decameron*. we are all so ludicrous and lousy with our miserable sex organs. I hope that if you read these stories, you will understand, not misunderstand the intent. I am down to one copy, but if you can't find any out there, let me know if you wish an inscribed copy, 'To Jim Roman,' etc. etc. whatever.

I am disappointed in your not responding to my mailing of *The Curtains Are Waving*, but hell, I *do* realize that Life does get in our way, sometimes. I have been just about out of my jughead mind for about a year and couldn't answer a damn letter to anybody. you must have thought I'd a gone to BRIGHTON, Eng. but I didn't write anybody. it was as if my head were chopped off. but now, strangely, things seem to be oozing back into place. I don't understand these mental blackouts and I'd rather not have them. I'm not a prima d. I don't play Arty. and basically I am a kind person, although it sounds unrealistic to say so. I think that finally and actually, there were too many people writing me at once and I simply gave up. I couldn't keep up. now I am corresponding again, but only with 3 or 4 and I am keeping it that way. and I feel better. I answer everybody but not at the length that I used to. [★ ★ ★]

all right then, fire engines going by. I am on FIRE! here they come! they are circling back. they are going to put me out just like a landlady who never read Rimbaud, or Bukowski. . . .

[To Jim Roman]

April 2, 1969

I think your Bukowski collection better than mine. somebody stole my only copy of my first book [★ ★ ★] and my only copy of 'The Genius of the Crowd.' but I'm told that this happens to all writers. those who come and beat on our doors and drink our beer and take our time – also steal our books.

[★ ★ ★] since you have shown such an interest I will be mailing you, in the next couple of days, one of the two hardcover Penguin Library editions that were airmailed to me. Dark gray binding, gold lettering on the spine; pages thread-sewn. they've really done a beautiful job, but I do want to take care in packaging and mailing. but it *will* arrive, autographed to you, as per usual. these books will not be on sale in American until July 1969. [★ ★ ★]

[To Jim Roman]

April 14, 1969

[★ ★ ★] I *do* want to get back to doing some painting with something or other – some kind of color on paper – there has been a long gap there. I jump from painting to poetry to prose, back and forth and in between with all three – my wives, my whores. speaking of which, the mother of my child is taking said child (aged 4) to New York City to live and it's going to make a hell of a cut into my feelings – the little girl and I vibe perfectly, but with the mother, it's something else, and I can't raise the child, don't know how, so there it is – stuck again with a sad and heavy smash of pain, but the game works that way – everybody gets it, you, me, everybody; we've just got to piece together and carry on with our bit of the play until the rotten stinking curtain is rung down. [★ ★ ★]

This letter announces the short-lived magazine, Laugh Literary and Man the Humping Guns, *that Bukowski co-edited with Neeli Cherry. 'We didn't get very good submissions,' Bukowski recalls, 'so we wrote most of the stuff ourselves, inventing the names of writers.'*

[To Carl Weissner]

April 23, 1969

you SENT the letters, baby, god bless your majestic koool spirit behind those shades!!!! I already hit the univ. for sum on manus. paintings books, other shit, but this is more money in the bank and since they are REALLY FUCKING with me on the rotten JOB – poor attendance, same old thing –

this will help keep me alive, and also Marina, and if the breaks keep coming I'll simply sit here over the typer and pour out the bullshit. I can write ENDLESSLY if I wish – and forgive me – but it all comes out pretty good. so, you'se a good Hun, babe. all my thanks. future letters yours – if they are worth a damn or not – I will not HIT you for letters again! so, you are great after all! I love your guts!

ho, and I am being a bit shitty in my way – I mean those who did not return letters upon my deathbed request – I *was* damn sick at the time – I no longer correspond with. so, I am a shit, you see.

I only have one copy of *Notes*, but would LOVE to see it in German – it would wobble my BRAINS!!! I will airmail you a copy soon as I can get another one. hard to find them. and some typos to correct. just read 4 of the stories for Columbia on record – yes, did 12 reels of poetry for APPLE, signed contract, got advance. guy coming over tomorrow with Columbia contract and advance. shit happening so fast I don't know where I am. also some experimental film co. wants to do *Notes of a Dirty Old Man* on file. coming over with contract next week. must be careful not sign away full movie rights. jesus christ, for a lousy post office clerk, things are sure happening. PENGUIN. and also two books coming up by BLACK SPARROW, plus a bibliography some poor shit's doing – a librarian – for which I will get automatic dollars. I might just have to finally *quit* the post office before they fire me. there is simply too *much* to do. – check for 'Fünfzehn Dollar' – Germany – for contribution *Acid* – 'At the End of Feet' and 'Lilies in my Brain' . . . what's going on, Carl? am I going crazy? I even win money on the horses! it would be the fairest DREAM OF DREAMS to be able to survive directly from the typer and continue to write anything and anyway I wanted to – which is the ONLY way I will do it . . . [★ ★ ★]

also editing a literary magazine – *Laugh Literary and Man the Humping Guns* – which should be out in 2 or 3 weeks. I was stuck with this when a rich backer turned out not rich but a runner from creditors . . . but liked the poems so much . . . had to go ahead and put mag out. hope to run it a while, tho leisurely, and not come out until the material is excellent enough to fill needed pages. which takes TIME. and how. [★ ★ ★]

[To Carl Weissner]

May 27, 1969

good you liked the dirty stories – they were easy to write – mostly after the races, tired, hitting on can after can of beer and smoking cheap cigars, sitting here under this lamp – there was this sense of ACTION – I knew that *whatever* I wrote it would be on the streets in a couple of days – no waste, no time-lag – hit the bull's eyes, BANG! and on to the next. once a week, week after week . . . it was a good piece of ass thing. now compare it – I have written two long stories, one – 'The Life, Birth, and Death of an Underground Newspaper' – send it to *Evergreen* – it has been two months – no answer. another story, 'The Night Nobody Believed I Was Allen Ginsberg,' has been resting with *Playboy* for 6 weeks. there's just no *movement.* even if the stories go, it is not the same fast-paced type of vibration. yes, *Open City* folded, and there was lot of shit involved for it all, and I wrote it in the *Evergreen* submission. Bryan phoned the other night, high, from Frisco, saying he wants to start another newspaper, this time sex, no politics, and so I might be back on the weekly column kick if he wasn't dreaming high. so, we'll see.

but, actually, the fact you want to translate the stories into the German is a high honor to me, no shit, it gives me the creeping chills to think of crawling back to the Fatherland like that – my own tongue, cut out – but you've got a good tongue, Carl, you speak for me, and gracious thanks for the miracle. The ESSEX HOUSE boys say, however you want to work it, Buk. so all's all right, only should it come off, they want a contract to sign, whatever it says. so I don't think that's too much bother. [⋆ ⋆ ⋆]

just heard from Martin on the phone – Blazek got 3 grand for his mag from the Coordinating Council of Little Mags. . . . about ten of them got grants. he says. says Martin. how much did you get, Carl? Martin says none of the good mags got anything. which means you got nothing. what is it, Carl? just one big ass-suck. all this poet-in-residence. all these grants. I suppose if I got one, though, I'd say it was all right. then there's Levertov who gets a yearly grant from the National Foundation of the Arts, has used up a year's grant, demands her next year's grant in advance. it wouldn't be so sickening, but these people just aren't that *good*, Carl. I mean with the word, putting it down, and maybe in a lot of other ways. me, they're still trying to fire me from the post office, trying to knock me all the way down to skid row. I may just quit. [⋆ ⋆ ⋆]

[To Carl Weissner]

[July 1969]

[* * *] don't make work much more. just stay up all night and drink and listen to the radio – switching around trying to get the little Schubert songs like I have now – only the other German who went mad and wrote nothing but *songs* – better, can't think of his name. drunk now yes. but I know with you that is all right. anyhow, sick early this morning. first the female mailman. postage due. a rotten magazine. I stand in the doorway in robe, my balls hanging out. but the word is out. he is nuts. you know. I go back to bed. telegram. Hoffman. *Evergreen*. can hardly read with eyes. wants to know if names, newspaper used in story true or not. reply collect. I try Western Union. there is only a fucking machine on the phone. how can I tell the machine that I want to send the fucking thing collect? no instructions about that given by machine. I drink two beers. keep dialing for live human. one hour later get one. I tell Hoffman, don't worry. no libel. I mean I tell the telegram woman. now Bach. thank Christ. o.k., I try to sleep again. big Hemingway. sleeping alone. 50 pound beergut. bad heart. and really a coward. a fine coward. and proud of it. I think too much. doorbell again. special delivery. the PROOFS. jesus christ. what's the rush? I drink another beer. PLEASE CORRECT THE PROOFS AND PHONE IN CORRECTIONS COLLECT. boy, am I Hemingway? uh. BEST, she signs. jesus, somebody knows that I am alive. I read the proofs. the 25 typewritten pages come to 9 or 10 long galley proofs. it is hot. 90 degrees. I am naked and sick in the center of the room. my knees hurt. I lean on a red pillow. uh uh uh, I read, uh uh uh uh I read, and I think, what the fuck? this stuff is not so good. what are they so excited about? well, I find some errors. dial collect. GROVE PRESS. no, *Evergreen*. everybody is mixed up. my balls are sweating on top of the red pillow. now I know that it is not so good being Hemingway. the telephone operator garbles my name: 'A Mr. Bublinskar calling collect.' I'm told that nobody is there. I wait 5 minutes. spell my name to the operator: B like in Bastard, U like in unguentine, K like in Kafka, O like on Ow, W like in Whore, S like in Siff, K like in Kafka's brother if he had one, and I like in the second letter of the city Winston-Salem. I got through. Susan Bloch. I got her. what a young and knowledgeable and sexy voice. she made me feel like an old pig. I'm not an old pig, am I? no, she made me laugh. kneeling on that red pillow fighting galley proofs.

there are some wonderful women in the world, Carl, but I never meet them. anyway, I finally went to bed and slept like, if not a dead Hem, at least better than a dead O. Henry. [* * *]

[To Carl Weissner]

[August 1, 1969]

los angeles, calif. it's Friday, I don't have a clown's calendar, but I think it's August First, 1969, HOT HOT, and good old cheap Sears Roebuck fan turned on my ass; well, not exactly, I sit in my shorts, aging, drinking beer, the windows open, and the look at me, 6 p.m., coming in from their little jobs . . . they have been drowned and shitted upon. well, they belong to my club . . .

hello carl:

good to hear; I'd though maybe the literary thumpers and back-scratchers had gotten to you and told you I was a pile of dog turds. but you are the quiet type; it didn't fit in my mind. I remember you behind those dark shades, just smiling evenly, that slight smile there all along. I read pretty good and I don't believe in poking into souls, but I thought, 'if Carl has turned, it is very strange. because usually is the *constant* talkers, the OPEN-HEARTS, that will leap from boat to boat when the waters seem to change: so good to hear – it keeps my score at 100 percent. [* * *] I am afraid that my time with the female is done, and there isn't any sadness. I've had enough sex experiences to write 400 more stories about sex experiences. like *The New York Review of Sex* sent me a 25 buck check about the time I stuck my head down there and saw the STRANGEST panties I ever did see . . . plus other things. they want to see more. well, I am full of bullshit, and years. and as the little money comes in from the writing, here and there, I simply give myself more leisure time, drink more, lay around, stare at the ceiling, walk over to the typer when it calls. my boss says, 'Bukowski, where have you been?' me, sitting there with a hangover and a new idea for a story. 'fuck it,' I tell him. 'I don't have any excuses. fire me!' he just shakes his head and walks away. he thinks that I am crazy. am I crazy, Carl?

just uncapped another bottle of beer with my short top. my landlord gives me TWO garbage cans while the others get one. the beerbottles. I am the true Hun, Carl. but even if I were mostly Polack, it wouldn't matter. I don't know how it works.

on 'Absence of the Hero,' good it went, it started as a very long matter but each time I read it I saw another line or another paragraph that didn't belong. I don't have a copy of the thing around so no longer know what I wrote. but, as I was writing the thing I had this idea that I was processing something down to where it BELONGED. it gets very slippery sometimes, and there you go over the EDGE, but I finally chopped it down to where I wanted it, and I knew I had what I wanted but I had to worry about *you* – there was a chance you might think that I was just throwing cold gravy out the window. it was not so. I fought the fucking thing all the way through like an octopus with an embracing pussy. so, I'm happy you picked up on the vibe strings. it's paranoia-reality; first one is one, the other the other; then they mix; everything become the same. when *Evergreen* #70 comes out – at least the proofs read #70 – my job is over at the post office. I exposed all their little interrogations in dark rooms under their human-skin lamps (America, the beautiful!) about how they didn't care for the type of thing that I wrote while drawing their bloody and sweaty pay-checks. of course, other things in there too. it runs quite long and is mostly comedy, like dying. I'll ship you a copy. you say so.

[★ ★ ★] I haven't eaten in 3 or 4 days, but that's nothing new with me. I still weigh around 220. was once down to 133. it's really much better to be light – for fucking, bumming, swimming, almost anything else. I guess the only edge a heavy man has is shitting – man, there's nothing like a heavy pooping fat stinking beershit your cheeks spread all over the silly bowl; looking down at your toes, cutting it loose! glory! then to get up and ADMIRE YOUR OWN TURDS! AH, SO MANY OF THEM! WHAT A GREAT MAN I MUST REALLY BE TO BE SO FULL OF SHIT!?!

strange thing – 3 critical studies of me arrived in the mail in about two days. one a long book, another an article in a sex mag, another some burblings about me in a thing called *A Bukowski Sampler*. really, the worst one was the one by the prof, the long book – he just went on winding-out the spool of literary criticism as he had been taught to do. and to make it more cajoling complete – he called the worst poems the best ones, the best ones the worst, and very bothered with the term 'surrealism,' I guess something they really jammed into his anus in college. the one in the sex mag was really the best; I got drunk with the guy all night one night so he had something to talk about that I told him instead of something he *imagined* through reading my crap. after getting a ph.d. you know? well, the *Sampler* thing was all mixed-up. they meant well, but, basically, they were too young and not enough had happened to them. I don't mean that you have to be OLD to write, but I do mean that if you *are* OLD and can still write and have sailed some bloody ships, you're got a little edge.[* * *]

[To Carl Weissner]

[September 16, 1969]

September 16, 2 a.m. plus listening to some symphonic piss, but even that is better than this day which preceded it, harassed by frightened little red-faced men about attendance, or lack of, thereupon, or arguing because I had not filled out the proper forms . . . what proper form? What proper form? I'd like to believe that the proper form is some type of existence that precludes being gunned down by idiots with brain cells the size of wasps and eyes that have the stink of the shit of their souls risen to the top iris, or whatever it is called . . . Sometimes I wish I knew the language better; then other times I know that this is dangerous, not dangerous, but trappish, wasteful, like dipping the fingers into cunt butter, then standing around for a couple of years licking out the droplets. what the hell am I talking about? I don't know. and that's good.

hello Carl:

not to insult, but your letter is the best gash of writing, straight on through that I have seen in some time. would like to use, will use in *Laugh Literary* #2 if you don't mind. #2 will be larger, easier to read with the eye, but emphasis still on CONTENT. # uno issue almost sold out, went very fast. I think that it is simply a matter of certain people knowing that your blood and guts are in the thing, instead of some kind of con. Most all of everything is con. But it seems that there *are* 500 people in the world who can tell the difference between con and the other. In the next issue, we are going to clown a bit, but the kind of laughter that comes up through the mouth after being hit with a sledgehammer. I believe that some names are going to be named and some assholes torn. But I am very very tired of the standardized type of little mag stuff. and after standing 8 or 10 hours a night talking with the dolts about who won the old ball game, or whether Namath has a right to own a bar full of thugs while quarterbacking for the

Jets – well, shit. I am not just going to turn out a little old ladies' magazine, I hope. the death-toll they count over me in their fucking pigs' pen is a pain that I have never been able to adjust to – and I am going to spit some shit back into somebody's eye – not out of vengeance – because some of what has happened to me is my own FAULT (or so I am told), but the lifejuice spit of a dying man will not, I hope, be without a vernacular of its own.

and as I work less and less in their pig pens, now, at least, for the time being – some luck comes my way – the fucking *Penguin* 13 – you pushing little buttons in the land of my birth – translating my slimy greasy cunt stories – and please take liberties – I trust your soul all the way through – you know what I mean [★ ★ ★]

I gave your letter to the two or 3 trusted that I know, and even those I do not entirely trust, and they laughed, each of them, reading certain phrases out loud. This is always the test: THE ULTIMATE TRUTH, NO MATTER HOW TRAGIC, THE ULTIMATE TRUTH ALWAYS MAKES A MAN LAUGH HIS BALLS OFF SIMPLY BECAUSE IT IS SO GOOD, SO ON THE MARK.

Having much luck with Dirty Old Man stories – some mag in Chicago bought reprint rights to 4 stories via Essex House for $250. [★ ★ ★] Just for kicks, one night, I didn't go to work, sat at typer, wrote thing, 7 typewritten pages, 45 minutes, called 'The Copulating Mermaid of Venice, Calif.' Some sex mag says it's worth $150 to me upon publication. But the beautiful thing is that I have not had to *compromise* my style. The post office may yet be told to go kiss its own ass. If it weren't for the child-support thing, I'd tell them now.

Meanwhile, certain poets drop around, mostly bad ones, complaining that they are misunderstood, blocked-off, black-listed, and some of it is true, but some of the fellows have simply forgotten how to write, or don't write, or pretend to, or play the Poet-game as a spiritual right to continual handouts from everywhere – $$$$, sex, adulation. and sometimes I get a little cruel, maybe jealous because they are living off the fat while I am hitting a timeclock, I tell them to try the steel mills and get their backbones back, but they pale at this – Christ, their little souls couldn't stand it. So, I relent, let off, get them some beers and listen to them, and next out come their poems – which most of them read to me out LOUD. They think that this improves the work.

And I say, no, I don't like it.

then they get pissed. after eating up the only 2 or 3 hours I have to do what I wish to do.

Then I tell them, look, man, I have to shit, shave, eat, make the fucking job.

And they leave off for someplace else, saying, 'Hey, Marty, let me have a twenty. You know, that Bukowski, he's a rotten son of a bitch . . .'

I can stand one poet a week but when they begin to arrive 7 days a week I begin to go a little crazy. listening to them, I can't even do the simple things – like – go to the laundry – get that one extra hour sleep I need – dump the garbage – get the stink out of the sink, the ring out of the bathtub, all the shit off the floor. and then come the others – the admirers – worse than the poets – with their drinks – and their softness and their ladies – you can't insult them – everything you say – no matter how vile – is funny. You could whip the whole roomful of them but they sicken you so you drink and drink and drink and drink, while all the time there's this idea in the center of your brain – the typewriter sits there. you can't make their women; they are fascinating and fascinated but frightened. What shit.

so I miss two or three days work, they don't fire me, I make no excuses and old black cunts press their flanks against me hardhard hard, say, 'Where ya been, Hank?'

'Drunk,' I say.

all of their faces are dumped and burned in pain, wasted, like mine. I think, go punch out. slam it home. no good.

No good. I always dream of my perfect one. Well, I don't mean that. just an ordinary little woman with nice knees and nice ankles who likes to put on high heels and nylons and drink and look at me from across the couch. and then, hours later, make love. Not a love to *prove*, just a love that has flowed into an easy evening. but most bitches are hunters, all the time gleaming gleaming, their cunts reaching forward like cages. ah, shit. can't I get off this sex thing?

Your letter – the camels, the arabs – the everything – easy to see why the Israelites won the last war. I have always thought that man's greatest inventions went like this:

1. The Bed.
2. The Shit and Piss disposal system (which, I understand, is beginning to back up, and fail).
3. The Atom Bomb.
4. The Hydrogen Bomb. and
5. the rubber. [★ ★ ★]

Accompanying money order and letter to Frances Smith, Marina's mother.

[To Marina Bukowski]

September 16, 1969

Hello Marina, little one:

Every time you phone me, it is so very good to hear your voice. You have the most beautiful voice in the world. Thanks very much for phoning me. I always feel good for days and days after you talk to me. And I feel that I will see you again some day and that keeps me going. Sometimes when I get sick I think about you and it makes me well again. PLEASE BE VERY CAREFUL WHEN YOU CROSS ANY STREET. LOOK *BOTH* WAYS. I think about you all the time and love you more than the sky or the mountains or the ocean or anybody or anything. Please stay well and happy and don't worry about me.

all my love, little one,
Hank.

At the end of November 1969 Bukowski resigned his position in the U.S. Postal Service and, encouraged by a promise of regular advance royalties from John Martin, took the risk of living solely by his writing.

[To Carl Weissner]

[Mid-]November 1969

[★ ★ ★] anyhow, so yes, I can't approach L.A. Freep, they hate my guts simply because of this and that and this and that, and various rumors, true and untrue, like I threatened to beat the shit out of a guy in a wheelchair one night . . . that's true, but I was joking and when guys 30 years younger began to run out of the house because I said they were next, I wondered, why please these chickenshits? so, with various other tales I could lay upon you, Carl, I am on the blacklist in this ass-sucking town, coteries town, big bloody cunt of nothing town . . .

also I am going crazy and can't stand the post office job any longer. I have one of two choices – stay in the post office and go crazy (I have been there eleven years) or stay out here and play at writer and starve. I've decided to starve. so at the end of Nov. I am going to resign my job at the p.o. so I need YOUR HELP! [* * *]

my child-support bag is only $45 a month plus this and that, and I hope to find a cheaper place to live. [* * *]

have sold some good stories coming down from *Evergreen* to the sex mags, so there will be various sources of income made mostly off this old machine [* * *]

so, after Dec. one, I will be on my own, and this typewriter will be a machine gun . . . as it was meant to be. this does not mean that I will be writing for money but for luck. a hell of a decision to make at age 50. . . . I toss a job away that most men would oh love. but I am not most men. [* * *]

my little daughter is so beautiful, Karl, Carl, you never met her did you? she's singing *London Bridge Is Falling Down* from the bedroom. the woman thinks London B. is corrupt. she's a radical. o.k. when the sun hops we will be the first to record it.

• 1970 •

[To Jim Roman]

January 11, 1970

[★ ★ ★] I am a member of the unemployed now with nothing but a typer and a couple of paint brushes to hold off the world. So keep your fingers crossed for me and hope the gods are on my side. There's my 5 year old daughter involved and if I lost her, that would do me in. But things sometimes have a way of working. There's no need to lay it down yet. There's a novel in mind and *The Days Run Away* . . . moving very nicely. but but but . . .

This letter is so gloomy, Jim, that I can't ever write it, finish it. I'll write when things are looking better.

[To Carl Weissner]

January 20, 1970

[★ ★ ★] I am out of the god damned post office and I am playing typewriter-boy and painter. If I fall flat it is my own fault – the child support, the rent, the utilities still come due, and I do love the child, would hate to lose her. 12 years on the job, and then to finally quit it, cold, half a century old. The first ten days I damn near went outa my skull – didn't know what to do with my hands, my feet, my mind. I almost cracked. And after a series of drunks at wild parties and alone, I ended up in bed deathly sick, shivering, depressed all the way to hell and almost to the kitchen butcher knife. I sweated it, staring at the ceiling, unable to sleep – shades down, I stared at the ceiling while being an inch from bottom. At the same time, the bathroom and kitchen sinks clogged up, and I vomited, trembling, into the toilet and it rained outside, and then some people came by with guitars and threw all the wine bottles, beer bottles, whiskey bottles in the trash, dumped the garbage. They made me laugh, they made me get off that stinking gloom bed. And I went out into the rain with them.

Nothing to eat for 3 or 4 days – my stomach raw. And I ended up drunk again . . .

Now I seem to have pulled together (I hope), and it seems to be going easier as each day goes by. I suppose it was a transition from the 12 year thing, and when you look at it, maybe ten days shot going from one to the other isn't too bad, what? Christ, I even give poetry readings now. [⋆ ⋆ ⋆]

See Charles Olson Reading at Berkeley, *a transcript of the reading discussed here, made by Zoe Brown and published by Coyote, San Francisco, 1966.*

[To Carl Weissner]

February 16, 1970

[⋆ ⋆ ⋆] Yes, I saw the transcript of the Olson reading in Berkeley. Frankly, man, it was sickening. He was begging to the audience, sitting in their laps like a baby. And his poems are so straight-laced. He broke out of his laces and slobbered all over everybody. He even begged people who were leaving to come back. Then a woman told him they had to close the auditorium at midnight, and he begged for a few minutes more, and then went on longer and longer. Something wrong with a man like that, sucking at the cunt of an audience. Thank god, I hate to read [⋆ ⋆ ⋆].

What the hell you doing reading the *Nola Express*? Lively little rag, though, courage, but young young. The govt. will finally bust them in half. All these undergrounds have this suicide complex. I think they really want to get spanked by papa instead of replacing him. I could be wrong. But sometimes they swing those roundhouse glory rights, and miss, when the steady left jab might take the whole fight. [⋆ ⋆ ⋆]

Dr. Renate Matthaei was editor for Verlag Kiepenheuer & Witsch, in Köln. The fake Henry Miller blurb invented by Weissner for the German edition of Notes of a Dirty Old Man *and that Bukowski finds 'quite accurate' reads as follows: 'Each line in Bukowski is infected by the terror of the American nightmare. He articulates the fears & agonies of that vast minority in the no-man's-land between inhuman brutalisation and helpless despair.'*

The novel Post Office *was eventually published in February 1971.*

[To Carl Weissner]

February 23, 1970

[★ ★ ★] glad you got hold of Dr. Matthaei, and I would prefer you to translate *Post Office*, of course. [★ ★ ★] The money thing *does* become important when writing is your only income and you want to go on writing without diluting your style or missing too many meals. Also, the beer bill rises when you sit by the typer near the window and things begin to move in toward you from out there.

I want to thank you for some of your suggestions – you've been a *great* moral support. In looking over the contracts in the drawer I see I've signed quite a few. There is that tangled word horror where I sold away movie rights to these guys for $50 while I was drunk. I think I told you about that. 2 year option. I've got to sweat another year and 5 months. That's on *Notes*. [★ ★ ★]

I think you'll like *Post Office*, maybe even better than *Notes*. There's plenty of sex in there for laughs and enough horror and madness to float the typescript to you across the Atlantic. I try to photograph rather than preach. [★ ★ ★]

I'm not too happy with the fake H[enry] M[iller] quote, and I would not tell Martin about it or he'd flip – maybe. But if you think it will make a difference in selling 2,000 or 5,000, go ahead. It's best that we survive. By the way, I like the blurb *itself*. Quite accurate. So what the hell, go ahead. [★ ★ ★]

[To John Martin]

February 23, 1970

I answered Weissner but I enclose his letter so you'll get some idea of the German scene. I told him to go ahead with the Henry Miller blurb but not to tell you or you'd flip, and now here I am sending you the letter. So you must pretend not to read the H.M. blurb part. These Germans may save my ass yet. I do trust Weissner because he lays everything in the open, and is one of the better writers in Germany, and I think can do a better job of translating than anybody. Also met him personally, you know.

Now you lay off the beer, keep your feet on the ground, Sparrow. Remember what ol' Franky D. said: 'We have nothing to fear but fear itself.'

[To Neeli Cherry]

[ca. April 12, 1970]

I figured they'd run you out of Germany fast enough. But you're living without working and that is an acceptable state. I sit here by the window, drinking coffee and rolling cigarettes and watching the long-legged nurses stroll home. They check their mailboxes and quickly lock themselves into their plastic cubicles. Let them; they shit, have monthlies, fart, scream. There's a new movement here now – The Women's Liberation Movement – there are a lot of clever lesbians in it and some man-haters, and they have certain piteous points – like their breasts, but damn if I don't think the ladies have rather ruled the cock-and-ball set right along. But they claim they are not represented with dignity – not enough female doctors, so forth, and then some guy says, there aren't enough female garbage collectors, and then it goes around and around. Everybody everywhere is screaming for dignity and representation but their minds and souls are mud and shit, and how can you give dignity to shit? Guy over here other day said, 'I think everybody who writes should have a guaranteed income.' Why just everybody who writes? I'd like to see most writers put into those ovens you were looking at. guaranteed. [★ ★ ★]

[To Carl Weissner]

April 14, 1970

great, my friend. I'm glad one of the Melzers finally stirred into action. [★ ★ ★]

sorry all this bitching and money talk shit, Carl. but it is part of the stew. but I felt all along that whether I got the advance from Meltzer or not would be the thing that made me or broke me. it's just one of those things, Carl. once I get rolling here, learn how to better operate the ship,

I feel I might go on, in spite of all. now that Meltzer is coming through the scene changes to one of hope. I mean hope of survival. there should be a way to get hold of my health, and the writing is coming along like a stampede – no dizzy spells there – wrote 35 *new* poems in the last 2 weeks. as good or better than any I have written. have also started a second novel, *The Horseplayer*. I am writing it in a more leisurely fashion than *Post Office*, which was quick-paced because I wanted it to be – because I didn't want to preach, only tell. first 2 chapters on the *Horseplayer* all right; in fact, the first chapter is a classic. I even had to laugh myself. I may never finish the H.P. or I might. Not pressing it.

sometimes I get in here, writing, writing, lounging, in trance-state; a couple of days go by and I realize that I haven't even been outside, and there I go – fresh air! sunshine! walking down the sidewalk, and then, friend, that first human face . . . [⋆ ⋆ ⋆]

The Days Run Away Like Wild Horses Over the Hills *was published on December 30, 1969.*

[To John Martin]

[? March–April 1970]

[⋆ ⋆ ⋆] I slipped off again, a week or so ago, but it was not nearly the agony trip that mid-January launch-out was. And each time I come back down, I am stronger again. These 2 good paintings today are an indication that the old Bukowski is coming back. Sardonic, easy – fucked-up but basically steering the wreckage. You won't be able to laugh at me over the phone any more as my voice quavers. Hitler is back. Thank God and the angels and the collected works of Turgenev!

The nurses are coming in now and I look at their legs and their asses and I love them. I am back at the old window. [⋆ ⋆ ⋆]

Yes, the Cal State thing. Felt shitty reading. I don't like it. It is just a survival sort of thing that must be done. But the guy who set it up said he had never heard such a good crowd reaction since . . . anybody. Well good, so I was lucky. And I did have the Sparrow brochures which I walked around handing out laughing, saying, 'Buy this, mothers . . .' If you have any ads left, ship me another bundle. Giving a small reading up at a rich dentist's place, booze and broads, lambs turning on spits in the fire, all that shit. But I will keep them off my soul, which is mine and mine only, next Sunday, but if you have any ads I will jam it to them. I am worried that you might have published too many copies of *Days* and I want to help you hustle them off. Right on, right on . . . Hey, I see where they called out the National Guard to protect my archives at the Un. of Santa B[arbara]. Good stout lads all!

[To John Martin]

[? April 1970]

meant to get these off yesterday, but 2 young guys by, and so there went a whole afternoon. they didn't like Henry Miller, they didn't like Pound, they liked Celine. then one of them handed me one of his things. I didn't like it.

so I'm coming in late with the work, but everything has its meaning. with these 2, I learned, mainly, there isn't any competition. one of them claimed you had to have connections to get published. I said that 2 things helped – talent and talent, the connections would take care of themselves. when I was young and it came back I threw it away. everybody thinks they are a genius; that's why they aren't.

when they left, after drinking my beer, or as they left, I said, 'I have Henry Miller's address if you want to drop by there.'

'that's an insult,' they said.

with these young guys it's always a pleasure to cut down the giants but the best way to cut them down is with your own work and I don't mean the work of your jaws. if Henry Miller had walked into the room, they would have shit and fawned all over him. the only reason they come to me is that I am the Image of the Loser, the Man who doesn't care, the Man who didn't quite make it, the man who will drink a beer with a bum. what they don't realize is that I *do* care, would like to do my work, and have the kindness or the cowardice not to cuss them and send them on their way. unfortunately, people like something in me, they can't let it go. I will simply have to work around it all and still do my work. my old theory while working ten to 12 hour nights and days in the factories and in the post office has always been, save what you can, don't give in. the theory stands now; whether my work holds up depends upon what is left of me.

and so that's kind of a bitch but that's o.k. because I know when I am bitching I am all right. [★ ★ ★]

[To Neeli Cherry]

May 10, 1970

little here. I am hanging on. just came off 2 weeks at the track, got way ahead, then gave it all back. I've made up my mind that I don't know anything about horses.

action in U.S.: student strikes at universities. Nix moved into Cambodia. National Guard fired on students at Kent State. wounded many, killed 4. then at Univ. of New Mexico, where I'm supposed to read this Friday night, the National Guard bayonetted ten. Prob. later in month I'm going to read at 2 colleges in Washington. I'm not like you. I hate to read. but no money coming in right now. the bank account is sagging. [* * *]

nurse pushing an old woman by in a wheelchair. it's sad, sad. I'll never get that old, something will kill me first. or maybe I'll bury you, spit on your grave from my head of white hair, rotten Andernach teeth grinning in the sun, rolling a cigarette and farting.

before the horse bit, wrote 50 new poems in 3 weeks, most of them quite good, maybe not from your viewpoint but from mine. and that's the one I go by. now I'll be in all the littles again just when they thought they had buried me. Blazek's gonna shit. there goes the old woman again. I'm running out of magazines to send to. even *Evergreen* took a poem; also lucked into *Stony-brook* – Creeley-land – with quite a number. there's little doubt that getting out of the post office has given me more time and energy. it's good, though it's hard sometimes facing my own mind 24 hours on 24. a job keeps you from thinking. [* * *]

p.s. – Martin going to publish novel. the Germans also want it. 3 companies interested. so I'm going to get up typescripts for each and take the highest bidder. I feel like Hemingway. gotta get a shotgun. [* * *]

[To John Martin]

[May 10, 1970]

sad letter. the system fell apart and I gave them their damned money back. worse was all the time wasted. well, that's out of my system anyhow. now back to playing the literary game. [* * *]

I can't agree with you on the dictionary idea for the novel [*Post Office*], but if you insist, we'll go ahead. keep writing down words. I think though that most of the terms are obvious, even to an outsider. but I'm glad enough that you are probably going to do the novel, so I'll compromise if nec. I do think the dictionary has a cheapening and commercial effect, however. Think it over a while. [* * *]

Lafayette Young had sent Bukowski a small gift of money. Niki is his daughter. Carson McCullers (b. 1917) was not *the daughter of Kay Boyle (b. 1903), whose story, 'Rest Cure,' was first published in* The First Lover and Other Stories *(New York, 1933).*

[To Lafayette Young]

May [?], 1970

I just read stuff, very little of it at that, only what goes for me, and so I am not an educated man in many senses. Did I *understand* you properly – via *Harper's Bazaar*, Nov. 1943, that Carson [McCullers] *was* the daughter of Kay Boyle? Too friggin' much, if true. Kay was a beautiful woman. Her style was way ahead of her time. I used to see many of her short stories in *Story*, where I was first published, 1944, just before my mad ten year drunk that almost took me out. Wasn't it Kay B. who wrote that short story, 'Rest Cure,' about the death of D. H. Lawrence? It would be very miraculous if Carson were actually the daughter, I mean had been, of Kay Boyle. Anyhow, I remember 'Rest Cure,' and if Kay Boyle didn't write it, she should have. As per her novels, they were not as tight as the stories. And comparisons are hell and unkind, but I'm afraid Carson outwrote mama. I'm afraid Carson McCullers just about outwrote everybody. I used to read Carson McCullers in bed in cheap rooms while I was starving and drinking wine and it was holy – my skin shivered and crawled and I didn't cry because I was too proud of her to cry.

Don't worry about alcoholism; it keeps us from committing suicide.

As per Niki and her 'The Lost Generation,' I hope she got it right. Those were interesting people, Gerty and Hem and Fitz and the gang. That gas station mechanic who called it the Lost Generation, though, was either an utter Romantic or he had nothing to compare it with.

There can't be any generation more LOST than our present one – being born into a war-after-war era, the Atomic Age, the Pollution Age, the Computer Age, all in one. They should be LOST, they know. There has never been another generation as knowing and as brave. They don't even call themselves lost. rather, they say, hell, let's straighten it out. Stay in there Niki. [★ ★ ★]

Black Sparrow Press had published Dorbin's A Bibliography of Charles Bukowski *in 1969. A videotape of the Bellevue reading mentioned below was published by Black Sparrow in 1988.*

[To Sanford Dorbin]

A Monday in June? yeh. 1970

Sandy fu Chris' sake:

[★ ★ ★] Took the train down to UNM and read there. drank there several days and threw off a drunken half-fuck. then back, and a plane up to Washington where I read at West. Wash. State College that night, got drunk, insulted the profs. got real sick drunk and was awakened in an upstairs bedroom at 8 : 30 the next morning and told we had a long ride to Bellevue for a reading at 11 : 30 a.m. good God Jesus. I kissed the prof's wife goodbye and we got in the car. stopped for refills. meanwhile, no eating. as approached college started heaving out the window. no time to stop. heaved right up into the parking lot where I staggered out and into the building and started reading, dead sick, and the bastards put me on video tape, and I got a few drinks down as I was reading and managed to bring it off. away to this cabin and more drinking and more drinking at the airport – I missed my plane while sitting in the bar over an hour early – finally got in only to find a certain lady wanted to see me and I stayed with her 2 nights, or she stayed with me, I mean, and more drinking, no eating – food, that is – and I finally put *her* on a plane, and then back and trouble getting straight, coming down, and it's easy for me to see why it killed Dylan Thomas, but I think if it ever happens again, I'll go a little easier. The readings came at a good time, a money-lag time. the sex mags, everybody, hollering 'tight money.' Even Norse lost 2 sponsors he's had for years – tight money, they say, and the market. so, it's a shitty time and the hustle is on. so understand, I am hanging to the branch; not with a rope, a thread . . . whatever, that means. . . .

on articles, well, yes, there's my name and somebody's done some work, but you know if I took the things seriously I would no longer know who I was – well, I don't anyhow – but I think you know what I mean. I mean if I were to comment on certain aspects of the article I'd feel as if I were talking about my cockhairs, my snot, my eyeballs, my brain, my heart, my gut, and I don't know anything about them. they operate me. I suppose I am not very clear today. I've been hav[ing] a 2 or 3 week battle with 12 or 14 Islanders who live in rotating shifts in the court in the center. we park on the front lawn. the landlord has lost control of this place, except to collect rent. the bastards keep blocking me in in hope to make me give up parking there so they can move in another one of their 6 or 7 cars. I am a bit outnumbered and they go to all means to block my car so I can't get out, even to parking across the front of me by using the apartment house driveway next door. I go crazy over shit like that. I've mailed in for a 9 inch switchblade. this morning I got them out of bed and made them move a car that had me blocked. I came back and got blocked again by another car. mad. I stop them one by one as they walk by the door. 'Hey, buddy, got a minute? I wanna have a little talk with you. What's wrong with you guys? Now, I'm not a hard guy to get along with. But why in the fuck??? . . .'

there's always some god damned thing. no women. or having a woman and having a lot of shit trouble with her. or hangover. or parking. or toothache. or money slipping away, or just the general stupidity and viciousness of the human race. I think I'm going to have to move the hell out of here. I can't fight them all. [⋆ ⋆ ⋆]

[To Neeli Cherry]

June 4, 1970

drinking beer, waiting for Marina to come over.

fridge shot. things getting tough. Knight-Adam hollering backlog. Out in *Evergreen* for a week now but no check from them. read within 2 weeks at Univ. of New Mexico, West. Wash. State College and Bellevue Community College. 660 total, no 600, but no travel expenses, and drinks, airflight, drinks, taxi, drinks in the airport, buying drinks for parties, almost lost on the deal. got laid a few times by sweet young things, tho. long drunken sweaty fucks. now back, still trying to get sober. bankroll diminishing. it looked so good for a while. I might have known. if you ever come back, look for me on skid row. this time you won't have to drive me down there. [★ ★ ★]

I can't beat the horses any more. I must stay away. I wish I were back in the post office. at least they dulled my mind and tired my body. now everything comes at me with knives out, there's no rest, no relenting. it's balls away. I'm on the cross.

In fact, I'm tired of writing. what's the use?

[To Neeli Cherry]

June [?18], 1970

fighting a battle with 14 Islanders who have suddenly possessed a court in the center. have sent in 3 bucks for a 9 inch stiletto. I may go but before I do, they will know that I have been here. And I'm not talking about poetry.

yes, I've had 2 or 3 good young fucks lately – the poetry con, you know – but now that it's over I hardly feel any different. it just doesn't work, and the strange idea has crossed my mind that a man may be able to exist quite nicely without sex at all. I like the color of their dresses, the way they walk, handle their buttocks, but I wonder if all the rest is needed? the sweating, the farts, the agony, the come, the declarations? the dirty sheets, the stink and the closeness?

the most beautiful woman is the one who walks past your window and then she is gone. [★ ★ ★]

ate at Norm's the other day, sirloin special dinner $1.35. found a seat at the counter, at the end, fine, nobody in the next seat, then just after I ordered here came this fag in and he sat next to me, ordered a coffee and he made that coffee last all through my meal. then he kept looking at me. I thought, next time he looks at me, I'm going to straighten him good. he looked again and I turned to look back, I was going to say, 'What the fuck you looking at?', but when I turned he looked straight ahead, quickly. then he jumped up and left. but I was finished eating. the mother had ruined my meal. [★ ★ ★]

[To John Martin]

June 22, 1970

[★ ★ ★] the boys are bad-mouthing you for publishing Forrest. one phoned and said he was on KPFK, unbelievably bad, and Cynthia fawned all over him. I said, 'oh yes, is that so?' somehow these poets seem to think that I am supposed to defend Black Sparrow, and I feel like doing so since you have done and are doing some good things for me. but, basically, you have a right to publish anybody you want to. I think of something John Thomas told me one night, 'No matter what you do, a certain number of people are going to dislike it, others will like it, and the vast majority will not give a damn one way or the other.' Once you understand this, the snipers will not make so much difference. [★ ★ ★]

Gerald Locklin had published Sunset Beach, *a book of poems from Hors Commerce Press, Torrance, California, in 1967. He has since published many further volumes.*

[To Gerald Locklin]

July 4, 1970

Hello G. Locklin:

yes, I was a bit pissed on your non-arrival [for a reading at The Bridge], having built you to the mob. I don't often step out to recommend a poet, but had seen your stuff in *Wormwood* and recognized a new tick and flare, a decent originality. for my money, which ain't much, but anyhow, for my money there are only 4 poets around doing it now – you, Ron Koertge, Bix Blaufus and, er, Bukowski. there may be others – I hope there are – but I haven't seen their work. and I get sent many magazines full of listless and stupid pages, so I'm glad you're there, anyhow, even if you get your dates mixed up. I have a prejudice against teachers, but if the work is strong enough, fuck it. Bix is going to teach somewhere in Oregon in a few months, and he's as real as catshit.

[★ ★ ★]

[To Carl Weissner]

July 5, 1970

[★ ★ ★] all in all, I seem to be surviving; of course, your getting Meltzer to come through was a big spiritual boost, the shot I needed and I sat down and rapped out 3 or 4 dirty stories, immortal, and some other shit. there's energy coming from somewhere because, for the time being, the days and the nights are mine, and if I fuck them up it's not nearly so bad as somebody else fucking them up for me with a time clock, you know.

this is a shitcan letter, it's so hot, fan on my ass, but it's not all bad, even got laid a few times lately. the ladies come by and knock on the door, and that's rather nice you know? even when I strike out I get a few grabs.

like I say, this is a shitcan letter but wanted you to know I think about you, you've done some good things for me, Carl, and all I do for you is holler and moan my troubles. so this is basically to let you know it's not all that bad. there's always PANIC especially when I hit the streets and look around or go into a barbershop or a supermarket. but that has always been there. I've learned more to live with my panic like a man sometimes learns to live with a bad woman. of course, now and then it gets too much, it can't be helped and one simply drinks until the pleasure of unconsciousness. you learn how to do that too.

so, it's o.k., the war is forever. [★ ★ ★]

[To Lafayette Young]

July 12, 1970

[★ ★ ★] you know, I almost go mad sometimes, like this year, total days fucked away and torn up. but all and all, it is better than it has been. I've gotten more writing done this year than any 3 years previous. it has to happen without a job in the way. now I get in the way, but it's realler, I can't blame any boss any wife any job any kid for ripping me up. I am the enemy, and it's good for laughs – sometimes. and the luck is good. like last night I was going to write myself a kind of grade b quicky short story for one of the underground papers that pays me 20 bucks a story. they are good people, so I don't try to write them shit. let's admit it, my grade b stuff is not too bad. so I rolled a cigarette and brought out the beer and turned on the radio to some symphony music and said, well, it'll take about an hour, I'll take it easy, enjoy it and get it in the mail. so what the hell happens? halfway through I see that I've got a grade a story and that makes the rest of the writing better too. so the undergrounds will have to wait – it's off to *Evergreen* or one of the sex mags and Bukowski is lucky again. It's called 'All That Pussy.' so all I need is beer and smokes and half a swing and I'm a writer. [★ ★ ★]

[To Neeli Cherry]

July 12, 1970

[★ ★ ★] so feel good picking your apples even if they are fucking up your head; at least you don't have to worry about foreclosure, all that shit. even I seem to be surviving, although there was a frightening dip in reserves a while back, it made me dig in, write a half dozen immortal short stories and a hundred new poems, almost all of them quite good. get me near the cross I SCREAM LITERARY. now Sunday, drinking beer, rolling smokes, sitting in this dirty place, barefooted, gut hanging out, watching the dead Sunday people walk by. I even eat at Norm's now and then when I am too lazy to cook, get that dollar thirty-five special and watch the waitresses' asses joggle about in their sweaty panties and the cook sweating and dazed and trapped over all that hot tin. found best to go in about 3 p.m. I feel like a millionaire. I don't drive but walk down and walk back, slowly in the sun, feeling like a jr. league Hemingway, spitting shreds of tobacco out of my mouth from that first cigarette, and watching the people rush about here and there in panic. [★ ★ ★]

[To Carl Weissner]

July 23, 1970

[★ ★ ★] read at Long Beach State College at noon yesterday, sober, with the sweat running down the arms. hard money. $50. they don't pay a man a damn until he leaves the state. also threw a young guy off my front porch a couple of nights ago. he was standing there pissing, a huge swath of curved piss right into the bush out there, and I get very tired of guys pissing on my porch – women never piss out there – so I picked the guy up and hurled him over the bush and into the night. he didn't return. [★ ★ ★]

yes, Martin has me worried. I'd prefer *Post Office* in its original raw form. of course I was a little bit out of my head when I wrote it, but it wasn't sloppy or lazy writing; it was written as it fucking well came out, and that meant turds and blood and the rest of the wash. I'm told that parts of it are in the present tense and parts in the past. that's all right with me. I know most of the rules of grammar but I'm not interested. he has inferred that he doesn't want to detract from my style, so there we are on the merry-go-round. he's a nice guy but he does treat me too much like an idiot. he admits I'm his best seller but at the same time he'd rather I wrote more safe shit. what the hell. well, maybe I worry too much. I'll go along with the single tense, but I feel the rest must stay. we'll see. I get depressed writing about it. [★ ★ ★]

[To Carl Weissner]

August 8, 1970

[★ ★ ★] The novel will be issued in the Fall, says Martin of Black Sparrow, which prob. means Winter, if I know publishers. Martin has done some good things for me and one thing he is worried about is that the Germans might get hot pants and bring out *Post Office* in Germany before it gets out here in America. He wants to be first. So I said, 'O.k., we'll simply tell them that the novel can't be released in Germany until it is released here. O.k.?' When I talk like that it gives me a feeling of immense power, as if I were some 1970 Hemingway instead of an old fuck who is trying to keep off of skid row. [★ ★ ★]

[To Carl Weissner]

August 20, 1970

[★ ★ ★] these people are on me again for the sound of my typewriter and I'm a little pissed tonight – not at you, old buddy. they make all kinds of shitty noises but a typewriter is verboten. was drunk one night and cussed them back – 'Yeah! You and your fucking dogs! Calling your dogs all the damned time! MICHELE! HERE MICHELE! Why don't YOU shut up all *that* shit noise!' I'd been drinking about a week, trying to forget my 50th birthday.

when I go out on the street Michele barks at me. 'Chew his leg off,' they tell the dog. I ignore that. bastards own the high-rise next door and are afraid the sound of typer will disturb their dear tenants. I dress in old clothes, need shave, red-eyed and hungover. they dislike me and my sounds and my looks very much. they like to see a man vanish at 6:30 a.m. then come back in in the evening, eat, flip on the tv. they have hours of leisure but all they do is sit on their steps and walk their dogs around and collect rents. I don't know what they are waiting for, what they want and I don't care. they want me. that's one place I would like to see burn. those people are completely dehumanized by their jobs and their walls. this society is unbelievable; they all do the same things, talk the same way, share the same hours, *look* alike (MY GAWD!), like and dislike the same things . . . never seen drunk in the streets, or in anything but freshly-laundered clothes. and they *don't like* my typewriter! what precious rum dum shit! what snail slime! what framed turds they are! they may have bellybuttons, elbows, assholes and all that . . . but they're completely DOWN THE RIVER, out of it, useless, worse than useless, not as good as a dead sparrow . . . may their asses rot on burning spiral points in hell FOREVER!!! fuck. [★ ★ ★]

[To John Martin]

August 25, 1970

hope you'll keep filing my stuff for me – I'll put you on salary some day – yeh. I have a rough first draft which I sometimes keep and which I sometimes lose, and also many poems sent out are never heard from again. so it's for the good of the Cause. my Cause.

I miss the horses – they kept my juices stirring and also put a little money in my pocket. Del Mar is just too far to drive without auto insurance. Garden Grove, where Marina is, is far enough. I just don't want a bunch of litigation on my neck for a freeway crash. that's not my idea of living. [★ ★ ★]

haven't heard from Weissner yet – wrote him at his Spanish address. I hear he's busy translating Warhol's 'a'. maybe I should have mentioned something about Carl's (that's Weissner) novel. his publisher sent it to me. I didn't. it's one of those cut-up Burroughs things and I've always been bored by those things, I can't help it. the publisher asked me to review it but I couldn't review it and be honest without hurting Carl's feelings. so there's always some shit. [* * *]

[To Carl Weissner]

August 31, 1970

[* * *] sitting here with a busted mouth after a week's drunk. really feel freaked-out, sick, pitiful. the blues, the depressive fits. I even wept, soundlessly. it's so much trouble just going on and a man gets tired of being brave.

anyhow, your letter cheered me. you have a way of saying kind things without bullshitting, and then your stuff is funny too, you know. anyhow anyhow I must guess that you are as desperate as I, only you take it better. fucking recession over here – god damned crap asses just don't want to let go of the buck. they *sit* on manuscripts now and when they finally accept them they delay payment until eternity. I'm speaking of the short story field. [* * *] so anyhow, this old rat's not dead yet. and the poems and stories keep popping out of my ears. this year I must have written 150 new poems, a novel and maybe 30 short stories. now all this stuff is not excellent but some of it is – sometimes I think I am just fucking away everything but the typer keeps doing it. and it comes out easy. tons and tons of shit. my machinegun sure – tattattattat a tattutuetutuetattutattu . . .[* * *]

[To Neeli Cherry]

September 1, 1970

[* * *] I may have to go to Greece and beg in the streets. recession here, everybody hanging to the buck. mags that used to pay right off don't anymore. one outfit has owed me $175 for 3 months. now they owe me 175 for a later acceptance. I can't live on OWE. all the other mags just sit on manuscripts for months – *Evergreen*, all of them. It's a real tight frightening situation. [* * *] lately people have been telling me I'm famous. a shit hell of a lot that does – the money's slipping away and I'm on the skids. I'm still hustling the poetry circuit – around here – for pennies. even read at a coffee house in Venice – $55. christ, I'm sweating raw pure blood. [* * *] my novel, *Post Office*, will be out in Nov. hope I get an advance. Black

Sparrow. man, the post office wasn't too bad. I thought the life of the writer would really be the thing. it's simply hell. I'm just a cheap twittering slave.

Univ. of Chicago writes they want me to read there in the fall. well, that's something. I'm fighting a slow desperate retreat, my mind, money, resources slipping away. [★ ★ ★] I have to write a lot of poems to keep from going crazy; I can't help it. I often write ten to 12 poems a day and then top the whole thing off with a short story. I may be going crazy but it has been all hell on production. I just hang on top of this typer and scream it out. wrote the novel in 20 days. 120,000 words, 30,000 of which I pulled out on the re-reading. one outfit in Germany tells me that they will buy the novel 'unseen.' *Notes of a Dirty Old Man* out in Germany, translated in the German. got a good review in *Der Spiegel* – equiv. to *Newsweek* here – one million circulation. photo and all. only they had me down as a native of Bavaria or something. poor Andernach. anyhow, for all this shit, there isn't any money showing.

meanwhile there's great violence in the streets here. men shooting each other, bombing each other. a guy tried to run me over in an empty parking lot last night. I just leaped aside in time. the stuff is catching. much hatred, confusion.[★ ★ ★]

Robert DeMaria was editor of Mediterranean Review, *published in Orient, New York, to which Bukowski had submitted some poems.*

[To Robert DeMaria]

September 2, 1970

'How come my x-wife thought Robert Graves was the greatest man alive?' Well, you see, my x-wife was a snob and she touted Robert Graves and other such cumbersome creatures because then people would think (she *thought* people would think), surely this little blonde creature must have BRAINS. Got it? O.k.

Definitely a pain to send poems to such places as Spain or England or hell because you have to get those International Reply Coupons and the clerks don't know what they are or how many you stick in, and I won't ask them. You know.

Will try you with another batch of poems soon. Your remark, on your last rejection, that my work was not carefully worked-out left me on high dry ground. Of course my work is not carefully worked-out and hastily written. that's the point. I write down what I need. poetry has long ago dulled me with its tricks and mechanics. or maybe the poems I sent you were just lousy. I write a lot of those.

[To John Martin]

September 4, 1970

like you know, you've been a big help to me, allowance, the Univ. of Santa Barbara thing, typewriter, paints, many things. And I can't expect you to worry about me day and night. don't want you to. you've got a one-man operation going that takes all your energy, and you've just finished straightening out my novel and mailing it off, so to bug you or put an extra weight on you is not my point. but it has been a real frozen mailbox lately. I don't know what the hell is going on out there (the magazines), and the bankroll is dipping, I'm far from starving to death, but can't help feeling concerned. I know how fast money goes when it's not coming in – the allowance is a lifesaver, of course, but I can't help thinking – and here I am bugging you – that the Blazek letters have been out about a year. It does seem an overlong time for no results. We had such a hell of a battle getting them from Blazek in the first place, if you remember. Also Dorbin told me he got paid his royalties on the Buk biblio. Didn't you tell me that I was also to get royalties on this? I know that there are answers to all this and that you are an honest guy, so I've hesitated. I realize that you are so damned busy with everything that you can't worry about my precious little irons in the fire – like I say, night and day, but hell, that mailbox worries me, and if you don't *ask* you don't find *out*. yeah, I know, I worry too much and I've got it made. o.k.

now I suppose I've spoiled your day. I'm Carol Bergé. writers are a shitty lot, I guess.

so here's another short story. don't rip it up but file it away as per usual, o.k? Celebrating Marina's birthday tomorrow so she won't have to come over on Labor Day. She'll be 6. good god. well, I'm doing a lot of writing but it's any good or not, I don't know. anyhow, I feel like writing and when I feel like writing there's some bit of warmth in the words. meanwhile, don't be pissed . . .

[To John Martin]

September 7, 1970

I WORKED labor day. see enclosed.

Marina had a nice cake Saturday, 6 candles but asked that we didn't sing Happy Birthday To You. the kid has some sharp. mama packed off to Synanon and we played for 8 hours. mostly she was Batman and I was Robin. then we painted, went for a long walk. then I played dummy, a familiar role.

where are your eyes? she asked. (I think of that sometimes too.)

and I'd point to my ears. my eyes? dose are my eyes.

no, no, Hank, *those* aren't your eyes! your eyes are here! (poking fingers into my skull)

hey, hell, kid, that hurts!

now, where are the pockets on your shirt?

pockets? shirt? well, I'm a pocket, you see . . .

no, Hank, look . . .

anyhow, it was a nice birthday, for Marina and for me.

and you're 40 and I'm 50 and my landlord's 60 (and built like a bull) and we're all going to die, and that's o.k. too. that gives us whatever beauty and power and grace we might have now. you know this. and, also, that this has been the most magic year of my life. it came late, but it will never be forgotten – even the horror of it. that's why I hang in now, fighting for a bit more horror. it may be beyond the imagination but by living carefully – fighting the slow retreat – I hope to squeeze out 3 or 4 years more before I have to get a job as a janitor or a dishwasher or go on relief. I'm sure you understand the picture, big Jawn, and even when the end comes down and I'm swinging that mop in the lady's crapper or facing some unloving creature across a desk in the frig. relief office, that the 2 or 3 good years will reside within me and they can't take those back. it's been a beautiful ball and a beautiful hell, and I'm talking too much.

when that brush gets too smooth in the tape machine, might as well replace it, you're going to get nothing but water on the tape and the frig. tape won't stick to the box. also when you're cutting a box down to size, cut *up* from the inside so you don't damage the merchandise.

the old shipping clerk, Henry.

[To Carl Weissner]

September 8, 1970

[★ ★ ★] I am coming out of about a month of deep black pure depression. one day I had to actually hold on to the mattress with my hands to keep from going into the kitchen where the butcher knife was. mixed-up situation, what? I've been in this court too long. stir-crazy. got to get out, walk somewhere, drive somewhere, do something. [★ ★ ★]

[To Carl Weissner]

September 18, 1970

[★ ★ ★] maybe I'm going crazy but I'm thinking of writing another one, *The Horseplayer*. a novel, I mean. don't know where I'll be able to dump it, but I guess write it first is the idea. in *The Horseplayer* though, once I write it, I will insist that all the bad grammar be left in and past and present tense be left in at the same time, if that's the way it happens to be. Martin claims that very few changes were made grammatically in *Post Office*, and I believe him, but I wish the few changes had not been made. everything counts. But I've read *Post Office* twice and even liked it better that 2nd time. that's a good sign. well, like I said, we'll see.

yes, most revolutionaries just love to talk and talk and talk. yes, there's a bomb now and then but sometimes I wonder *which* side plants those. my revolution is a one-man revolution and almost everybody is the enemy. I may not be doing a great deal of damage, but at least I'm not bullshitting. [★ ★ ★]

[To Carl Weissner]

September 21, 1970

[★ ★ ★] After a bit of a dry spell, things are looking up over here. A few sales to the mags for stories and even got *paid* for some poems. jesus. also doing a series of columns, short, called 'Hairy Fist Tales,' for *Fling*, a Chicago sex rag. [★ ★ ★]

You know, I've tried the starving writer bit. I guess it works with many. I write better with a few bucks in my pocket. Give me a half mile lead on the wolf and I'm tough as hell. I call it STAYING ON TOP OF THE GAME. This doesn't mean that I write for money; this means that I'll have money so I'll be able to *continue* writing. Of course it's going to end, but since I gave away the first 49 years of my life, this part is very strange. Indeed. this morning I stood on the front lawn, sun coming down, I was barefoot, nobody around, all these highrises, everybody off somewhere on their fucking crosses, and I stood there in the sun, haven't shaved in two weeks, hair uncombed, ripped shirt, 4 buttons missing from the fly of an old pair of army pants somebody had given me, and I smoked a cigarette and grinned into the world, knowing its shit and its blood and its plan, but I was in this special space somewhere for a moment, and it was quite good, quite. by god. of course, the butcher knife is still in the kitchen and I keep it good and sharp on the stone steps and that's part of it too. STAY ON TOP OF YOUR GAME, BABE, STAY ON TOP OF YOUR GAME. and a little bit of luck is nice too, but don't look for it.

[To Lafayette Young]

October 25, 1970

[* * *] I have to drink and gamble to get away from this typewriter. Not that I don't love this old machine when it's working right. But knowing when to go to it and knowing to stay away from it, that's the trick. I really don't want to be a *professional* writer, I wanna write what I wanna write. else, it's all been wasted. I don't want to sound holy about it; it's not holy – it's more like Popeye the Sailor Man. But Popeye knew when to move. So did Hemingway, until he started talking about 'discipline'; Pound also talked about doing one's 'work.' that's shit, but I've been luckier than both of them because I've worked the factories and slaughterhouses and park benches and I know that WORK and DISCIPLINE are dirty words. I know what they meant, but for me, it has to be a different game.[* * *]

[To Lafayette Young]

October 28, 1970

[★ ★ ★] frankly, most editors look at the writer as some kind of idiot, and in many ways he is. I've met quite a few of them and I've been taken on some deals myself. the writer, the real writer is only concerned with writing, writing that NEXT thing. you know, it's quite like that good fuck you (or I) had 3 months ago. who cares? it's tonight's or tomorrow's or the last one that counts. it's NOW. NOW IS THE ONLY LIVING BREATHING REALITY. when somebody tells me, 'Bukowski, I really liked that poem "The Priest and the Matador,"' I say, 'yeh.' who cares? I'd just as soon piss on it. that's why at poetry readings I read only the stuff – with one or two exceptions – that I've written in the last month or two. everything else leaves me dead and I read it dead. [★ ★ ★]

jesus christ, I've even been printed in the Dutch. DRONKEN MIRAKELS & ANDERE OFFERS. just got book in mail today. nicely done offset. Title means something like DRUNKEN MIRACLES AND OTHER IMMOLATIONS. combo of two poems 'Rain and Transport' plus 'Kaka and other Immolations.' I was only sent one copy so can't send any to you or Jimmy [Pitts] or Katz, who have all been very good to me in my times of hell shit fire gloom. but don't think issued in many copies (really don't know) but if I may sound like a prick, it will prob. be a collector's item worth maybe 25 or 50 bucks in a couple of years. see, there we go talking money again? see how they suck us in? let's be careful. it's just a funny odd book and you can probably get it for a buck as a curio piece for the crapper. let's take it that way. no price listed. if you get one, mail to me, I'll sign it. [★ ★ ★]

Linda King, whom Bukowski met in late 1970 and who was 'destined to become Hank's longtime girlfriend,' had four sisters who shared her literary bent. See Hank, pp. 211 and 216.

[To the sisters King]

October 30, 1970

My dear sisters King (or however it has been changed):

you have put much energy and time into writing me; I have no way of knowing, but I would judge that you are both living together, off of child support, something went wrong with the men, but the courts are fair, aren't they? hmmm? very well, diddle with Bukowski. wouldn't it be nice to put him in our female cage and poke him with sticks?

kill a coward and be
brave. that's
unity.

look, girls, it's nice to have you visit. I like girls about. an old dog like me should. and I do. just to look at. but even sex, that's no big go to me. after 2,000 pieces of ass, what's one more to me? one more strip of tinsel on a tired xmas tree. I pay child support, voluntarily, and gladly, I love my daughter. but sex to me is almost so much bog. I mean, you do it, that's nice, and then it's over and then what have you got? 2 chunks of flesh looking at each other and waiting and resting for the next trip. I write about sex like I write about anything else – mainly because I think it's tragic and funny. if you want to know more about the game, do try reading *The Decameron* by Boccaccio. *Notes of a Dirty Old Man* or all my poetry are nothing compared to his explicit laughing understanding of the thing. he's in your public library. me, I'd rather just talk to women or rather listen to them than fuck them. if I must fuck them, they must do most of the work, most of the coaxing. maybe I am queer? call me queer if that makes you feel better. they always call strong men queers. I've heard Hemingway mouthed as a queer. this is society's way – they won't leave a man alone. I'm a loner. I want to do my work, drink my beer and die. It's nice when the ladies knock on my door and are pretty, as both of you are, and giggle. but actually there's only one thing less predictable than a horse and that's a woman. don't bet on either one unless you want to take odds-on when you should be getting one hundred to one on your chances.

about dumbness (stupidity), ya got me all wrong – how can I have anything against it, when I don't know anything about it?

now, girls, let me get back to my business. you must realize that I am just an old guy with no visible means of support? now let me turn on that red light out there and spread my cheeks with vaseline . . . ok?

your in deepest penetration
and understand and love
and looove and broken
ladders

Robert Head and Darlene Fife were the editors of NOLA Express, *an underground paper published in New Orleans.*

[To Robert Head and Darlene Fife]

[? October 1970]

have been drunk for some weeks . . . this is no brag shit thing . . . don't like it . . . mind very heavy, fog-shit, you know. but grass and various other shit . . . speed, so forth, not worth a cat's ass. death of Hendrix did not bother me. Janis Joplin death particularly saddening, terrible to me because to put it shittily, I related to her. she had the courage of a mountain, understand? don't worry about vocal chords . . . wrote an 8 or ten page tribute to the guts of Joplin but so filled with love, I had to destroy. [★ ★ ★]

Listen, you know I am high here or I wouldn't go on like this with this shit . . . yes, got 2 copies of . . . what was it . . . the issue . . . I asked for. many thanks. the archive shit pays off. I'm lucy, not lucy, lucky. or maybe I'm Lucy? eh? all right. they used to have a thing called Lucy and Desi Arnez, perfectly sickening . . . barely remember it, but knew right away, 2 people sucking at anything they could get at any price and fooling everybody, almost every body. That Desi Arnez, he had such a bad band (that's what they used to call them in those days: 'bands'), how'd he ever get hold of Lucy? And, so what the hell, Lucy just began to look sillier and sillier, playing stupid parts, eyelashes getting longer, and more lipstick on and more slapstick on, and I don't know, this isn't hatred, it's just high, and I knew the cocksuckers of the world would bring them down, so fake them, so fake all, the final gods are very hard to fool. all right, how did I get into this garbage except to explain what it is? [★ ★ ★]

If you guys can line me a couple of readings in N.O. to cover plane fare and room and booze, would be nice . . . would like to meet you both just for chicken-ass kicks . . . no hatred. have long gotten over hatred drunks when I used to clean out houses full of people. now quite gentle even when totally loaded. took me a long time to learn. [★ ★ ★]

[To John Martin]

November 1, 1970

[★ ★ ★] they tell me your Wakoski is reading at Pomona College Dec. 7, flying in from N.Y. She has a nice loose and human style which I think she learned from me, but that's all right. if she has a weakness, it is the inability to write a good short poem. but few people can. Jeffers couldn't. Pound could. In fact, the shorter he got the better he got. I always liked him for that. But when he got long – *The Cantos* – he shit himself. the test of a good poet is one who can write any number of short good poems. W. C. Williams did it once, as we know. I haven't done it, prob. won't. I'm not a great and yet the greats bore me terribly. there really haven't been any strong people on earth yet and maybe that's the way the game is built. an ant is an ant and what can you do with an ant? there's an occasional flash of something now and then, but the guy who flashed hardly comes up with any more. it's hardly right, is it? when the fucking soul is trying so hard? and then you end up looking at a face like Nixon's and he's the same guy who flunked you in English I and with as little reason.

but there have been strong men – the same ones I have mentioned – Fyodor Dos, Celine, Artaud, Kafka . . . arising out of the billions and billions and zeroes produced and reproduced, almost for nothing – I do suppose that there have been stronger men, but circumstances simply drowned them away from future communication with the centuries. or, you take a man really strong enough, he can look around at the age of *four*, take some instrument and kill himself. swimming pool, anything else. [★ ★ ★]

[To John Martin]

November 6, 1970

[★ ★ ★] just think, someday after I'm dead and they start going for my poems and stories, you will have a hundred stories and a thousand poems on hand. you just don't know how lucky you are, babe. remember Marina. shouldn't be so serious, I know, but she is to be my literary executor, or whatever you call it. all royalties should go into a *trust* for her until she reaches the age where she is entitled to it. That name is Marina Louise Bukowski. [★ ★ ★]

all very serious, I know, and all the poems and stories may well rot, but it is a dark afternoon, and one thinks certain things . . .

[To Neeli Cherry]

November 20, 1970

[★ ★ ★] Guggenheim, all those prizes and grants – you know how they go – more money is given to people who already have money. Shit, I know a prof, friend of Corrington's, can't write a cat's ass . . . he wins a prize every year . . . usually the same one . . . and he goes off to some island and works on some project, meanwhile still getting paid half salary for doing nothing at the Univ. he's supposed to be teaching at. on one of his island trips he put together an anthology, even put me in it, but didn't even have the decency to send me a copy. 'Old Man, Dead in a Room,' he used. now, that took a lot of imagination, didn't it? I'll be an old man dead in a room soon enough as long as they keep baby-spooning these literary idiots. [★ ★ ★] I don't even know where to get the *papers* he fills out to win his shitty prizes. and if I did, they'd only write back, 'Sorry, but . . .'

well, it all helps keep me pure, yeah. [★ ★ ★]

[To Lafayette Young]

December 1, 1970

[★ ★ ★] it was good meeting you, you know that, and thanks for all . . . that fine motel bit, the transport, you . . . all that. you are a gentle and easy man . . . I hate to see them laying it into you down there . . . hope you've come out of it by now and are eating a little . . . but your family lays it into you because they love you, man; nobody understands an alcoholic . . . I started drinking young . . . at 16 and 17, and the next morning I'd always get it – those looks, that hatred. of course, my parents hated me anyhow. But I remember saying to them one morning: 'Christ, so I got drunk . . . You people treat me like a murderer . . .' 'That's it! That's it!' they said, 'what you've done is worse than murder!' they meant it. well, what they meant was that I was socially disgracing them in front of the neighbors, and there might be an excuse for murder, but for drinking . . . never, by god, no! They must have meant it, because when the war came on, they urged me to join the murder . . . it was socially acceptable. [★ ★ ★]

[To John Martin]

December 15, 1970

[★ ★ ★] Celine's *Castle to Castle* a horrible book. Of course, they really kicked his ass . . . threw him in a stinking pit . . . cancer ward afterwards . . . stole all his books and manuscripts, kicked the shit out of his motorcycle . . . what a grand chance he had to lay it into them by being objective . . . but he had to bitch and rail right down to the last stitch. he had all the tools to crucify the sons of bitches, but he couldn't do so: too close to his belly-button. well, it's too late.

all right, everything here is a mess too. papers all over the floor. gloom like spiderwebs. I seem caught in my own corner. It's round ten. and they're pushing me off the stool. I'm behind on points. Face of a madman. lace on left glove undone. can't see out of eyes. who started all this shit anyhow?

p.s. – next day – yesterday's phone call was nice but now that we're off the free $100 per month, life will get grimmer. christomighty yeah. so we've got to start scratching. [★ ★ ★]

[To Lafayette Young]

December 21, 1970

well, the amateur drunks have taken over and will hold this town until Jan. 2 . . . driving on the wrong side of the street, running red lights, bellowing the same songs. figs of people, twigs of people, shits of people . . . MERRY CHRISTMAS, HAPPY NEW YEAR. Christomighty, yeah.

I drove down to get Marina today – Santa Monica – we're still in tune. The few people who knew always laughed at me because I talked to her like an adult. I still do. she's 6 now but it's the same as when she was two or three. this had nothing to do with trying to elevate her mental hygiene – I'd be the worst for that. the worst one, I mean. but she's gotten used to talking to me and I've gotten used to talking to her and we listen to each other; we're serious about it but we laugh a lot too. like today, we decided to get some wrapping paper [★ ★ ★] and I said, 'Now, look, Marina, see all those people trying to get into the Thrifty drugstore parking lot? The lot is already full and they are just going to sit there for hours, or maybe ten or twenty minutes waiting for somebody to pull out so they can park. So, we're not going to do that. We'll just park across the street a half a block away and *walk* in.' Which we did. [★ ★ ★]

Marina was so beautiful and happy at her grammar school xmas program . . . Christ, all she wants is love, to be *noticed* . . . she glows and I glow back; it's almost unbearable . . . not to bring out the crying towel, but both my parents hated me. But that has nothing to do with it: she brings the miracle to me, and *I* respond.

O.k. man, to hell with kids and Christmas talk. [★ ★ ★]

[To John Martin]

December 23, 1970

[★ ★ ★] There have been some pretties coming around in their minis, flashing me all that leg, smiling from the couch. I just sit there and glower, thinking of the trap. 'I'm through with women,' I tell them. 'My pecker still gets hard now and then but a little cold water takes care of the problem.' They just laugh. They think I'm joking. 'Oh, hehehe, you're *so* funny!'

One of them wants to sculpt my head at her place. I told her, 'O.k., give me a ring sometime in Jan. or Feb. and I'll trot on over. Where we gonna sculpt? In the bedroom?'

'Oh no, we have a nice secluded place in the backyard . . .'

Thanks for not sending me the Creeley xmas card. Not to be a bitch, but after I've read one of his poems I really don't know what he's said, and then my next reaction is, 'O, what the fuck. Forget it.'

Hello to my dear telephone-relay message girl, my Barbara; don't ruffle the Sparrow's feathers, he's been bitten and smitten by the poet lice . . .

hang in.

[To John Martin]

December 27, 1970

have been crawling through one of those depressive fits that seem to fall upon me. please believe me, I am not trying to play the sensitive Artist bit – that's sickening. I only wish it wouldn't happen. It's just like all the walls fall down upon me. I've almost analyzed it – it happens mostly after I have been on a drunk with 2 or more people. I don't understand it – I can drink more, all by myself, and don't even awaken with a hangover.

[★ ★ ★] 1970 was my most magic year. the horrors increased and the joys, and the typewriter became more real, instead of an afterthought. I don't know how much longer I can g.d. sluff off those most real ghosts with sharp teeth . . . age and booze dull the soul . . . But the post office would have killed me within 2 more years. my thanks to both you and Barbara for understanding a lot of it. [★ ★ ★]

AFTERWORD

It's easy, reading these letters, to see why Bukowski's correspondents saved them. Apart from the sometimes striking idiosyncrasies of format which gave them an unusual impact (and which we mostly can't see in book form), their often searing vividness – a stream of feeling and suffering more than stream of consciousness – gives them an impact which must have been easy to recognize. Besides, during these years all of those addressed in the letters printed here were aware of Bukowski's poetry and already valued it for similar vividness of impact.

Bukowski's letters have an unusual immediacy, compared to those of other noteworthy modern literary correspondents. (Think of Lawrence, Pound, Fante, or Creeley and Olson; all are variously fascinating as letter writers but give infinitely less by way of self-portrayal.) Bukowski seems, with trusted correspondents, to pour himself forth with little forethought or purpose other than to render his immediate experience. Only a small minority of surviving letters have a mainly conventional kind of purpose – answering or posing questions, conducting literary business. More often, even when the letter accompanies submissions of poems or other writing, there is a full outpouring of the self in its present situation, generally incorporating notations of the immediate mundane circumstances: people passing or working outside, activities in the apartment, toothache, hangover, radio sounds, etc.

It is a cliché to lament the decline of the personal letter in our telephone age, but Bukowski never doubted its value. 'I think the letter is an important form,' he writes early on.

> You can touch about everything as you run around. It lets you out of the straightjacket of pure Art, and you've got to get out once in a while. Of course, I don't restrict myself as much in the poem as most do, but I have made this my business, this freedom with the word and idea [★ ★ ★]. (22)

He escapes from the straightjacket of pure Art, we note, not by self-indulgence but by a *discipline* ('my business') of writing designed to earn the freedom with word and idea. Yet even so, the personal letter offers a welcome further relief: no worries about unity, shaping a whole, or revision, for instance. Still, it's a form it would be dangerous to grow self-conscious about. When Tom MacNamara proposed quoting from both past and future Bukowski letters, Bukowski sensed a danger.

> Letters? god damn, man, let's be careful. all right at outset, esp. for tightheads who have been working in sonnet form, writing critical articles, so forth; it gives them (letters) the facility and excuse for wallowing in the easiness of their farts and yawns without pressure. [* * *] then the next thing you know instead of being an o.k. thing, a natural form, it simply becomes another form for the expulsion of the creative, artistic, fucked-up Ego [* * *] and soon a lot of the boys end up working as hard or harder on the letters than they do on their poems. wherever the payoff lies, what? (103)

Self-consciousness and posing are the enemy, in all their guises and whether in writing or personal behavior. It is his suspicion of such posing that makes much traditionally admired literature unpersuasive to Bukowski:

> 'I have just read the immortal poems of the ages and come away dull. I don't know who's at fault; maybe it's the weather, but I sense a lot of pretense and poesy footwork: I am writing a poem, they seem to say, *look* at me!' (14)

(His recurrent jeering at the coteries and mutual admiration societies of the 'creative writing' crowd provides many amusing passages of invective throughout the decade.) Against such falseness there is unself-conscious 'natural form,' whether of the letter or of the kind of poem Bukowski writes. Bad poetry, false poetry, is the self-important ego on display: 'I am not primarily a poet, I hate god gooey damned people poets messing the smears of their lives against the sniveling world [* * *].' (47)

The letter form is liberating when unself-consciously undertaken – and undertaken at the typewriter, essentially. Technology helps, not inhibits, his epistolary self-expression. To Kaye Johnson he explained: 'you know, u really kant get the ingress into a WORD without the typer, the typer is the carver, the ax, the cleaver, the thing with the mouth that hollers about the bloody dice. it machineguns the mind out of penury. fuck the pen.' (75) When his machine broke down, he said he felt 'like a man without a cock having a spiritual hard-on and nothing to ram it home with. I can't spin anything without the keys, the keys have a way of cutting out the fat and retaining the easiness.' (101) Bukowski's handwritten letters are done in large printing and seem laborious; the machine allowed him speed and copiousness with less effort.[1] Spontaneity meant occasional whimsical spellings (and infrequent misspellings), it meant free play with capitalization (almost always the first person pronoun retains its capital, however) and sometimes with layout. But Bukowski is surprisingly fastidious about punctuation, consistently using the semi-colon in the traditional way, for example. Spontaneity also allowed improvisation in vocabulary: we find quite a few nonce words and coinages enlivening these letters, with only rarely a loss of intelligibility. The improvisation co-exists with a certain purity of diction: taboos on obscenity, of course, are not respected, but there is a remarkable absence of clichés, catch pharases, or ephemeral slang.[2] Perhaps most strikingly, spontaneity meant a rich inventiveness of imagery, as in the phrases just quoted.

The Bukowski letter, then, has something in common with the 'spontaneous prose' described by Kerouac in 1957.[3] Or it may be seen as a kind of performance art, an improvisation analogous to that of a jazz soloist. The mood of the moment, whether exhilarated or suicidal, comradely or belligerent, is the essential subject matter. Bukowski kept no carbons of his letters, and writing with self-abandonment meant that he often professed not to remember what he had said in prior letters (as in interviews, phone calls, etc.). Responding to earlier prospects of seeing some of his letters in print, Bukowski agreed enthusiastically: 'I'd like to see what I have written too' (September 30, 1965; to Blazek). But even without knowing what he might have said, he always gave permission to present the authentically embodied self warts and all, with no censorship: 'I've got nothing to hide,' he told the Webbs. 'That I drink or play the ponies or have been in jail is of no shame to me.' (31)

If the letters render and project a self with striking vividness and uninhibited fullness, we can yet remark on how narrow the focus is, how painfully constricted the life. The constriction is the price of the intensity. For Bukowski in the sixties, after periods of omnivorous reading in earlier years and after decades of wandering (see *Factotum*), the *Racing Form* would seem to be the main reading material, the hated job alternating with drinking-and-writing and playing the horses the main activities. For the now settled Bukowski, it was a period of intense physical and mental suffering and intense productivity. Writing poems and letters – he tells us as much – was what kept him from suicide or insanity: that and drink. A man too self-conscious and inarticulate to enjoy most forms of face to face meeting, especially with literary people, he found in his intense exchanges with a few kindred spirits (Jon Webb, Doug Blazek and Carl Weissner most notably) the sense of community that we all need, and the impetus to keep writing. Russell Harrison puts this well:

> the very fact that Bukowski is engaged in an extensive and ongoing correspondence is significant. It bespeaks a social need that we would not at first suspect in a writer who, in his fiction and poetry, has placed an unusual emphasis on his protagonist as an isolated individual, a loner. That the correspondence was important is evidenced by his promptness in responding.[4]

Bukowski told Wantling in 1965, 'Sometimes I am corresponding with 15 or more people at once, but finally after I work them over a few rounds they have their way and edge off.'[5] By 1967 he was slacking off a bit: 'it's all right to be a good guy and to send 12 page drunken letters to 40 different people but after a while there just isn't enough Bukowski to go around any more.'[6]

Writing letters fed the impulse to write poems and indeed sometimes (especially to Blazek) the letters themselves modulate into verse as they go. And while Bukowski was never too much interested in literary chitchat, criticism, theory, or analysis, the letter form allows him to throw off a number of passing evaluative remarks about other writers, from Hamsun and Kafka to Ginsberg and Creeley, and about his sense of what literature is for, what makes it good. He never quotes Pound's phrase to name the function of literature: 'nutriment of impulse' (indeed he rarely quotes at all), but he seems to agree with it. Clearly he hates any sense of literature as an accomplishment or of literary education as what gives polish to a man or woman. The literature that matters is what keeps you from dying. If he seems (to someone like me, of more conventional tastes) narrow in the range of his appreciation, he makes up for it in the passionate existential seriousness of his approach: 'Poetry must be forgotten; we must get down to raw paint, splatter. I think a man should be forced to write in a roomful of skulls [⋆ ⋆ ⋆]' (14) Such an impatience with literature as 'belles lettres' ('this fiddle,' in Marianne Moore's phrase) has a long pedigree. Wordsworth, for one, the revolutionary who wanted to write like 'a man speaking to men,' would have agreed.

A final word should be said on the consistency and integrity of the self so vividly and dramatically presented in this book. The man who cheerfully quotes Popeye's 'I am what I am' reminds me of Lawrence's jaunty citing of 'The Miller of Dee':

> There was a jolly miller once,
> Lived on the River Dee.
> He laughed and sang from morn till night,
> No man more blithe than he.
> And this the burden of his song
> Forever used to be:
> I care for nobody, no not I,
> Since nobody cares for me.

It hardly needs saying that the insoucient attitude in both cases is only one element of a more complex stance in the world, balanced by (perhaps protective of) other instances of great sensibility. Bukowski was never without sensitivity to the uniqueness of the person he was addressing. The letters to Ann Menebroker, among those here present, are particularly revealing in this respect: their delicacy of tone contrasts markedly with the more macho strutting sometimes heard (e.g. in a letter to Marvin Malone of August 1962, a letter which refers crudely to the same Menebroker he could write so self-revealingly to). More painfully amusing, as revealing different 'voices' of Bukowski's letter writing, is the early series sent to the publisher of his first chapbook, E. V. Griffith, progressing from the impersonal to the totally exasperated to the abjectly apologetic. Towards the end of the decade we find an extremely long letter to Carl Weissner provoked by his comic embarrassment at having identified Weissner in a snapshot as a girl. The tenderness of feeling for his baby daughter is another recurrent note that fills in the self-portrayal. So does a remark he made in response to the joy given him by the Webbs' publication of his second large scale book collection. '[A] book like this lifts my life up into light whether I deserve it or not,' he writes, adding:

> I used to have a theory that if I could just make one person's life happy or real that would have been otherwise, then my own life would not have failed. It was a good theory but a few whores ran me through the wringer for it, but I do think that for a while a few of them enjoyed not being spit on for a while, and so this made it o.k. for me. (77)

We come back to the literary vocation which in the long run is what makes these letters valuable to a wider public than their addressees. '[* * *] it's up to a man to create art if he's able, and not to talk about it, which, it seems, he's always more than able.' (174) Deprecating, as usual, his own public persona, Bukowski writes:

> I say or do nothing brilliant. The most brilliant thing I do is to get drunk – which any fool can do. If there is any dramatics in me, it must wait on the Art Form. If there is any ham in me it must wait on the Art Form. If there is any D. H. Lawrence in me it must wait on the A. F. (25)

It was D. H. Lawrence who said, 'Art speech is the only speech,' and these declarations by Bukowski put the emphasis finally in the same place – on the achieved writing. The ability to be buoyantly stoic, to declare, 'I have nothing to hide and anything I say in a letter goes anywhere anytime, and if they don't like the taste of it, let them suck empty beer bottles' (86), is a liberating and enabling self-sufficiency. The letter writer and the poet are a single, coherent entity. One result is that, while we may find a difference of emphasis and tone in references to the same person over time, we don't find here the kind of bad faith recently noticed in the letters of Philip Larkin:

> a warm and appreciative letter to X is followed, often on the same day, by a warm and appreciative letter to Y in jeering dispraise of X, and so on. Bad faith was a form of good faith; it meant that Larkin was still keeping his options open.[7]

Bukowski's letters give us a whole self in many moods. His courage and endurance and sheer hard work at his writing are exemplary. He told a correspondent that 'it is good to have your own courage but it is also good to take hope and courage from the ways of others. this I haven't been able to do until lately.' (185) The encouragement he found in his correspondence can be shared by us. 'I wrote letters to many in those days,' he has said, 'it was rather my way of screaming from my cage.' It is gratifying for the reader of these sometimes agonized 'screams' to know that the decade ends with his escape from the Post Office into a successful career of living by his writing alone.

– Seamus Cooney
Western Michigan University
Kalamazoo, Michigan

NOTES TO AFTERWORD

[1] He had to suffer the complaints of his neighbors, though, and was forced to agree not to type after 10 p.m. in his first apartment.

[2] Neeli Cherkovski made a similar point about Bukowski's diction: 'In the heart of the sixties he remained untouched by hippie terminology, employing it only sarcastically to prove a point' (*Hank*, p. 189). Curiously, one of the few literary allusions to familiar quotations that I have spotted in these letters is to Spenser's remark that Chaucer is 'a well of English undefiled' (Bukowski calls the Cantos 'a well of Pounding unrecognized' [5]). (Another allusion is to the last lines of Eliot's *Prufrock*.)

[3] See Jack Kerouac, 'Belief and Technique for Modern Prose' and 'Essentials of Spontaneous Prose' (1957), reprinted in *New American Story*, ed. Donald M. Allen and Robert Creeley (New York: Grove Press, 1965), pp. 269–271.

[4] Unpublished paper by Russell Harrison.

[5] Letter of June 23, 1965, not otherwise excerpted in the present volume.

[6] To Louis Delpino, August 2, 1967.

[7] Jonathan Raban, *The New Republic* (7/19–26/93), p. 35.

Index